YELLOW	GREEN/BROWN		
Within yellow are included a few flowers that are orange.	Green flowers may have green petals or may lack petals altogether or drop them so soon after the flower opens that the overall impression is green or, occasionally, brownish.		
Wood Spurge *107* **xv** 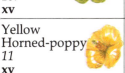	Common Orache *47* **xii**	Enchanter's-nightshade *93* **viii**	0–2 petals irregular flowers
Yellow Horned-poppy *11* **xv** 	Procumbent Pearlwort *39* **xii**	Hedge-bedstraw *167* **viii** 	4 petals regular flowers
Yellow Corydalis *13* **xv-xvi** 	Wild Liquorice *69* **xii**	White Dead-nettle *159* **viii**	4 petals irregular flowers
Yellow Iris *211* **xvi** 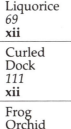	Curled Dock *111* **xii** 	Star-of-Bethlehem *207* **ix**	3 or 6 petals regular flowers
Small Balsam *57* **xvi**	Frog Orchid *215* **xiii**	Lesser Butterfly-orchid *217* **ix** 	3 or 6 petals irregular flowers
Perforate St John's-wort *31* **xvi-xvii** 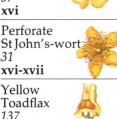	Stinking Hellebore *3* **xiii**	Upright Hedge-parsley *97* **ix-x** 	5 or 7 petals regular flowers
Yellow Toadflax *137* **xvii**	Common Figwort *139* **xiv**	Sweet Violet *27* **x**	5 or 7 petals irregular flowers
Lesser Celandine *9* **xviii xxvii-xviii** 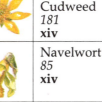	Heath Cudweed *181* **xiv**	Mountain Avens *81* **xi**	8 or more petals regular flowers
Daffodil *211* **xviii** 	Navelwort *85* **xiv**	Bindweed *133* **xi**	tubular

THE MACMILLAN FIELD GUIDE TO
BRITISH WILDFLOWERS

Franklyn Perring and Max Walters
Photographs by Andrew N. Gagg

Grange
BOOKS

Published by Grange Books
An Imprint of Grange Books PLC
The Grange
Grange Yard
London SE1 3AG

First published in 1989 by THE MACMILLAN PRESS LTD
London and Basingstoke

This edition 1994

ISBN 1-85627-636-8

Printed and bound in Slovakia

CONTENTS

INTRODUCTION

We have written this *Guide* to help our fellow botanists – especially we hope the next generation. We have tried to put across from our experience what it is we are looking at when we identify a species. By time and place alone a species like cow parsley on roadside verges in May can be named with certainty at 40 mph, although it belongs to that troublesome family, the *Umbelliferae*, whilst others which are small and difficult to see from a distance need much closer inspection – looking at the tip of a sepal with a lens or counting the number of stamens. The photographs have been chosen to reflect the need for different approaches to different species – and this is a unique aspect of this book. From the outset we have been able to ask our photographer to take the picture which we wanted, to show you what to look for and we are delighted that we found such a gifted plant photographer to work with. Andrew Gagg combines the triple attributes of being a technically brilliant cameraman, having an artist's eye for composition *and* being a very sound field botanist as well.

However there are situations where even his skill in meeting our demands could not quite be met on film. So, here and there, we have inserted line drawings to bring out some important detail, often just the thing you need to look for with a lens. Here again we have been fortunate to have an illustrator with such wide botanical experience as Michael Hickey.

This *Guide* does *not* include all the flowers which grow wild in the British Isles, but it does include all those which you are likely to find unless you are visiting very special places for rare or local species. We have used our extensive knowledge of looking for plants over the last 50 years and our work in preparing the *Atlas of the British Flora* to ensure that our selection is as objective as we can make it. We have also omitted from this volume all trees and shrubs except for a few low-growing or twining woody species, and we have left out rushes, sedges, grasses and ferns: these may be the basis of a second volume.

Franklyn Perring
Max Walters

Photographer's Acknowledgements
Thanks are due to the many people who have given their unending help in obtaining the photographs for this book, in particular; Mr R.W. Arthur, Dr H.J.M. Bowen, Mr J.J. Day, Mr F. Fincher, Mr A. Fraser, Mrs G.M. Gent, Dr G. Halliday, Mrs S.C. Holland, Miss K.M. Hollick, Mr L.J. Margetts, The late Miss E.D. Pugh, Mr E.G. Philp, Mr Jeremy Roberts, Mr M.G. Rutterford, Mrs J.M. Roper, Dr I.C. Trueman, Mrs M. Wainwright and last but not least my wife Christine.

Additional photographs have been supplied by the following to whom thanks

are also due: Mr G.R. Carter *Ophrys insecifera* p.217, Prof J.H. Fremlin *Saussurea alpina* p.193, Mr A.L. Grenfell *Bupleurum subovatum* p.97, *Pyrola media* p.117, *Lamium moluccellifolium* p.159, *Anthemis arvensis* p.185, Mr A.R.G. Mundell *Veronica fruticans* p.143, Dr F.H. Perring *Cerastium diffusum* p.37, *Medicago polymorpha* p.61, *Sison amomum* p.99, *Oenanthe crocata* p.101, Dr M.C.F. Proctor *Lavatera arborea* p.51, *Trifolium glomeratum* p.65, *Loiseleuria procumbens* p.115, Mr P.D. Sell *Veronica alpina* p.143, *Hieracium holosericeum* p.201.

Andrew N. Gagg

GLOSSARY

achene a small, dry, single-seeded fruit with its own stigma.

annual a plant that produces flowers and seeds and dies within a year.

auricle small projections, often overlapping, at the base of a leaf.

biennial a plant that produces flowers and seeds and dies within 2 years.

bract the reduced, leaf-like part of a plant beneath the flower-stalk on which one or many flowers grow.

bulbil a small bulb found in the axil of a leaf or amongst the flowers of an inflorescence.

capsule a dry fruit consisting of 2 or more seed-containing compartments, round or quadrangular in cross-section.

entire leaf one in which the margin is neither toothed nor cut.

follicle a dry fruit of one carpel which opens along one side.

gland a small, globular object, often on a short stalk, containing sticky or aromatic substances.

nectary a small area of tissue at the base of a petal exuding a sugary substance.

ovate shape like the outline of a hen's egg – mainly used to describe leaves.

ovoid egg-shaped, often used to describe fruits.

palmate leaf one in which there are more than 3 leaflets arising from a single point.

panicle a much branched inflorescence markedly decreasing in size upwards.

perennial a plant that lives for more than 2 years and usually produces flowers and seeds each year.

pinnate leaf one in which there are more than 3 leaflets arranged in 2 rows along a common stalk. They may have a terminal leaflet (inparipinnate) or lack one (paripinnate).

receptacle a flat, convex or concave area at the top of a stem from which the parts of the flower arise.

spike a simple inflorescence with all the flowers in a column on very short stalks.

stipule a leaf-like appendage at the base of a leaf-stalk where it joins the stem and sometimes attached to it.

tendril a part of the leaf or stem modified to act as a climbing organ.

tubercle a round or oval swelling on the face of a sepal or fruit.

umbel an umbrella-shaped arrangement of flowers in which all the flower-stalks arise from a single point at the top of a stem. There are usually 2 layers.

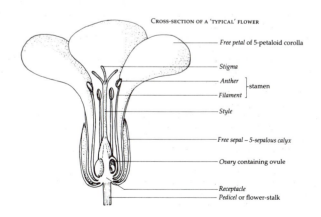

CROSS-SECTION OF A 'TYPICAL' FLOWER

Free petal of 5-petaloid corolla

Stigma

Anther ⎤ stamen
Filament ⎦

Style

Free sepal – 5-sepalous calyx

Ovary containing ovule

Receptacle

Pedicel or flower-stalk

HOW TO USE THIS GUIDE

The order of plants in this *Guide* is that normally adopted by British Floras. Families of plants are indicated by headings or by running heads at the top of each page. Each family is divided into a single genus or number of genera. A genus is a group of species which tend to look alike. A family is a group of related genera that have features in common indicating a common ancestry.

The experienced

If you are a fairly competent botanist with a good grounding in wildflowers you may be able to recognise the family or genus your unknown specimen belongs to and therefore go directly to the appropriate section of the *Guide*, either via the Index (p.222) or by knowing the family order, which follows that now used in the standard British Floras such as *Excursion Flora of the British Isles* (Clapham, A.E., Tutin T.G., and Warburg E.F., 3rd edn, 1981). For two of the larger families or groups, carrot and yellow members of the daisy family, keys to species have been provided. They begin on p.xxvii.

The inexperienced

If the unknown specimen does not readily bring to mind a family or a genus, this *Guide* provides you with a key in two parts (a general identification key beginning on p.viii and a special identification key on p.xxvii) to help you find the one or two pages on which it is likely to appear and in many cases the exact species.

1 Start with the endpapers inside the front and rear covers (they are both the same). Look at the headings of the rows along the left hand side and decide on the colour of the flowers, noting carefully the definition of the colours given there.

2 Count the petals (or apparent petals) and decide, with the aid of the drawing, which column has the flower nearest to your specimen. *N.B.* Other flower shapes

which fit may be found elsewhere in the vertical column above or below.

3 When you have found a 'match' of colour and petal numbers/shape, the numbers in the box in which it occurs will either take you to the further keys in the body of the *Guide* or, in a few cases, directly to the correct species.

4 The identification keys work by asking you to look at the headings in the first, extreme left column. When you have decided which one agrees with your specimen, proceed to the entries in the second column next to the one selected, and make a further selection, working in order downwards. Repeat the performance in the third column if necessary: the answer (the page number usually to a particular genus or species) will be next to your selected statement in the fourth (last) column.

5 With each photograph we have provided a short description. This complements the picture by drawing attention to those features of the plant which, in our experience, are the most important for a certain identification. To give added point we have put the most significant characters in **bold** type. If the picture looks right and the **bold** characters agree you may be confident of a correct identification.

6 To help your understanding of the text we have tried to avoid technical language when plain English is equally explicit: however, there is a basic number of terms we could not avoid – these, and a drawing of a 'typical flower' may be found on p.v.

EXAMPLE 1

Your 'unknown' specimen has greenish, apparently 4-petalled irregular flowers. Beginning with the endpapers, the pealike flower is similar to the wild liquorice illustrated. You are directed to p.xii. In the left-hand margin you will find a similar illustration under '4 petals, irregular flowers'. To the right there are drawings of 2 kinds of leaves: the lower one is divided into several pairs of leaflets and, if this matches your specimen, it suggests that it is indeed wild liquorice. This takes you to p.69 where you will find the photograph and be able to check the description with the text.

EXAMPLE 2

Your 'unknown' specimen has yellow, regular flowers with 4 petals. It is similar to the yellow horned-poppy on the endpapers which appears where the column of 4 petals, regular flowers, meets the row for yellow but lacks the long 'horn' and is more like the dame's-violet which is illustrated in the blue/violet box opposite. Your specimen probably belongs to the cabbage family rather than the poppy family. You are directed to the 'yellow pages' of the general identification guide which begin on p.xv. In the left-hand margin you will find the same illustration of the yellow horned-poppy under '4 petals, regular flowers'. To the right there are several choices and, if your 'unknown' has separate petals, 6 or fewer stamens and a pod opening from the bottom which is about 3 times as long as broad, it will certainly be a member of the cabbage family and you are taken to pictures and descriptions which begin on p.12.

Equipment

Whilst pictures and some details of shape and number may be adequate to name most species, there are some where measurements and the ability to see features not visible to the naked eye are essential. So, to be a complete botanist and make the most of this *Guide*, buy yourself a ×10 lens and a clear plastic centimetre ruler.

If in difficulty, lenses are available from Botanical Society of the British Isles Publications, 24 Glapthorn Road, Oundle, Peterborough PE8 4JQ.

White Flowers

2 petals	*Enchanter's-nightshade p.92*		
4 petals regular flowers Petals joined	Leaves narrow – whorled		*Squinancywort and Bedstraws pp.166–9*
	Leaves ovate – opposite		*Gipsywort p.152 Small Teasel p.172*
Petals separate	Pods' length over 3 times width	Leaves opposite	*Pale Willowherb p.90*
		Leaves alternate or spirally arranged	*Crucifers pp.20–3*
	Pods' length less than 3 times width	Leaves undivided	*Crucifers pp.16–19*
		Leaves divided into segments	*Meadow-rue p.8 Crucifers pp.14–19*
		Leaves narrow – needle-like	*Procumbent Pearlwort p.38*
4 petals irregular flowers	Leaves alternate	Flowers with round winged pods	*Wild Candytuft p.16*
	Leaves opposite	Flowers with tubular calyx	*Labiates pp.154, 158–61*
		Flowers with narrow pods	*Eyebright p.146 Bear's-breech p.150*
		Flowers with broad pods often with 2 segments	*Speedwells pp.140, 144*
	Leaves trifoliate	Flowers in heads	*Clovers pp.62–7*
		Flowers in spikes	*White Melilot p.62*
	Leaves pinnate		*Bird's-foot p.70 Vetches p.72*

	Leaves much–divided			*Fumitories p.12*
	No green leaves			*Toothwort p.148*
3 or 6 petals regular flowers	Leaves divided		*Dropwort p.76*	
	Leaves simple and broad		Water plants	*Water-purslane p.88* *Water-plantains and Frogbit p.202*
			Land plants	*Butcher's-broom p.206* *Ramsons p.208*
	Leaves arrow-shaped		*Arrowhead p.202*	
	Leaves narrow		*Scottish Asphodel and Fritillary p.204* *Star-of-Bethlehem p.206* *Leeks p.208* *Snowflake and Snowdrop p.210*	
3 or 6 petals irregular flowers	Flowers large, over 1cm long		With spurs	*Butterfly-orchids p.216* *Spotted-orchids p.218*
			Without spurs	*Helleborines p.212*
	Flowers small, under 5mm long		*Lady's-tresses pp.212–15* *Small-white Orchid p.216*	
5 or 7 petals regular flowers Stamens many	Fruits many – dry		*Wood Anemone p.2* *Water–crowfoots pp.6–9* *Meadowsweet p.76* *Barren Strawberry p.78*	
	Fruits many – succulent		*Brambles p.76* *Strawberries p.80*	
	Fruits few – like cheese in box		*Mallows p.50*	
Stamens 10 or less	Leaves lobed or divided once, or feathery		Flowers in loose branched clusters	*Saxifrages p.86* *Black Nightshade p.134* *Dwarf Elder p.170*
			Flowers in umbels	*Carrot Family pp.94–105*

White Flowers (contd)

5 or 7 petals regular flowers	Leaves trifoliate		Flowers solitary		*Wood-sorrel p.56*
			Flowers in spikes		*Bogbean p.126*
Stamens 10 or less (contd)	Leaves undivided		Stem leaves without stalks – opposite		*Pink Family pp.32–43* *Blinks p.44* *Fairy Flax p.50* *Red Valerian p.172*
			Stem leaves in pairs around stem		*Springbeauty p.44*
			Stem leaves in whorls of 5–6		*Chickweed Wintergreen p.122*
			Stem leaves without stalks – alternate		*Stonecrops p.84* *Knotgrass and Bistort p.108* *Brookweed p.122* *Gromwells p.132* *Giant Bellflower p.164*
			Stem leaves with stalks		*Grass-of-Parnassus p.88* *Bindweeds and Knotweeds p.108–11*
			Leaves only at base – covered in glands		*Sundews p.88*
			Leaves only at base – *not* covered in glands		*Wintergreens p.116*
5 or 7 petals irregular flowers	Flowers with spurs		*Sweet Violet p.26* *Pale Toadflax p.136*		
	Flowers without spurs		Fruits' length over 2 times width		*Water-dropworts pp.100–3*
			Fruits' length less than 2 times width		*Spreading Hedge-parsley p.96* *Ground-elder p.100* *Hogweed and Carrot p.104*

8 or more petals or many flowers in heads	Single flowers with many separate petals		*White Water-lily p.8* *Mountain Avens p.80*	
	Many flowers together in compact heads	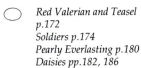	Leaves smooth-edged or toothed but not divided	*Red Valerian and Teasel p.172* *Soldiers p.174* *Pearly Everlasting p.180* *Daisies pp.182, 186* *Sneezewort p.184*
			Leaves much divided	*Chamomiles and Mayweeds p.184* *Feverfew p.186*

Tubular flowers – lobes less than 1/10 length of tube 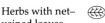	Climbing plants with bell-shaped flowers		*Bindweeds p.132*
	Trailing shrubs with oval leaves		*Bearberry p.114* *Cowberry p.116*
	Herbs with net–veined leaves		*White Comfrey p.128* *Thorn-apple p.134*
	Herbs with parallel–veined leaves		*Lily-of-the-valley and Solomon's-seals p.204*

Green or Brown Flowers

0–2 petals	Flowers with central stalked fruit with 3 segments		*Spurges p.106*
	Flowers not as above	Leaves opposite	*Blinks p.44* *Sea-purslane p.46*
		Leaves alternate	*Oraches p.46*
		Leaves absent	*Glassworts p.48*
4 Petals regular flowers Petals joined	Leaves narrow and/or whorled		*Plantains and Shoreweed p.162* *Wild Madder p.168*
	Leaves oval or roundish		*Mistletoe p.92* *Plantains p.162*
	Leaves divided		*Moschatel p.170*
Petals separate	Leaves narrow – needle-like		*Pearlworts p.38*
	Leaves oval		*Pellitory-of-the-wall and Nettles p.112* *Herb-Paris p.206*
	Leaves roundish		*Golden-saxifrages p.86* *Mountain Sorrel p.110*
	Leaves pinnate		*Salad Burnet p.82*
4 petals irregular flowers	At least upper leaves in opposite pairs		*Spurges p.106* *Wood Sage p.160*
	Leaves pinnate		*Wild Liquorice p.68*
3 or 6 petals regular flowers	Leaves narrow		*Arrowgrasses p.202* *Star-of-Bethlehem p.206* *Sweet-flag p.220*
	Leaves broad – opposite		*Water-purslane p.88* *Mercuries p.104*

	Leaves broad – alternate		Plants climbing	Black Bryony p.210
			Plants not climbing	Docks p.110–13
3 or 6 petals irregular flowers	Flowers large, over 1cm long		With 4 lobed 'man-like' lips	Common Twayblade p.214 Man Orchid p.220
			Not as above	Broad-leaved Helleborine p.212 Bird's-nest Orchid and Frog Orchid p.214
	Flowers small, under 5mm long			Lesser Twayblade p.214
5 or 7 petals regular flowers Stamens 10 or less	Leaves circular with central stalk		Navelwort p.84 Marsh Pennywort p.94	
	Leaves ovate		Leaves opposite	Sea Sandwort p.40 Blinks p.44 Sea-purslane p.46 Serrated Wintergreen p.116
			Leaves alternate	Goosefoots p.44 Sea Beet p.46 Pale Persicaria and Water-pepper p.108
	Leaves narrow		Leaves opposite	Cyphel and Annual Knawel p.42
			Leaves alternate	Sea-blites and Prickly Saltwort p.48 Bastard-toadflax p.92
	Leaves heart-shaped or arrow-shaped		Oraches p.46 Black Bindweed p.108	
	Leaves lobed or once divided		Lady's-mantles p.82 Ivy p.94 Rock Samphire p.100 White Bryony p.104	

5 or 7 petals regular flowers (contd) Stamens many	Leaves at top of stem undivided		*Stinking Hellebore p.2*
	Leaves at top of stem divided		*Green Hellebore p.2*
5 or 7 petals irregular flowers	Leaf teeth blunt	∿∿∿	*Water Figwort p.138*
	Leaf teeth sharp	⋁⋁⋁	*Common and Green Figwort p.138*
8 or more petals or many flowers in heads	Leaves opposite		*Bur-marigolds p.174*
	Leaves alternate		*Cudweeds p.180* *Canadian Fleabane p.182*
	Leaves much-divided		*Pineappleweed p.184* *Mugwort p.186*
Tubular flower lobes less than 1/10 length of tube	Leaves circular with central stalk		*Navelwort p.84*
	Leaves much-divided		*Parsley-piert p.82*

Yellow Flowers

0–2 petals	Flowers with central stalked fruit with 3 segments		*Spurges p.106*	
	Flowers not as above		Leaves much divided	*Goldilocks Buttercup p.4* *Meadow-rues p.8* *Greater Bladderwort p.150*
			Leaves opposite	*Wood Sage p.160* *Cow-wheats p.146* *Honeysuckles p.170*
			Leaves arrow-shaped	*Italian Lords-and-Ladies p.220*
4 petals regular flowers Petals separate	Stamens 6 or less		Pods' length over 3 times width opening from top	*Roseroot p.82* *Evening-primrose p.92*
			Pods' length over 3 times width opening from bottom	*Crucifers pp.12–15, 20–5*
			Pods' length less than 3 times width	*Great Yellow-cress p.22*
	Stamens numerous		*Poppies or Greater Celandine p.10*	
Petals joined	Whorled leaves' length *c.*2 times width		*Crosswort p.166*	
	Whorled leaves' length *c.*10 times width		*Lady's Bedstraw p.166*	
4 petals irregular flowers	Leaves absent or reduced to spines		*Gorses p.58*	
	Leaves opposite		Flowers with 5-toothed calyx	*Yellow Vetchling p.74* *Labiates pp.156, 160*
			Flowers with 4-toothed calyx	*Yellow-rattle p.146* *Yellow Bartsia p.148*

xv

Yellow Flowers (contd)

4 petals irregular flowers (contd)			Flowers with central stalked fruit with 3 segments	*Spurges p.106*
	Leaves alternate		*Dyer's Greenweed and Petty Whin p.58*	
	Leaves trifoliate		Flowers in heads	*Medicks p.60 Sulphur Clover p.62 Trefoils p.66*
			Flowers in spikes	*Melilots p.62*
	Leaves in fives		*Bird's-foot-trefoils p.68*	
	Leaves pinnate		*Kidney Vetch p.68 Horseshoe Vetch p.70*	
	Leaves feathery		*Yellow Corydalis p.12*	
3 or 6 petals regular flowers	Leaves circular in outline		*Winter Aconite p.2 Yellow Water-lily p.8 Yellow-wort p.124*	
	Leaves linear – net-veined		*Golden Dock p.112*	
	Leaves linear – parallel-veined		*Bog Asphodel p.204 Yellow Star-of-Bethlehem p.206 Yellow Iris p.210 Sweet-flag p.220*	
3 or 6 petals irregular flowers	Leaves oval and toothed		*Balsams p.56*	
	Leaves oval and smooth-edged		*Musk Orchid p.214*	
	Leaves much-divided		*Wild Mignonette p.24*	
5 or 7 petals regular flowers	Stamens many		Leaves circular, floating	*Yellow Water-lily p.8*

			Leaves narrow, alternate		*Spearworts p.6*
			Leaves oval or round, opposite		*Common Rock-rose p.28* *St John's-worts pp.30–3*
			Leaves lobed, circular in outline		*Buttercups pp.4–7* *Cinquefoils p.78*
			Leaves pinnate, lobes divided		*Silverweed p.78* *Agrimonies p.80*
			Leaves trifoliate		*Tormentil p.78* *Sibbaldia p.80*
	Stamens 10 or less		Leaves alternate		*Stonecrops p.84* *Yellow Saxifrage p.86* *Hare's-ear p.96* *Pale Persicaria p.108* *Changing Forget-me-not p.130*
			Leaves opposite		*Pimpernel and Loosestrife p.120* *Fringed Waterlily p.126*
			Leaves in rosette at base		*Primrose and Cowslip p.120* *Mulleins p.136*
			Leaves lobed or once divided		*Alexanders p.96* *Henbane p.134*
			Leaves much divided		*Carrot Family (Umbelliferae) pp.98–105*
			Leaves trifoliate		*Yellow-sorrels p.56*
5 or 7 petals irregular flowers	Flowers with spurs		*Pansies p.28* *Common Toadflax p.136* *Fluellens p.138*		
	Flowers without spurs		Green plants with round, opposite leaves		*Monkeyflower and Musk p.140* *Honeysuckles p.170*
			Yellow/brown plants with scale-like leaves		*Yellow Bird's-nest p.118* *Broomrapes p.148*

Yellow Flowers (contd)

8 or more petals or many flowers in heads ✳	Single flowers with many separate petals ✳	Leaves undivided and rounded in outline ◯	Lesser Celandine p.8 Yellow-wort p.124
		Leaves deeply lobed 🍀	Globeflower p.2
		Leaves succulent – boat-shaped ▷	Hottentot-fig p.44
	Many flowers together in compact heads 🌾	With no conspicuous ray florets ⊕	Bur-marigolds p.174 Groundsels p.176 Ploughman's-spikenard p.178 Cudweeds p.180 Sea Aster p.182 Tansy and Mugwort p.186
		With both ray and disc florets ✿	Ragworts and Groundsels pp.174–77 Leopard's-bane p.176 Elecampane, Golden-samphire and Fleabane p.178 Goldenrod p.182 Corn Marigold p.186 Carline Thistle p.188
		With ray florets only ✸	Nipplewort, Cat's-ear, Hawkbits and Oxtongues p.194 Goat's-beard, Lettuces and Sow-thistles p.196 Dandelions and Hawk's-beards p.198 Hawk's-beard and Hawkweeds p.200

Tubular flowers lobes less than 1/10 length of tube	Flowers with frill at base of tube	Wild Daffodil p.210
	Flowers without frill at base of tube	Comfreys p.128

Blue Flowers

2 petals	Milkworts p.28				
4 petals regular flowers	Petals separate		Dame's-violet p.22		
	Petals joined		Field Gentian p.126		
4 petals irregular flowers	Leaves pinnate		Tares p.70 Vetches p.72 Marsh Pea p.74		
	Leaves opposite		Flowers with broad pods often with 2 segments		Speedwells pp.140–5
			Flowers with tubular calyx		Labiates pp.154–61
3 or 6 petals regular flowers	Petals separate		Pasqueflower p.2		
	Petals joined		Bluebell and Squills p.206		
3 or 6 petals irregular flowers	Violet Helleborine p.212				
5 or 7 petals regular flowers	Leaves undivided		Leaves opposite		Pale Flax p.50 Periwinkles p.124 Gentians p.124–7
			Leaves alternate		Borage, Green Alkanet and Bugloss p.128 Forget-me-nots p.130 Bellflowers p.164
			Leaves both opposite and alternate, lies prostrate on beaches		Oysterplant p.132

Blue Flowers (contd)

5 or 7 petals regular flowers (contd)	Leaves pinnate	🌿	*Jacob's-ladder p.126*			
	Leaves otherwise divided	🌿	*Flowers with spurs*	🌿	*Columbine p.8*	
			Flowers without spurs	🌿	*Meadow Crane's-bill p.52*	
5 or 7 petals irregular flowers	Flowers with spurs	🌿	*Violets p.26 Common Butterwort p.150*			
	Flowers without spurs	🌿	*Monk's-hood p.2 Viper's-bugloss p.132*			
8 or more petals or many flowers in heads	Leaves opposite	🌿	*Scabiouses p.172*			
	Leaves alternate	🌿	*Flowers with radiating petals*	🌸	*Asters p.182 Chicory p.192*	
			Flowers without radiating petals	⬤	*Sea-holly p.94 Round-headed Rampion and Sheep's-bit p.164*	
Tubular flowers lobes less than 1/10 length of tube	*Grape Hyacinth p.206*					

Red or Purple Flowers

0–2 petals	Leaves opposite		Crested Cow-wheat p.146 Honeysuckles p.170		
	Leaves arrow-shaped		Lords-and-Ladies p.220		
	Leaves much-divided		Meadow-rues p.8		
4 petals regular flowers	Petals joined		Mints p.152 Thymes p.154		
	Petals separate		Poppies p.10 Great Burnet p.82 Heather p.114		
4 petals irregular flowers	Leaves opposite		Flowers with tubular calyx		Labiates p.154–9
			Flowers with narrow pods		Eyebright p.146 Bartsias p.148 Bear's-breech p.150
	Leaves alternate – grass-like		Grass Vetchling p.74		
	Leaves spirally arranged		Rose-bay Willowherb p.90		
	Leaves trifoliate		Lucerne p.60 Clovers pp.62–5		
	Leaves pinnate		Without tendrils		Kidney Vetch and Purple Milk-vetch p.68
			With tendrils		Vetches pp. 70–5 Sea Pea p.74
3 or 6 petals regular flowers	Leaves absent at flowering		Meadow Saffron p.204		
	Leaves narrow		Crowberry p.118 Fritillary p.204 Stinking Iris, Crocus and Montbretia p.210		

3 or 6 petals regular flowers (contd)	Leaves arrow-shaped		Sheep's Sorrel p.110		
	Leaves opposite or in 3s		Mossy Stonecrop p.84 Purple-loosestrife p.88		
	Leaves alternate		Wood Dock p.112 Martagon Lily p.204		
3 or 6 petals irregular flowers	Flowers without spurs		Dark-red Helleborine p.212		
	Flowers with long narrow spurs		Fragrant Orchid p.216 Pyramidal Orchid p.220		
	Flowers with short thick spurs		Orchids and Marsh-orchids p.218		
	Flowers with lower lips like insects		Bee, Fly and Spider Orchids p.216		
5 or 7 petals regular flowers Stamens many	Leaves lobed		Common Mallow p.50		
	Leaves pinnate		Marsh Cinquefoil p.76 Water Avens p.80		
Stamens 10 or less	Leaves undivided, opposite or in 3s		Petals separate		Red Campion p.32 Purple Saxifrage p.86 Purple-loosestrife p.88 Scarlet Pimpernel p.122
			Petals joined		Autumn Gentian p.126 Red Valerian p.172
	Leaves undivided, some, at least, alternate		Petals separate		Orpine p.82
			Petals joined		Hound's-tongue p.128 Deadly Nightshade p.134 Venus'-looking-glass p.164
	Leaves strongly toothed or lobed		Crane's-bills p.52 Henbane and Bittersweet p.134		

	Leaves once or more divided		Crane's-bills p.52 Stork's-bills p.54		
5 or 7 petals irregular flowers	Flowers with spurs		*Snapdragon and Toadflaxes p.136*		
	Flowers without spurs		*Blood-drop-emlets p.140* *Ivy Broomrape p.148*		
8 or more petals regular flowers or many flowers in heads	Single flowers with many separate petals and succulent, boat-shaped leaves		*Hottentot-fig p.44*		
	Many flowers together in compact heads		Leaves opposite		*Red Valerian and Teasel p.172*
			Flowers with radiating petals		*Asters and Blue Fleabane p.182* *Knapweeds p.192* *Fox-and-cubs p.200*
			Flowers without radiating petals		*Burdocks p.188* *Thistles pp.188–93* *Knapweeds and Saw-wort p.192*
Tubular flowers lobes less than 1/10 length of tube	Dwarf shrubs with needle-like leaves		*Bell Heather p.114* *Crowberry p.118*		
	Herbs with smooth-edged, oval leaves		*Common Comfrey p.128* *Foxglove p.140*		

Pink, Rose or Lilac Flowers

4 petals regular flowers Petals joined	Leaves narrow	⬭	*Squinancywort p.166*			
	Leaves oval in whorls		*Field Madder p.166*			
	Leaves opposite		*Vervain p.150* *Mints pp.150–3*			
	Leaves in rosette at base		*Hoary Plantain p.162*			
Petals separate	Pods over 3 times width		Leaves opposite		*Willowherbs pp.88–91*	
			Leaves pinnate		*Sea Rocket p.14* *Cuckooflower p.20*	
	Pods less than 3 times width		*Opium poppy p.10*			
4 petals irregular flowers	Leaves opposite		Flowers with tubular calyx		*Labiates pp.154–61*	
			Flowers with broad pods often with 2 segments		*Speedwells p.142*	
	Leaves trifoliate		Flowers solitary in leaf axils		*Restharrows p.58*	
			Flowers in clustered heads		*Clovers pp.64–7*	
	Leaves pinnate		Flowers in loose spikes		*Sainfoin p.70* *Everlasting-peas p.74* *Louseworts p.146*	
			Flowers in clustered heads		*Crown Vetch p.70*	
	Leaves much-divided		*Common Fumitory p.12*			

3 or 6 petals regular flowers	Leaves narrow, less than 7mm long		Crowberry p.118	
	Leaves narrow, over 10cm long		Flowering-rush p.202 Wild Onion, Field Garlic and Chives p.208	
	Leaves less than 3 times width		Water-plantains p.202	
3 or 6 petals irregular flowers	Flowers with spurs		Flowers long-stalked	Indian Balsam p.56
			Flowers stalkless in spikes	Common Spotted-orchid and Early Marsh-orchid p.218
	Flowers without spurs		Bee Orchid p.216	
5 or 7 petals irregular flowers Stamens 10 or less	Leaves absent, twining plant		Dodder p.134	
	Leaves undivided		Stem leaves without stalks – opposite Plants erect	Pink Family pp.32–5 Pink Purslane p.44 Centauries p.124 Cornsalads p.172
			Plants creeping	Sand Spurrey and Sea-Spurries p.42 Trailing Azalea p.114 Bog Pimpernel and Sea-milkwort p.122 Twinflower p.170
			Leaves without stalks – alternate	Hairy Stonecrop p.84 Bistorts and Redshank p.108 Chaffweed p.122 Lungwort p.130
			Some leaves with stalks	Pink Purslane p.44 Bistorts p.108
			Leaves in rosette at base	Sea-lavenders and Bird's-eye Primrose p.118
			Leaves lobed or once divided	Crane's-bills pp.52–5 Stork's-bills pp.54 Valerians p.170

5 or 7 petals irregular flowers (contd)	Leaves trifoliate		*Bogbean p.126*
	Leaves much-divided or feathery		*Herb-Robert and Stork's-bills p.54* *Water-violet p.120*
Stamens many	Leaves lobed		*Mallows p.50*
	Leaves with 3 or 5 leaflets		*Brambles p.76*
5 or 7 petals irregular flowers	Flowers with spurs		*Violets p.26* *Pansies p.28* *Toadflaxes pp.136–9* *Lesser Snapdragon p.138* *Pale Butterwort p.150*
	Flowers without spurs		*Water Lobelia p.164*
8 or more petals regular flowers or many flowers in heads	Leaves absent		*Dodder p.134*
	Leaves opposite		*Valerians p.170* *Cornsalads p.172*
	Leaves large, basal		*Butterbur and Winter Heliotrope p.178*
Tubular flowers lobes less than 1/10 length of tube	Climbing or trailing herbs with heart-shaped leaves		*Bindweeds p.132*
	Trailing shrubs with oval leaves		*Bilberries and Cranberry p.116*
	Trailing shrubs with narrow or needle-like leaves		*Bog-rosemary and Cross-leaved Heath p.114*
	herbs with oval leaves		*Russian Comfrey p.128*

SPECIAL 'KEYS' TO TWO FAMILIES

The two families for which these extra 'keys' are provided are those in which, in our experience, most field botanists have real difficulty in recognising species or genera, and in which recourse to the standard technical floras may still leave them feeling baffled.

Like the General Identification Keys (see pp.viii–xxvi) the special keys begin with the headings in the first, extreme left column. For further explanation see *How to use this Guide* on p.vi. *Note* that phrases in brackets in the third column merely corroborate your choice in the second column: if – we hope this is rare – the phrase does not agree with your specimen, there is something wrong.

S.M. Walters who prepared these keys, would like to express his indebtedness to that excellent book by John Hayward entitled *A New Key to Wild Flowers* (Cambridge University Press, 1987). It will be obvious to users that much has been learned in terms of presentation from Hayward's book.

Daisy and Dandelion Family (Compositae), yellow flowered

The key includes all yellow-flowered 'daisy-like' and 'dandelion-like' *Compositae* – technically those with heads of both ray and disk florets and with heads of ray florets only. *N.B.* Colt's-foot has very few disk florets and may be incorrectly looked for among dandelions.

Heads of yellow disk florets and yellow ray florets ('daisy' type)	Heads single on long stems	Stem with bracts only	Colt's-foot p.176
		Stem with leaves:	
		heads more than 6cm	Elecampane p.178
		heads 4–6cm	Leopard's-bane p.176 and Corn Marigold p.186
	Heads grouped in various ways	Hairless plants (sea coast)	Golden Samphire p.178
		Leaves clasping stem	Common Fleabane p.178
		Heads in narrow spikes	Goldenrod p.182
		Not as above	Ragworts and Groundsels p.174–6
Heads of yellow ray florets only, on a leafless stem ('dande-lion' type)	Plant with runners	(Leaves white-felted beneath)	Mouse-ear Hawkweed p.200
	(Copious milky juice when broken)		Dandelions p.198
	Stem unbranched with bracts near head	Leaves not grass-like	Hawkbits p.194
	Stem usually branched with scattered bracts	Scales present between florets in head	Cat's-ear p.194
		Bracts numerous near heads	Autumn Hawkbit p.194
		Not as above	Hawkweeds p.200

Heads of yellow ray florets only, on a leafy stem ✻	Achenes with no pappus	Heads many, small, stalked	*Nipplewort p.194*
	Stems with prickles or bristles	Stout, branched plants	*Oxtongues p.194*
	Stems with copious milky juice when broken	Heads with 5 ray florets	*Wall Lettuce p.196*
		Heads with several ray florets	*Lettuces, many Sow-thistles and Goat's-beard p.196*
	Stems with little visible milky juice when broken	Involucral bracts in 2 distinct rows, the outer much shorter than the inner	*Hawk's-beards p.198*
		Involucral bracts not in 2 distinct rows	*Hawkweeds p.200*

N.B. Very small specimens of the smooth hawk's beard (a common plant) may not have developed stem-leaves. Beware ! The **dunce's-cap shaped fruiting heads** are diagnostic.

Carrot Family (Umbelliferae)

Flowers in umbels with bracts and bracteoles (see p.94). Fruit splits into two 1-seeded carpels.

Note:

The small Marsh Pennywort, *Hydrocotyle,* is very different from other members of the family. Its round leaves with central stalks are unmistakable in wet places. The other easily-recognised *umbellifer* is the Sea-holly *Eryngium* (p.94); it has **spiny** leaves and heads of flowers. All others are keyed here.

Yellow or Greenish-Yellow Flowers	Hairy plant (all other yellow flowered members are hairless)	(Common on roadsides on limy soils)	*Wild Parsnip p.104*
	Shiny, rather fleshy-leaved plants (mainly sea-side)	Ripe fruits dull black	*Alexanders p.96*
		Ripe fruits greenish or purplish	*Rock Samphire p.100*
	Small annual with undivided leaves	(On saltmarshes and by tidal rivers)	*Slender Hare's-ear p.96*
	Leaves very finely divided into thread-like segments	(Plant with 'fennel' smell)	*Fennel p.102*
	Leaves with more or less triangular segments	Plant with 'celery' smell	*Wild Celery p.98*

		Plant with 'parsley' smell	*Garden Parsley p.98*
	Leaves with narrow segments	(Only faint smell)	*Pepper-saxifrage p.102*
White Flowers	Fruit narrow and cylindrical (more than 2cm)	(Annual weed)	*Shepherd's-needle p.94*
	Fruit bristly	Bracts divided	*Wild Carrot p.104*
		Bracts entire or absent	*Bur Chervil p.94 and Hedge-parsleys p.96*
	Stem with purple spots	Stem rough, hairy	*Rough Chervil p.94*
		Stem smooth, hairless	*Hemlock p.96*
	Leaves simple	Stem leaf surrounding stem	*False Thorow-wax p.96*
		Leaves palmately lobed	*Sanicle p.94*
	Larger leaves 3-pinnate	Leaves with white blotches: plant smelling of aniseed	*Sweet Cicely p.96*
		Small, northern grassland plant with finely-cut leaves	*Spignel p.102*
		Common plant found by road-sides in spring	*Cow Parsley p.94*
		Marsh or water plants	*Water-dropworts pp.100–103 and Milk-parsley p.104*
	Leaves ternate or 1–2 pinnate	Tall robust plants with thick stems: On roadsides and waste places	*Hogweeds p.104*
		In marshes or water: stem purplish	*Wild Angelica p.102*
		Leaves 1-pinnate	*Greater Water-parsnip p.100*
		Leaves 2-pinnate (rare) Small or medium-sized plants	*Cowbane p.98*
		Shiny-leaved plant of northern coasts	*Scots Lovage p.102*
		Not as above – see next page	

White Flowers Small or medium-sized lowland plants with ternate or 1–2 pinnate leaves	Leaves 'yarrow-like' with fine segments, appearing whorled	(Rather rare, only in the west)	*Whorled Caraway p.98*
	Marsh or water plants	Bracts many, leaf-like	*Lesser Water-parsnip p.100*
		Bracts usually absent	*Apium species p.98*
	Plants of roadsides, grassland or arable land	Annual weed with long vertically-hanging bracteoles	*Fool's Parsley p.102*
		Leaf-segments broad; Leaves ternate	*Ground-elder p.100*
		Leaf-segments broad; leaves pinnate; no bracts or bracteoles	*Greater Burnet-saxifrage p.100*
		Leaf-segments broad; leaves pinnate; both bracts and bracteoles	*Corn Parsley p.98*
		Leaf-segments narrow; bracts 2–4	*Stone Parsley p.98*
		Leaf-segments narrow; bracts 0 (1); bracteoles 2–5	*Pignut p.98*
		Leaf-segments narrow; no bracts or bracteoles	*Burnet-saxifrage p.100*

THE SPECIES

Diocotyledons

All but the last 20 pages of this book are devoted to the
Diocotyledons. They have leaves which are generally not
parallel-veined like the Monocotyledons and their flowers
are typically in 4s or 5s not in 3s. Technically the character
which gave the name is that there are a pair of seed-leaves
(cotyledons) in the germinated seedling, not the single one of
the Monocotyledons.

Buttercup Family (Ranunculaceae)

The Buttercup Family is very variable having flowers not only with the unjoined 'petals' in 4s (meadow-rues) or 5s (buttercups) but in 6s (pasqueflower) or numerous (marsh-marigold). The number of carpels varies from 3 (hellebores) to numerous (buttercups): however they do all have a large number of stamens. Flowers may be regular and circular (buttercups) or irregular and obviously oriented in one direction (monk's-hood). Thankfully the generic characteristics are clearer than the family ones.

Marsh-marigold
Caltha palustris
Distinguished from all other 'buttercups' by the **large flowers, up to 5cm across, and glossy, kidney-shaped, deep-green leaves**. Flowers of 5–8 petal-like sepals, all yellow. The unopened golden buds were once gathered and used as a substitute for capers. Each flower produces up to *c.* 10 follicles up to 1.5cm long.

Identifiable from a distance as large clumps of golden yellow on stream banks in spring and early summer. Also in marshes and woods throughout British Isles to over 1000m.

P   50cm   Spring and summer

Globeflower
Trollius europaeus
The only 'buttercup' with **flowers up to 3cm across, more than 5 'petals' and leaves deeply divided into 3–5 toothed segments**. The 'petals', which are really sepals, never fully open retaining the globe-like shape. Sepals hide the 5–15 narrow true petals which have nectaries at the base. Each flower produces many transversely wrinkled follicles up to 1.2cm long.

Damp upland meadows, mountain woods and ledges. Throughout Britain from Gwent northwards, generally over 300m. Only in NW Ireland.

P   60cm   Summer

Stinking Hellebore
Helleborus foetidus
The 'winter green' hellebore distinguished from *H. viridis* by having **leaves at top of stem undivided** and without teeth and by the numerous 1–3cm diameter **globe-shaped, drooping, not open, flowers**. Each flower has 5 greenish petaloid sepals with a reddish-purple border and 5–10 nectaries at the base attractive to bees, numerous (30–50) stamens and 2–5 (usually 3) wrinkled follicles. Plant emits an unpleasant odour if bruised.

Scattered in lime-rich woods and scrub of lowland England: a rare garden escape elsewhere.

P   80cm   Early spring

Green Hellebore
Helleborus viridis
The smaller of the two hellebores with **stems and leaves developing narrow–toothed segments**. Each plant has only 2–4 flowers which have 5 yellowish-green **sepals spreading almost flat** and lacking any reddish-purple border. The plant has only 2–4 flowers which have 5 yellowish-green **sepals spreading almost flat** and lacking any reddish-purple border. The (usually) 3 follicles are not wrinkled as in stinking hellebore.

Local in damp lime-rich woods and scrub in lowland England: garden escape elsewhere.

P   40cm   Early spring

Winter Aconite
Eranthis hyemalis
Recognised from a distance as a sheet of gold beneath bare trees in January and February. Close up notice **each stem has a solitary terminal flower surrounded by a ruff of 3 stalkless, deeply-lobed leaves**. Flowers have 6 petaloid sepals and *c.* 30 stamens, and produce *c.* 6 stalked, brown follicles up to 1.5cm long. After flowering a single, circular, lobed and stalked leaf grows from the tuberous rhizome below ground.

Introduced and scattered through lowland Britain.

P   15cm   Winter

Monk's-hood
Aconitum napellus
The spikes of **helmet-shaped, mauve flowers on tall stems with divided, fan-shaped, stalked lower leaves** and stalkless upper leaves are unmistakable. Each flower is made from 5 sepals, the upper forming the monk's-hood which hides 2 petaloid nectaries. Below is a large cluster of stamens surrounding 3 carpels which develop into hairless follicles up to 2cm.

The native variant grows on shady stream sides in SW England and S Wales. Cultivated forms often occur as garden escapes.

P   1m   Early summer

Wood Anemone
Anemone nemorosa
Sheets of white flowers carpeting woodland floors before the trees are in leaf readily identify this species: confirmed by the **sepals**, sometimes pink-tinged, **varying in number between 6 and 9 and the 3 divided stem-leaves in a whorl below the solitary stalked flower**. 1 or 2 larger leaves develop from the base after flowering and persist to mid-summer when the rest of the plant has withered.

Woods, hedgebanks and in mountains to 800m throughout British Isles but rare in southern Ireland.

P   30cm   Spring

Pasqueflower
Pulsatilla vulgaris
The beautiful, **bell-like, violet flowers up to 5cm across in lime-rich grassland in April and May** are unmistakable. Each 6-sepalled flower is on a short stalk above a whorl of woolly, deeply-divided, sessile leaves. Larger, carrot-like, leaves form a rosette at the stem base. Flowers start upright showing many bright yellow anthers, droop with age but, when fruits are ripe, the stalk elongates pushing feathery achenes up for wind dispersal.

Old chalk and limestone grassland in central and E England north to R Humber.

P   30cm   Spring

Caltha palustris

Trollius europaeus

Helleborus foetidus

Helleborus viridis

Eranthis hyemalis

Aconitum napellus

Anemone nemorosa

Pulsatilla vulgaris

Buttercups

Buttercups have regular flowers with 3–5 sepals and, usually, 5 yellow petals (sometimes more or none) each with a nectar-secreting pit near the base. There are always a large number of stamens and single-seeded fruits (achenes).

Meadow Buttercup
Ranunculus acris
The tallest of the 3 common buttercups, immediately **recognised in flower or fruit by the unfurrowed, hairy stalk below each flower which is only c. half the diameter of bulbous or creeping buttercup: the sepals are upright encircling the petals**. Vegetatively distinguished by the basal leaves divided and roundish in outline, and the absence of both a bulbous base to the stem and runners.

Throughout British Isles in damp meadows. On mountain ledges up to 1200m in Scotland.
P 90cm Late spring and summer

Creeping Buttercup
Ranunculus repens
The most widespread of the 3 common buttercups, **recognised by the furrowed, hairy stalks below each flower and sepals encircling the petals**. Petals vary in number from 4–13, most frequently 5 or 6. Vegetatively distinguished by basal and lower stem-leaves with a long-stalked middle lobe, absence of a bulbous base to the stem and long surface runners, by which it forms large circular patches in grassland.

Throughout British Isles in 1000m in wet meadows, damp woods, sand-dunes and gravel pits and quarries.
P 60cm Spring and summer

Bulbous Buttercup
Ranunculus bulbosus
The least frequent of the 3 common buttercups, **identified by the furrowed, hairy stalks below each flower and sepals turned down encircling the stalk**. Vegetatively recognised by basal and lower stem leaves with long-stalked middle lobe, the absence of runners and by the bulbous base to the upright stem which may still be found when the rest of the plant dies down in mid-summer.

Dry, especially lime-rich, pastures to 550m throughout British Isles.
P 45cm Late spring and early summer

Corn Buttercup
Ranunculus arvensis
One of 2 buttercups with fruits covered in spines or hooked bristles but distinguished from small-flowered buttercup by 5-petalled **flowers up to 1.2cm across with spreading sepals on unfurrowed, hairy stalks. Spines on fruits over 1mm long**. Vegetatively recognised by the hardly divided, spoon-shaped, stalked lower leaves and the upper leaves deeply 3-lobed and stalkless: all more or less hairless.

Once common in cornfields throughout lowland England but much reduced by weed-killers.
A 70cm Summer

Hairy Buttercup
Ranunculus sardous
Similar to bulbous buttercup with **sepals turned down to surround the furrowed stalk** but an annual, lacking the bulbous base to the stem and recognised by the **pale yellow flowers with fruits** which are not completely smooth but **have a ring of tiny tubercles next to the well-marked green border**. The whole plant is hairy like small-flowered buttercup but most leaves are triangular in outline and deeply 3-lobed to the midrib.

Infrequent weed of damp places, especially near the coast throughout lowland Britain.
A 45cm Summer and autumn

Small-flowered Buttercup
Ranunculus parviflorus
The **bristles all over the fruits** are much shorter than those of corn buttercup and **strongly hooked at the tip**. The **flowers**, up to **only 6mm across, with 5 or fewer tiny petals are on furrowed, hairy stalks with sepals turned back**. The whole plant is hairy and all the roundish leaves are lobed half way to the mid-vein or more: the lower into 5 main segments, the upper in 3.

Scattered in arable fields and dry open grassland throughout lowland England, Wales and SE Ireland; frequent only in SW.
A 40cm Late spring and early summer

Goldilocks Buttercup
Ranunculus auricomus
Differs from all other buttercups in having most **flowers with few petals: some with none**, others 1 or 2, whilst 5 may be found only occasionally. Where petals are missing the sepals may be coloured yellow in their place. **Leaves** also distinctive: **the lower stalked, roundish or kidney-shaped**, toothed or shallowly lobed; the upper deeply 3–5 lobed, reduced to linear segments below the hairy, unfurrowed flower stalk.

Woods and shady hedgerows to 500m throughout British Isles but rare in north and west.
P 40cm Spring

Ranunculus acris

Ranunculus repens

Ranunculus bulbosus

Ranunculus arvensis

Ranunculus sardous

Ranunculus parviflorus

Ranunculus auricomus

Greater Spearwort
Ranunculus lingua
Spearworts are 'buttercups' with long, narrow, undivided leaves with few teeth on the margin. Greater spearwort has **large glossy flowers up to 5cm across on tall stems** normally growing with their feet in water. All the leaves have a bluish sheen and those at the base, which are blunt and heart-shaped, disappear before flowering. The **flower stalks are hairy but unfurrowed**.
Widely scattered throughout the lowlands of British Isles in marshes and fens but much reduced by drainage.
P 1.2m Summer and early autumn

Lesser Spearwort
Ranunculus flammula
Distinguished from greater spearwort by the small **flowers, less than 2.5cm across**, on short **stems rarely exceeding 50cm**. The **flower stalks are furrowed but only slightly hairy**. Plants are often prostrate at the base and spread by runners which root at nodes. The leaves, which lack any bluish sheen, have a burning taste, hence the Latin name *flammula* – a little flame. Both spearworts are poisonous to cattle.
Common in wet places throughout British Isles to 900m.
P 50cm Summer and early autumn

Celery-leaved Buttercup
Ranunculus sceleratus
A plant of bare mud recognised by its **glossy leaves, 5-sided or kidney-shaped** in outline and divided into 3–5 toothed lobes. The fleshy, hollow, branched, hairless stem arises from the centre bearing very **small flowers only c.1cm across** on furrowed, hairy stalks. After the petals fall each **flower** produces **an oblong head with 70–100 tiny fruits**. A poisonous plant – all parts produce blisters if they touch the skin.
Muddy pond, stream and ditch sides throughout lowland British Isles.
A 60cm Late spring to autumn

Crowfoots and Water-crowfoots

Crowfoots and water-crowfoots are 'buttercups' with white flowers which nearly always have their 'feet' (and often their 'bodies' as well) in or near water.

Ivy-leaved Crowfoot
Ranunculus hederaceus
This is the more widespread of the 2 crowfoots which lack finely dissected submerged leaves, and the only one normally found in central and eastern Britain. Distinguished from round-leaved crowfoot by the **ivy-shaped leaves, with their lobes broadest at the base**, where there are often dark marks, and the **small flowers up to 6mm across** with petals scarcely longer than sepals.
On mud and in shallow water throughout British Isles to 650m in Wales.
A or P 10cm Summer

Round-leaved Crowfoot
Ranunculus omiophyllus
This other crowfoot lacking finely dissected submerged leaves is distinguished from ivy-leaved crowfoot by the **circular to kidney-shaped leaves with their lobes broadest in the middle**, never with dark marks at the base, and by the **larger flowers up to 1.2cm across** with petals twice as long as sepals
A species of the oceanic fringe of Western Europe found mainly in southern Ireland and S and W Britain, to 1000m in Wales.
A or P 10cm Summer

River Water-crowfoot
Ranunculus fluitans
One of 2 water-crowfoots found in fast-flowing water which may lack floating leaves. *R. fluitans* has **submerged leaves up to 50cm** with parallel divisions **2–3 times forked and overlapping the next leaf up the stem**. *R. penicillatus* which may have some floating leaves, **has submerged leaves up to 25cm** with the divisions arranged in a fan-shape **not usually overlapping the next leaf up the stem**.
Rivers and streams. *R. fluitans* rare outside the English lowlands. *R. penicillatus* widespread and dominant in Ireland.
P 6m long Summer

Thread-leaved Water-crowfoot
Ranunculus trichophyllus
A water-crowfoot of slow-moving or stagnant water, **lacking any floating leaves** and recognised by its **small flowers, less than 1cm across** with non-overlapping petals, and the **fan-shaped submerged leaves**. After flowering the stalks of the seed heads rarely exceed 4cm and they end in a hairy receptacle.
Shallow ponds, ditches and streams throughout the lowlands, mainly coastal in the west.
A or P Prostrate Late spring to mid-summer

Common Water-crowfoot
Ranunculus aquatilis
A water-crowfoot of slow-moving or stagnant water with **floating leaves** which **have lobes with pointed teeth**, as well as finely dissected submerged leaves. **Flowers** are small, **less than 1.8cm across**, with **fruiting stalks** which **rarely exceed 5cm** and do not taper towards the top.
The commonest water-crowfoot, found in ponds, ditches and streams throughout the lowlands of the British Isles especially on hard rocks.
A or P Prostrate Late spring and early summer

Ranunculus lingua

Ranunculus flammula

Ranunculus sceleratus

Ranunculus hederaceus

Ranunculus omiophyllus

Ranunculus fluitans

Ranunculus trichophyllus

Ranunculus aquatilis

Pond Water-crowfoot
Ranunculus peltatus
Another water-crowfoot of slow-moving or stagnant water with finely dissected submerged leaves but with kidney-shaped **floating leaves** which **have lobes with rounded teeth**. The **flowers** are larger than common water-crowfoot, **up to 3cm across**, with **fruiting stalks** which **reach 15cm** and taper towards the tip.

Shallow lakes, ponds and slow streams throughout the lowlands, more frequent on soft rocks.

A or P Prostrate Late spring and summer

Lesser Celandine
Ranunculus ficaria
A 'buttercup' with **glossy, heart-shaped leaves** and **bright yellow flowers with 8–12 petals** but only 3 sepals. Two common forms occur which can be distinguished when flowering is over: one has little white bulbils where the leaf-stalk joins the stem and usually lacks fertile seeds, the other has no bulbils but develops good seed. The former is abundant as a garden weed or in plantations whilst the latter is more usual in old grassland and native wood-lands.

Common throughout British Isles.

P 25cm Spring

Common Meadow-rue
Thalictrum flavum
Recognised by the **flowers** which, though lacking coloured petals, are made conspicuous by growing **in bunches with erect bright yellow anthers** on long slender filaments which flutter in the breeze. Each flower has 4 narrow white 'sepals' which soon fall. Differs from other meadow-rues in the **terminal leaflet** being **longer than broad** and the **fruits less than 2.5mm**.

Marshes, fens, and the banks of streams and rivers in the lowlands; rare in Scotland.

P 1m Summer

Alpine Meadow-rue
Thalictrum alpinum
Clusters of shiny leaves with 3-lobed leaflets on mountain rock look not unlike the fern, wall-rue, but in bloom this meadow-rue can be identified by the **slender, leafless, unbranched flowering stem** with about 10 flowers, each first drooping, later erect. Flowers have bright yellow anthers contrasting with pale violet filaments, and develop **fruits up to 3.5mm**.

Rocky slopes and ledges to *c.* 1300m in the mountains, descending to sea-level in the far north.

P 15cm Summer

Lesser Meadow-rue
Thalictrum minus
Also in the lowlands with a **branched flowering stem** like common meadow-rue but distinguished by its **separate, not bunched, flowers with drooping**, not erect, **stamens**, its **terminal leaflets as broad as long** and its **fruits up to 6mm**. A very variable plant – the form on sand-dunes in the north and west, with flowering stems branched at or below the middle, is sometimes regarded as a separate species.

Scattered in dry lime-rich grassland and rocks, damp places by streams and sand-dunes.

P 50cm Summer

Columbine
Aquilegia vulgaris
An unmistakable plant familiar to most gardeners. Each drooping **flower has 5 spurred petals**, with the spurs uppermost, **arranged like doves** sitting **round a feeder**: the alternating sepals resemble the wings. Hence the name 'columbine' which comes from the Latin *columba*, a dove.

Occurs as a native on lime-rich soils in wet woodland and damp grassland to 500m in the Lake District but also scattered on roadsides as an escape from cultivation.

P 1m Early summer

White Water-lily
Nymphaea alba
When in bloom there can be no mistaking the large floating **flowers up to 20cm across with 20–25 petals**, the outermost longer than the sepals. Before flowering it can be separated from yellow water-lily by its **round leaves with a split almost to half-way**: after flowering the spongy **berry-like fruit sinks below the surface**. In N Scotland and W Ireland a form occurs with small flowers only 5–12cm diameter.

Lakes and ponds to 350m: commoner than yellow water-lily in the north.

P Underwater stems to 3m Summer

Yellow Water-lily
Nuphar lutea
The large **flowers up to 6cm** are unmistakable: the 5–6 'petals' are sepals which hide the many spoon-shaped true petals inside. The flowers do not float but stand on stalks above the surface. Before flowering separated from white water-lily by its **oval leaves 'split' only ⅓ way across**: after flowering the large **flask-shaped fruit** (the brandy-bottle, which gives the plant another name) **ripens above the water**.

Lakes, ponds and slow-moving water throughout British Isles to 500m.

P Underwater stems to 2m Summer

Ranunculus peltatus

Ranunculus ficaria

Thalictrum flavum

Thalictrum alpinum

Thalictrum minus

Aquilegia vulgaris

Nymphaea alba

Nuphar lutea

Common Poppy
Papaver rhoeas

All our poppies have large flowers with **4 coloured petals, crimped in bud, inside 2 green sepals which fall off when the flower opens**. In the middle of the flower is a mass of dark stamens and the ovary, which develops into the familiar **pepper-pot capsule** from which the tiny seeds are shaken out through holes round the 'lid'. The common poppy has an **almost spherical capsule**, and its **petals** of rich scarlet colour **often have a dark blotch at the base**.

Throughout most of British Isles on newly-disturbed ground and waste places, formerly seen regularly in masses as a cornfield weed. In the north and west it is less common than the long-headed poppy.

A   60cm   Summer

Long-headed Poppy
Papaver dubium

Like the common poppy, but with paler, **unblotched** scarlet **petals** (see photograph) and a **long, smooth club-shaped capsule** (see drawing).

This poppy often grows with the common poppy, but is generally commoner in north and west Britain.

A   60cm   Summer

Prickly Poppy
Papaver argemone

Like common poppy and long-headed poppy, but with smaller flowers, and a **long capsule with prickly hairs** (see drawing).

Less common, but found in most of lowland England and Wales, extending to Scotland and Ireland.

A   40cm   Summer

Opium Poppy
Papaver somniferum

This poppy is unmistakable, with its **very large, pale lilac petals**, usually with a black blotch at the base, and its wavy, bluish-grey leaves.

It is not a native, but was formerly grown, mainly in the East Anglian fens, for the production of opium, and is still seen commonly in gardens and occasionally on waste ground throughout much of Britain.

A   1m   Summer

Welsh Poppy
Meconopsis cambrica

A **perennial** almost hairless herb with **yellow flowers**, differing from the true poppies mainly in the capsule which splits near the top into short teeth to release the seeds. The basal leaves are long-stalked and divided into pointed segments.

Very familiar in gardens, where it brightens many a shady corner as a ground-cover, but quite local as a native plant, in damp, shady and rocky places in SW England, Wales and Ireland.

P   50cm   Early summer

Yellow Horned-poppy
Glaucium flavum

One of the most handsome of our sea-shore plants, with **large yellow 'poppy flowers'** succeeded by **long, narrow, curved fruits** ('horns'), which split almost to the base when ripe into 2 parts. The leaves and stems are bluish-grey.

Locally common, mainly on shingle, round the coasts of W and S England and Wales, extending up the W coast to Arran and the E coast to Berwick: rare and decreasing in Ireland.

B or P   80cm   Summer

Greater Celandine
Chelidonium majus

The common name of this plant is misleading; it is not related to the lesser celandine (see p.8) and indeed does not much resemble it, except in flower colour. It is obviously a poppy relative, with its **yellow 4-petalled flowers** and rather bluish-grey stems and leaves. The long thin fruit splits from the base into 2 parts. The **stems when broken exude a bright orange poisonous juice**.

A doubtful native, occurring on banks and walls throughout lowland England and Wales, in scattered localities up to N Scotland and in much of Ireland.

P   80cm   Early summer

PODS

Papaver rhoeas

P. dubium

P. argemone

Papaver rhoeas

Papaver dubium

Papaver argemone

Papaver somniferum

Meconopsis cambrica

Glaucium flavum

Chelidonium majus

Fumitory Family (Fumariaceae)

Corydalis and fumitory are herbs, often climbing, closely related to poppies but have a watery, not milky or coloured, juice and tubular flowers with 2 kinds of petals, the outer 2 horizontal with a spur or sack at the base, the inner vertical and often joined. Fumitories have one-seeded pods and petals with dark tips, corydalis many-seeded pods and no dark tips to petals.

Climbing Corydalis
Corydalis claviculata
An annual with slender, brittle stems and much divided **leaves with blunt segments and tendrils** at the end by which it scrambles up hedges and over walls. The **flowering stalks have** only c. **6 flowers up to 6mm long**: petals cream, the outer with a short spur. The **2–3 seeded pods** are held erect.

Mainly on acid soils in woods and on shady banks up to c. 500m: rare in areas of low rainfall.
A   80cm   Summer

Yellow Corydalis
Corydalis lutea
A clump of pale green, **much divided leaves** growing out of the mortar of an old wall producing **stalks with 6–10 yellow flowers up to 1.8cm long** will be this species. Introduced as a garden plant from S Europe. The large black shiny seeds are attractive to ants which may carry them up to new crevices.

Widespread throughout the lowlands, especially in towns; rare in Ireland.
P   30cm   Late spring and summer

White Ramping-fumitory
Fumaria capreolata
A scrambling annual with much divided **leaves with pointed segments and lacking tendrils**. The flowering **stalks have c. 20 flowers up to 1.2cm long**. The **single-seeded pods** are **on short stalks which curve down** as the flowers age and wither.

Cultivated and waste ground and hedgebanks mainly near S and W coasts; rare except around the Moray Firth in Scotland.
A   1m   Late spring and summer

Common Fumitory
Fumaria officinalis
An upright weed with feathery grey-green leaves. The **flowering stalks have often over 20 pink flowers up to 8mm long**, the bare **stalk below much shorter than the part with flowers. The single-seeded pods remain upright after flowering.**

The commonest fumitory in arable fields and gardens in the lowlands but may be replaced in the west by common ramping-fumitory (*F. muralis*) **with 15 or fewer flowers on a stalk with the bare part below longer than the part with flowers.**
A   40cm   Late spring to autumn

Cabbage Family (Cruciferae)

Members of the cabbage family are recognised by their flowers with 4 free petals and sepals, 4 or 6 stamens, and pods made into 2 chambers by an often silvery divider.

Rape
Brassica napus
In spring-time rape now turns the lowland landscape into yellow squares where it is grown for the oil from its seeds. Escapes from cultivation are easily confused with wild turnip from which it may be separated by the **pale-yellow petals 1.1–1.8cm long**, and the **flower buds overtopping or equalling the flowers**, as clearly shown on the stems without pods in the foreground of the photograph.

Road verges and waste places throughout the lowlands.
A   1m   Late spring and summer

Wild Turnip
Brassica rapa
Turnips are also cultivated, mainly as a winter food for sheep which are folded in the crop in winter. Difficult to separate from rape but usually with **deep yellow petals less than 1.1cm long** and **flowers overtopping or equalling the buds**. However beware! – the buds of rape may abort so that the flowers then overtop them and it looks like wild turnip. Petal length is the best character.

Widespread escape from cultivation on roadsides and in waste places.
A   1m   Late spring and summer

Corydalis claviculata

Corydalis lutea

Fumaria capreolata

Fumaria officinalis

Brassica napus

Brassica rapa

Black Mustard
Brassica nigra
There are 2 kinds of mustard, black and white. They are difficult to separate in flower but easy in fruit. Black mustard has **erect 4-sided pods clinging to branches** held at a wide angle to the main stem. These pods **produce** the **reddish-brown seeds** which are the main source of the condiment. More mustard is used throughout the world than any other flavouring.

Lowland England, especially stream and river banks and coastal cliffs in the south-west and Wales.
A 1m Summer

White Mustard
Sinapis alba
The **pods** of white mustard are unmistakable: they **end in a flattened, often sabre-shaped, curved beak which equals or exceeds the seeded part**. The **pods** are **held away from the branches** which are at less than 45° to the main stem. The pods **produce yellowish seeds** which are often mixed with black mustard before being crushed to produce the oil of mustard. Also grown as a green manure or fodder crop.

Weed of arable and waste land throughout the lowlands.
A 80cm Summer

Charlock
Sinapis arvensis
Similar to white mustard but the **pod has a straight not curved beak** which is only **a little over** half as long as the seeded part. Before pods are mature **distinguished from white mustard by the simple and stalkless, not divided and stalked, upper leaves, and from black mustard by the spreading not half erect, sepals**.

A troublesome weed of cornfields throughout British Isles to 500m, now controlled by weed-killers but seeds persist in the soil for 50 years.
A 80cm Late spring and summer

Radishes

Radishes are distinguished from other crucifers **by their hairy cylindrical pods, over 3 times as long as broad, which break up into one-seeded joints**. Their **sepals** are **erect** surrounding the long claws of the petals. (*N.B.* the sepals are not spreading as in charlock, with which it may be confused in flower.)

Wild Radish
Raphanus raphanistrum
Wild radish has petals varying from yellow to lilac or white, often with darker veins on a paler ground. The **pods have up to 8 joints** and a **terminal beak 4–5 times the length of the top joint**.

An arable weed throughout the lowlands, especially on acid soils; the yellow-flowered forms are commonest in the north and west.
A 60cm Late spring and summer

Sea Radish
Raphanus maritimus
A taller and more handsome plant than wild radish forming extensive colonies on the driftline of sandy or rocky shores. Distinguished by the **pods** which **have**, usually, **only 3 or fewer joints** with the **beak less than twice the length of the top joint**. Normally yellow-flowered but a white form has been recorded in the Channel Isles.

Sea-shores, but very rare on the east coast north of the Wash.
B or P 1m Summer

Annual Wall-rocket
Diplotaxis muralis
Also called 'stinkweed' because of the nasty smell produced by rubbing the leaves. Distinguished from other crucifers by the **pods much longer than their stalks, ending in a short seedless beak**, by the **change in angle upwards where pod and stalk join** and by the 2 rows of seeds. Perennial wall-rocket (*D. tenuifolia*) has **pods longer than stalks and stems hairless below, not stiffly hairy as in annual wall-rocket**.

Rocks, walls and waste places throughout the lowlands but rare in the north.
A 60cm Summer

Sea-kale
Crambe maritima
Found almost entirely on shingle beaches where it is easily recognised by its **bluish-green, cabbage-like leaves** and large **clusters of pure-white flowers with a dark centre**. These develop into **spherical, one-seeded pods** which are distributed by wind and sea: they can float in salt water for over 20 days and still germinate.

A rare coastal plant absent from most of Ireland and the northern half of Scotland. Once more common: decline perhaps due to former exploitation as a vegetable.
P 60cm Summer

Sea Rocket
Cakile maritima
One of the most frequent shoreline plants distinguished by the way it often grows in colonies and by its smooth, **fleshy, lobed leaves** and lilac or white petals. Flowers develop **2-jointed pods, the upper twice as long as the lower, which is often seedless and stalk-like**. The pods are dispersed by floating in the sea yet they remain viable.

On sand and shingle all round the coast of British Isles. Northern forms commonly have leaves without lobes.
A 45cm Summer

Brassica nigra

Sinapis alba

Sinapis arvensis

Raphanus raphanistrum

Raphanus maritimus

Diplotaxis muralis

Crambe maritima

Cakile maritima

Pepperworts

Pepperworts have white flowers and belong to a group of crucifers, including shepherd's-purse, with **short pods** and **a narrow division between the 2 seed-chambers**. In pepperworts the pods are **winged or keeled** and look like old-fashioned ladles.

Field Pepperwort
Lepidium campestre
Readily distinguished from all other British pepperworts by the **ripe pods** which are **densely covered in small scale-like bumps** and from Smith's pepperwort by the **very short style** which **scarcely projects beyond the top of the wings**, and the **yellow undehisced anthers**.

Dry grassland, walls, banks and arable fields throughout the lowlands but commonest in south and east.

A or B   60cm   Late spring and summer

Smith's Pepperwort
Lepidium heterophyllum
The only pepperwort with ladle-shaped, winged pods which have a **long style, over 1mm**, projecting well beyond the notch at the top. Before flowering can be distinguished from field pepperwort by the **stout woody perennial rootstock**, and **stems** often **branched** well **below the middle** (above the middle in field pepperwort), and the **red to purple undehisced anthers**.

Dry banks and disturbed grassy places; infrequent in the east, reaching 450m in central Wales.

P   45cm   Late spring and summer

Swine-cresses

Swine-cresses are small prostrate plants with white flowers, the only common crucifers **in which there is a central group of flowers** and the rest of the flowering stalks arise opposite a leaf, not in its axil as is normal.

Lesser Swine-cress
Coronopus didymus
Distinguished from swine-cress by the generally more ascending habit, flowers with **petals shorter than sepals or absent**, only 2 (not 6) stamens, and much less warty **pods, shorter than their stalks**, with a **clear notch at the top**. The leaves give off an unpleasant smell when crushed and are not recommended for salads.

Lowland arable fields and waste places mainly in the southern half of British Isles: an introduction which is still spreading.

A or B   30cm   Summer and autumn

Swine-cress
Coronopus squamatus
Recognised from a distance by the rosettes of fern-like leaves in gateways and other trampled areas. The flowers, with **petals longer than sepals**, develop into **pods longer than their stalks**, each with 2 one-seeded halves covered in warts which look as though they have been carved from wood. The fruit has **no notch at the top**. The leaves are bland and have been used in salads.

Abundant S and E of a line from R Humber to R Severn; rare and mainly coastal elsewhere.

A or B   30cm   Summer and autumn

Hoary Cress
Cardaria draba
Recognised at a distance as large, white, fluffy **low-growing patches near the front of roadside verges**. Closer up distinguished by the **wingless, heart-shaped pods** which led to its scientific name, *Cardaria*, from the Greek, *kardia*, a heart. Introduced in 1809 it spread rapidly because it not only reproduces by seed but also by root buds which break off and develop into separate plants.

Throughout the lowlands but especially common S and E of a line from R Humber to R Severn.

P   90cm   Late spring and early summer

Wild Candytuft
Iberis amara
A rare plant now found **only on** chalk soils in central England as far north as Cambridgeshire, and along the North Downs. Recognised by the large white **flowers up to 8mm across** with the **2 outer petals twice as long as the inner**, by the **winged pods notched at the top** with a **style about equalling the notch**, and by the large reddish-brown seeds up to 3mm diameter, one in each segment of the pod.

Bare places **on the chalk** such as arable fields, railway banks and rabbit-infested areas.

A   30cm   Summer

Shepherd's Cress
Teesdalia nudicaulis
With wild candytuft (q.v.) one of only 2 British crucifers with **2 of the 4 petals longer than the others**. Clearly separated from candytuft by the tiny **flowers c. 2mm across**, by the **wingless pods** with a **very short style**, and by the small, pale brown seeds less than 1.2mm diameter, 2 in each segment of the pod. Recognised before flowering by the rosettes of leaves which look in what looks like a piece of jig-saw.

Thinly scattered throughout British Isles **on sand or gravel** to about 450m on Mull.

A   40cm   Spring and early summer

Lepidium campestre

Lepidium heterophyllum

Coronopus didymus

Coronopus squamatus

Cardaria draba

Iberis amara

Teesdalia nudicaulis

Field Penny-cress
Thlaspi arvense

The tiny white flowers under 6mm across develop into **10p-sized pods** which form a conspicuous spike. Each pod has a **deep notch at the top** with a very **short style in the bottom** and consists of 2 valves attached to a thin central partition. Unlike *Lunaria annua*, in which the partition is in the same plane as the pod and the same size, the **partition** in penny-cress **is at right angles to the pod** and little remains when the valves fall.

Arable fields and waste places throughout the lowlands.

A 60cm Late spring and summer

Alpine Penny-cress
Thlaspi alpestre

Forms **rosettes of spoon-shaped**, sparsely-toothed **leaves** from which develop **short stems with leaves clasping them**. The white, 6-stamened flowers develop into **winged fruits** which are **hardly notched** but have a **prominent style up to 2mm long**. A very variable species with a range of notch shapes and style lengths: the variant in the Mendips has lilac flowers.

Limestone and other basic rocks in western and northern Britain; frequent only in the north Pennines.

P 40cm Spring and summer

Shepherd's-purse
Capsella bursa-pastoris

As this plant is in flower and fruit throughout the year it can always be recognised by its **heart-shaped pods** said to resemble the kind of purses carried by medieval shepherds round their waists. A more modern image is of a delta-winged aircraft. Without flowers or pods it may be recognised by the **leaf rosettes**, (usually **with large terminal lobes**,) and **stems with leaves clasping them**.

A very variable and almost ubiquitous weed of arable fields and waste places up to 500m in Scotland.

A or B 40cm All year

Scurvygrasses

Scurvygrasses are distinguished from other crucifers by their fleshy leaves and their rugby-ball-shaped pods which have 2 rows of seeds in each half (*a back-row and a front-row?*).

Common Scurvygrass
Cochlearia officinalis

Separated from other species by the **heart-shaped basal leaves**, the **stalkless upper stem-leaves** clasping the stem and the almost **round, pea-sized pods** on stalks at a wide angle to the stem.

A very variable plant of sea-banks and salt-marshes all round the coast except the extreme south-east; also on dry banks and stream sides inland rising to 900m in the Scottish Highlands.

B or P 50cm Spring and summer

Danish Scurvygrass
Cochlearia danica

Distinguished from other scurvygrasses by the small **flowers up to 5mm across** which are usually **mauve** or whitish, the **stalked stem-leaves** and the **basal ones ivy-shaped**, and the pea-sized pods on stalks about 45° to the stem.

Widespread all round British Isles on sandy and rocky shores and on banks and walls near the coast; occasional as an introduction inland, especially on railway lines.

A 20cm Winter and spring

English Scurvygrass
Cochlearia anglica

Differs from other scurvygrasses in having large **flowers up to 1.4cm across** and **pods** up to 1.5cm long which, **in cross-section**, are **3–5 times wider in one direction than the other** with the 2 halves **divided by a narrow partition c. 1.5mm across**. The **basal leaves** are not heart-shaped but **taper gradually into a long stalk**: the **upper stem-leaves** are **stalkless** and clasp the stem.

Muddy shores and estuaries all round the coasts of British Isles except the far north.

B or P 35cm Spring and summer

Common Whitlow-grass
Erophila verna

A tiny plant recognised by the **basal rosette** of hairy, slightly **toothed leaves** and **leafless flowering stalks**, rarely more than 10cm high, with white, 4-petalled flowers up to 6mm across, each petal divided to about half-way. The flowers produce **short, round pods, rugby-ball-shaped** on walls and paths inland, football-shaped on sand-dunes. The silvery partition between the segments of the pod persists long after the seeds have been shed.

In dry open places reaching 750m in the Pennines.

A 20cm Spring

Horse-radish
Armoracia rusticana

Readily identified by the long, undivided, often yellowish-green, **lower leaves, with a wavy-toothed margin**, which grow in clumps in tall grass. Some of the **stem-leaves may be divided** like the teeth of a coarse comb. Develops tall, much-branched spikes of white **flowers** which **rarely set seed** in our climate. Introduced from the Near East and grown as a condiment in gardens from which it has escaped.

Roadside verges and river banks throughout the lowlands.

P 1.2m Late spring and early summer

Thlaspi arvense

Thlaspi alpestre

Capsella bursa-pastoris

Cochlearia officinalis

Cochlearia danica

Cochlearia anglica

Erophila verna

Armoracia rusticana

Bitter-cresses

Bitter-cresses **have white flowers**, with **petals twice as long as sepals**, which develop into **long narrow pods**. They have leaves divided into oval or rounded segments which have a bitter but not disagreeable flavour and may be used in salads.

Large Bitter-cress
Cardamine amara
Close to cuckooflower in appearance but the **flowers** are white and **do not exceed 1.2cm across with purple** (not yellow) **anthers**. Differs from the other 2 bitter-cresses by the **creeping and rooting stems at the base**, the absence of a rosette and the **oval**, rather than round, **coarsely-toothed leaf segments**.

Wet areas like springs and flushes up to 500m in Scotland; locally frequent but absent from SW England, NW Scotland and most of Wales and Ireland.
P 60cm Spring and early summer

Wavy Bitter-cress
Cardamine flexuosa
A **biennial and often perennial** plant with only a few basal leaves in a **loose rosette** and **numerous**, **(4–7) stem-leaves**. Distinguished from hairy bitter-cress by the more **zig-zag stems** and, when in flower, by the **6** (not 4) **stamens**, though 2 of them are often small and difficult to see.

Shade-loving plant of stream banks and damp woods throughout British Isles to 1200m in the Highlands.
B or P 50cm Spring to autumn

Hairy Bitter-cress
Cardamine hirsuta
An **annual with a slender taproot**, a **well-developed basal rosette**, and a **straight stem with few**, **(1–4) leaves**. Despite its name, not hairier than the wavy bitter-cress and most easily separated from it by the **4** (not 6) **stamens** and, in fruit, by the **ripe pods which 'explode'** from the bottom upwards when touched.

Usually in dry places on bare ground, walls and rocks throughout British Isles to 1200m in the Highlands.
A 30cm Spring and summer

Cuckooflower
Cardamine pratensis
Recognised from a distance in early spring when it turns wet meadows and marshes lilac, as the cuckoo starts to call. The **leaves are similar to water-cress** in taste and **shape** and may be eaten in their stead. Like the bitter-cresses (q.v.) but with **flowers up to 1.8cm across** and **petals 3 times as long as sepals**. The large patches, which are occasionally white, are said to resemble linen bleaching in the sun which could be the origin of the other name, lady's-smock.

Wetlands throughout British Isles to 1000m in N Wales.
P 60cm Spring

Winter-cress
Barbarea vulgaris
Distinguished from other crucifers by the **deeply lobed**, usually **hairless, dark green, shiny leaves with a large terminal leaflet**, by the **small** yellow **flowers** and the **4-angled, thin, upright pods** up to 3.2cm long **with a persistent style** up to 3.5mm. Formerly known as Herb St Barbara after the saint whose day was in December when the leaves were most appreciated as a winter salad.

Throughout the lowlands on river banks, in ditches or on roadsides.
B or P 90cm Spring and summer

Northern Rock-cress
Cardaminopsis petraea
A mountain flower with a **basal rosette of long-stalked, divided leaves with a large terminal lobe**, covered in **branched hairs**, and **spoon-shaped**, slightly toothed, **stem-leaves on short stalks**. The white or purplish **flowers up to 6mm across** develop into long, narrow, unbeaked, flattened pods up to 3cm long.

Lime-rich mountain rocks to 1250m in N Wales, Scotland and in 2 isolated localities in Ireland; occasionally lower down on river gravel.
P 25cm Summer

Hairy Rock-cress
Arabis hirsuta
Distinguished from all other white-flowered crucifers by the **stiff, erect stems**, rising from a **basal rosette** with **stalkless upper leaves clasping the stem** and the whole plant **covered in forked hairs**. The tiny white flowers up to 4mm across, with petals twice as long as sepals, develop into erect flattened pods with a distinct midrib.

Lime-rich soils on dry banks, rocky slopes and sand-dunes throughout British Isles to 900m in Scotland.
B or P 60cm Summer

Cardamine amara

Cardamine flexuosa

Cardamine hirsuta

Cardamine pratensis

Barbarea vulgaris

Cardaminopsis petraea

Arabis hirsuta

Water-cress
Nasturtium officinale
The familiar leaves and the marshy or watery habitat make this one of our easiest plants to identify – up to a point. There are in fact 2 species and a hybrid which have similar leaves, however they are separable in fruit. *N. officinale* has **ripe pods** which are usually **straight, over 2mm across**, with **2 rows of seeds with 7–12 depressions across their width**: narrow-fruited watercress (*N. microphyllum*) has, usually, **curved pods under 2mm across**, with **one row of seeds with 12–18 depressions across their width**. The hybrid (*N. x*

sterile) has **ripe pods with 4 or fewer seeds** (see drawing).
Throughout lowland British Isles, to 450m in the Pennines.
P   60cm   Spring to autumn

PODS

Nasturtium officinale

N. microplyllum

N. x sterile

Yellow-cresses
Yellow-cresses are plants of damp places with **divided leaves**, related to water-cress, but with small, **yellow flowers up to 6mm across** which develop into long **pods with segments not clearly marked with veins** (see drawings).

Creeping Yellow-cress
Rorippa sylvestris
A perennial with **flowers up to 5mm across** with **petals twice as long as sepals**, which develop into **thin pods over 9mm long**. Recognised also by its stem-leaves which are deeply divided to the midrib, with each segment strongly toothed.
Wet ground by streams, occasionally as a roadside or garden weed. Widely scattered throughout lowland British Isles.
P   50cm   Summer

Marsh Yellow-cress
Rorippa palustris
An annual with tiny **flowers up to 3mm across**, with pale-yellow **petals hardly longer than the sepals**, which develop into short, **fat pods up to 1cm long**, over 3 times as long as broad. Recognisable also by the stem-leaves which are not divided to the midrib and have 'ears' (auricles) at the base, half clasping the stem.
Wet ground where water stands in winter such as pond margins. Throughout lowland British Isles to 300m in the Pennines.
A   60cm   Summer and autumn

Great Yellow-cress
Rorippa amphibia
A handsome perennial with **flowers up to 6mm across**, with bright-yellow **petals twice as long as sepals**, which develop into **pods under 5mm long**, less than twice as long as broad. The stem leaves are not divided to the midrib but are often shallowly lobed and distinctly toothed. However the basal leaves, if they develop under water, are deeply cut into linear segments.
Locally abundant by and in ponds, ditches, streams and rivers in lowland England, Ireland and the eastern borders of Wales.
P   1.2m   Summer

Dame's-violet
Hesperis matronalis
A garden plant which has escaped and become naturalised. Recognisable by its tall spikes of large, unveined, **violet or white flowers up to 1.8cm across** on stalks equalling or longer than the sepals, and by the **deeply 2-lobed stigma** with the **lobes erect**, not spreading as in the wallflower. Flowers smell of violets, especially on evenings with high humidity. *Hesperis* is Greek for a plant that flowered in the evening.
Hedgerows, verges and plantations scattered throughout the lowlands of British Isles.
B or P   90cm   Late spring and summer

Treacle Mustard
Erysimum cheiranthoides
A tall weed **covered in branched hairs** with many long, narrow leaves and clusters of small yellow **flowers, with petals twice as long as sepals, up to 6mm across** which develop into upright, **matchstick-shaped pods**, square in cross-section. The seeds were used in medieval times as one of the 72 ingredients needed to make 'Venice treacle', a famous cure for worms and an antidote for all other animal poisons.
Common in arable fields and waste places in E England; scattered and generally rare elsewhere.
A   90cm   Summer

Nasturtium officinale

Pods

Rorippa amphibia

R. palustris

R. sylvestris

Rorippa sylvestris

Rorippa palustris

Rorippa amphibia

Hesperis matronalis

Erysimum cheiranthoides

Wallflower
Cheiranthus cheiri
This familiar garden plant, which was introduced from Greece in the medieval period, has escaped and become widely established on rocks and old walls, especially of ruined castles and monasteries. In these places the **flowers** are always **single** and **bright yellow** in colour: garden varieties range from white through orange to deep red. Distinguished from other crucifers by the **long, cylindrical pods** and the **stigma with 2 spreading lobes** at the top.

Scattered throughout the lowlands.

P   60cm   Spring and early summer

Garlic Mustard
Alliaria petiolata
Recognised by the hairless, **heart-shaped**, strongly-veined, **shiny leaves** which give a strong **smell of garlic when crushed**. Also well-named 'Jack-by-the-hedge' for it is commonly seen as a long line of white against the bright green of the bursting leaves of a hawthorn hedge in spring. Later in the year the **upwardly curving** remains of the **pods and** their **stalks** are still unmistakable.

Hedgerows and woodland margins throughout the lowlands to 300m in the Pennines.

B   1.2m   Late spring and early summer

Hedge Mustard
Sisymbrium officinale
Another 'mustard' most readily recognised by its pods. Apart from black mustard (q.v.) it is the only common, yellow-flowered crucifer with **pods clinging closely to the branches**: it is distinguished from that plant by the tiny **flowers, less than 3mm across**, and the, usually, hairy pods which taper from base to tip on **branches at right-angles to the stem**. This wiry branching makes identification of the dead skeleton possible even in winter.

Hedges, roadsides and waste places throughout the lowlands to 300m in the Pennines.

A   90cm   Summer

Tall Rocket
Sisymbrium altissimum
This yellow crucifer with medium-sized flowers up to 1.1cm across is distinguished by its **upper leaves deeply divided into long, narrow segments**. The flowers develop into **long, straight, hairless pods, up to 10cm**, which are held **at an angle of c. 45° to the stem**: by this time the basal, pinnate leaves are dead.

An introduced weed established in the lowlands but very rare except in England.

A   1m   Summer

Thale Cress
Arabidopsis thaliana
Like whitlow-grass (p.18) this is an annual with a **basal rosette of hairy, slightly toothed leaves**, but the petals are not divided to halfway, the almost leafless stems may reach 50cm, whilst the **pods**, which are held **at a wide angle to the stem**, are **long and narrow up to 1.8cm**.

Walls, rocks and bare places in dry, often sandy, soils throughout British Isles to 700m in Scotland.

A   50cm   Late spring and early summer

Flixweed
Descurainia sophia
An erect, annual crucifer with tiny, pale yellow **flowers up to 3mm across** and greyish-green **leaves, deeply divided into hundreds of 2 × 1mm segments**, the lower covered in star-shaped hairs. The flowers develop into narrow **pods up to 2.5cm long curving upwards at an angle to their very slender, c. 1mm, stalks**.

An introduced weed of arable fields and waste places scattered throughout the lowlands but only common in East Anglia.

A   90cm   Summer

Weld and wild mignonette
Weld and wild mignonette belong to a small family, the *Resedaceae*, members of which have **irregular flowers**, with **many stamens** and a mixture of **2–8 large and small, variously divided petals**, which develop into a **capsule with an opening at the top**.

Weld
Reseda luteola
Weld has an almost **unbranched stem** bearing **simple, glossy, wavy-margined leaves** and **flowers with 4 sepals and 4 variously cut petals**, the **lower petal reduced to a single strap-like lobe**. Also known as dyer's greenweed, weld is one of the longest-used and best plants for obtaining a fast and brilliant textile dye. The flowers turn on their stalks following the sun by day.

Waste places and dry banks, especially on lime-rich rocks, throughout lowland British Isles.

B   1.5m   Summer

Wild Mignonette
Reseda lutea
Distinguished from weld by the shorter, usually **branched, stems** bearing **much-divided and lobed leaves** and **flowers with 6 sepals and 6 variously cut petals**, the 2 **lower petals divided into 3 strap-like lobes**. Mignonette, French for 'little darling', originally referred to a scented garden species, *Reseda odorata*, a native of N Africa.

Waste places and disturbed ground, especially on lime-rich soils. Common throughout the English lowlands but local and mainly coastal in the West.

B or P   75cm   Summer

Cheiranthus cheiri

Alliaria petiolata

Sisymbrium officinale

Sisymbrium altissimum

Arabidopsis thaliana

Descurainia sophia

Reseda luteola

Reseda lutea

Violets and Pansies (Violaceae)

Violets and pansies are amongst our most familiar wild and garden flowers. The flowers are built on a unique plan; the 5 petals are unequal, with an upwardly-projecting upper pair, a lateral pair and a fifth, broader petal which bears a spur behind. The fruit is a capsule splitting into 3 parts and the relatively large seeds bear an oil body attractive to ants which disperse the seeds (see drawings).

Sweet Violet
Viola odorata
This favourite flower of February and March is found in **white** and **violet coloured forms**. It is easily recognised by its **sweet scent** and by the **long, strawberry-like runners** which produce new plantlets. The wild plants are commonly white-flowered.

Native in hedgerows, woodland etc., especially on chalk and limestone, in much of England, Wales and central Ireland; not uncommonly found in Scotland and the rest of Ireland as a probable garden escape.
P   10cm   Winter and early spring

Marsh Violet
Viola palustris
Recognised by its **pale lilac flowers round in outline**, and by the **almost circular leaves**.

Common in acid bogs and marshes throughout British Isles except some eastern and Midland counties of England. The only violet you will see growing with bog-moss (*Sphagnum*).
P   10cm   Late spring to summer

Hairy Violet
Viola hirta
Easily distinguished as the only **obviously hairy** violet, with **spreading hairs on the leaf-stalks**. The flower is scentless, a paler violet in colour, and the leaves are more triangular in shape than those of the sweet violet.

Native in grassland, especially on chalk or limestone, from mid-Scotland southwards, and locally common in England; rare in Ireland.
P   5cm   Early spring

Viola – flower

Viola – capsule

Common Dog-violet
Viola riviniana
Most wild violets belong to this species which varies in size and shape of flower. The common woodland form has quite large 'wide-awake looking' flowers, but dwarf plants with much smaller flowers are found on heathland and grassland. The **spur is pale in colour**, and **never darker than the petals**. In fruit, the **5 persistent sepals have quite large appendages, projecting backwards**.

Common throughout British Isles, from sea-level to high mountains, avoiding only very wet soils.
P   15cm   Spring

Early Dog-violet
Viola reichenbachiana
Resembles woodland forms of the common dog-violet, but has narrower petals, **a spur darker than the petals**, and much **smaller sepal-appendages in fruit**. Where both species grow together, the early dog-violet flowers some 3 weeks before the other, often in March.

Native in woods usually on chalk or limestone; common in S, C and E England, but found also north to the Scottish lowlands and rarely in Wales and Ireland.
P   10cm   Spring

Heath Dog-violet
Viola canina
A rather uncommon plant, best distinguished from the common dog-violet by its **much truer blue flower** with a **greenish-yellow spur**, and rather narrower, **triangular leaves which are thick in texture**.

Scattered throughout British Isles, in a variety of unshaded habitats, never in woodland. Fenland plants are much taller and with thinner leaves than those on exposed heaths.
P   20cm   Late spring

Viola odorata

Viola palustris

Viola hirta

Viola riviniana

Viola reichenbachiana

Viola canina

Mountain Pansy
Viola lutea
Pansies differ from true violets in having the 2 lateral petals directed upwards (giving the flower a very characteristic appearance shown in the photograph) and also in having rather large, leaf-like stipules. The mountain pansy, which can be yellow, purple or a mixture of the two, is the most handsome of our wild pansies. It has a **long creeping underground stem** and **handsome large flowers up to 3cm**.

Locally common in grassland in hilly districts of N and W Britain; very local in Ireland.
P   10cm   Summer

Wild Pansy
Viola tricolor
The wild pansy is very variable in flower colour, being purple, yellow and white in various combinations. It differs from mountain pansy in being **tufted** and in having **smaller flowers up to 2.5cm**. Some variants are annual and occur as weeds on acid or neutral soils. Others are perennial, sometimes on sand-dunes.

Recorded throughout British Isles, on suitable soils.
A and P   15cm   Spring and summer

Field Pansy
Viola arvensis
Like the wild pansy, but with a smaller flower to 2cm, usually **cream-coloured**, in which the **petals are often shorter than the pointed sepals** (This is clearly seen in the sideview of the flower in the photograph.)

A common annual weed of neutral or limy soils found throughout British Isles.
A   15cm   Spring and summer

Milkworts (Polygalaceae)
Milkworts are small perennial plants with blue, pink or white flowers which resemble pea-flowers (*Leguminosae*, pp. 58–75) but are not related to them. **The sepals are very unusual: 2 are very much larger than the other 3, and coloured, enclosing the rest of the flower**. The fruit is a **flat, winged capsule** which splits at the edge to liberate a single seed in each of the 2 compartments (see drawings).

Common Milkwort
Polygala vulgaris
A common and variable plant, with slender stems bearing **alternate leaves**, the upper narrow and acute, and a loose few-flowered inflorescence. The **flowers are quite commonly blue, pink or white on different plants**.

In grassland throughout British Isles.
P   20cm   Summer

Heath Milkwort
Polygala serpyllifolia
Like the common milkwort, but with slenderer stems, with **some lower leaves opposite**, and **smaller, usually blue flowers.**

In heathland and acid grassland, avoiding limy soils, throughout British Isles on suitable soil.
P   15cm   Summer

Chalk Milkwort
Polygala calcarea
Quite different in habit from common milkwort and heath milkwort, with broad **lower leaves forming an irregular rosette** from which the short, unbranched flowering stems arise. The **flowers are usually crowded, and of an intense blue** (paler blue forms are rare).

Locally in chalk and limestone grassland in S England from the Cotswolds eastwards; rare in S Lincolnshire.
P   15cm   Summer

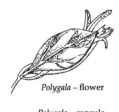

Polygala – flower

Polygala – capsule

Common Rock-rose
Helianthemum chamaecistus
Rock-roses in a range of colours are very familiar garden flowers. We have only one common species of this mainly Mediterranean family (*Cistaceae*).

A dwarf shrub, easily recognised by its **large, yellow, 5-petalled flowers with numerous stamens** on **trailing stems with narrow, opposite leaves**. At the leaf-bases are small, narrow stipules.

Common throughout most of Britain (except N and W Scotland) on chalk and limestone, ascending to 600m; only known from one locality in Ireland.
P   30cm   Summer

Viola lutea

Viola tricolor

Viola arvensis

Polygala vulgaris

Polygala serpyllifolia

Polygala calcarea

Helianthemum chamaecistus

St John's-worts (Hypericaceae)

Most of our St John's-worts are herbs, sometimes with a slightly woody base: only 2 species are shrubby.

All St John's-worts have simple, opposite leaves, often with translucent dots (glands). The flowers are large, 5-petalled, with the stamens grouped in 3 or 5 bundles.

Tutsan
Hypericum androsaemum
A **half-evergreen small shrub** with **stalkless, oval leaves**, and yellow flowers in small groups, each with 3 large and 2 small sepals. The **fruit is a red, finally purplish-black berry**. All other species have capsules which split when ripe.

In woods and hedges, more common in Ireland and W Britain than in the east, and absent from NE Scotland.
P (shrubby)   1m   Summer

Rose-of-Sharon
Hypericum calycinum
An evergreen small shrub with **long creeping rhizome**, distinguished from tutsan by its **very large, solitary flowers up to 8cm across**, and its **dry, capsular fruit**.

A garden plant originally from Turkey and SE Bulgaria, but very extensively planted for ground cover and often naturalised, especially in S England.
P (shrubby)   60cm   Late summer

Perforate St John's-wort
Hypericum perforatum
A **hairless** plant, **spreading by rhizomes**. The flowering stems are erect, **with 2 raised lines, and pairs of stalkless leaves**, usually narrowly oval, **with many translucent dots**. The flowers are about 2cm across, with rather pointed sepals. The leaves are very variable in shape, but always have abundant dots (hold up against the light!).

Common in grassland and waste places, especially on limy soil, throughout England, Wales and S Scotland, but rare in C and N Scotland; widespread in Ireland, especially in the centre.
P   80cm   Summer

Imperforate St John's-wort
Hypericum maculatum
Like the perforate St John's-wort, but with **4-angled stems, leaves with very few or no dots, petals with numerous black dots or streaks**, and blunt sepals.

A locally abundant plant of wet grassland and wood margins, occurring throughout British Isles, mainly in Wales, W Midlands and S Ireland.
P   80cm   Summer

Square-stalked St John's-wort
Hypericum tetrapterum
Like the perforate St John's-wort but with **slender runners, winged, 4-angled stems**, and smaller flowers (*c.* 1cm) with paler yellow petals. Best distinguished from the imperforate St John's-wort by its dotted leaves and pointed sepals.

A common plant of wet grassy places and damp woodland throughout most of British Isles, but absent from much of N Scotland.
P   80cm   Summer

Trailing St John's-wort
Hypericum humifusum
A pretty, **trailing, hairless** plant with **very slender stems with 2 raised lines**, small, more or less oblong, blunt leaves and **small flowers up to 1cm across**.

Fairly common, especially on heath and moorland, and confined to acid soils, throughout British Isles.
P   20cm   Summer

Slender St John's-wort
Hypericum pulchrum
Well-named (in Latin) 'beautiful', this is an attractive plant with **smooth, erect, often reddish stems and hairless, heart-shaped leaves clasping the stem in pairs**. The **petals are yellow with reddish tinges**, and have a **row of black glands at their edges**, and the sepals are blunt, and similarly edged with black glands.

Somewhat local on acid soils, usually in rather dry grassy places, but found throughout British Isles except in inland E Anglia.
P   60cm   Summer

Hypericum androsaemum

Hypericum calycinum

Hypericum perforatum

Hypericum maculatum

Hypericum tetrapterum

Hypericum humifusum

Hypericum pulchrum

Hairy St John's-wort

Hypericum hirsutum

Easily distinguished from all the other species (except the marsh St John's-wort: see below) by having **obvious hairs on the stems and both sides of the leaves**. The flowers are similar in colour (pale yellow) to those of the square-stemmed St John's-wort (with which it often grows in wet woodland in England), but are somewhat larger (*c*. 1.5cm across).

Common in damp woodland on basic soils in lowland England, but rare in the west, and absent from most of Wales, W Scotland and Ireland.

P   80cm   Summer

Pale St John's-wort

Hypericum montanum

A handsome St John's-wort, with simple **smooth, rigid, hairless stems** topped by a **dense head of pale yellow, fragrant flowers**; below the flowers there is a long stretch of leafless stem before the uppermost pair of leaves, which clasp the stem.

Occasional, usually on chalk or limestone, in England and Wales. Absent from both Scotland and Ireland.

P   60cm   Summer

Marsh St John's-wort

Hypericum elodes

Quite different in appearance from all other St John's-worts, this remarkable plant is **woolly-hairy, with soft, prostrate, stems** closely set with pairs of almost **round leaves**. The flowers, which betray the relationship of this unusual plant. Often seen in a mat growing in water, where the thick hair-covering prevents the plant from being wetted when submerged.

Found in bogs and acid marshy places, mostly in the west and south of Britain; locally common in the west of Ireland.

P   10cm   Summer

Pink Family (Caryophyllaceae)

The sticky stems that give a common name to some of these plants are found in some species of both *Lychnis* and *Silene*, and the only technical difference, based on the number of teeth into which the ripe capsular fruit splits at the top, is really so difficult to work that they have been grouped together.

Red and White Campion

Silene dioica and *S. alba*

The red campion is one of our best known wildflowers. In May and June it makes a lovely picture in hedgebanks and wood margins with white greater stitchwort (p.38) and bluebells (p.206). The **red petals are deeply 2-lobed**, and the **leaves are quite broad**.

The white campion is similar in size and shape, but quite different in where it grows. Its handsome, **pure white, evening-scented flowers** may be seen in waste places or as a weed. Often described as an annual, the plants frequently over-winter, but it is not a long-lived perennial like the red campion.

Both campions are **dioecious**

(i.e. **with separate male and female plants**); in our photograph of the white campion the female flower is easily distinguished by the much fatter calyx (see drawing).

Red campions are common over much of Britain, but rather rare in W Scotland and much of Ireland. They are almost absent from Cambridgeshire. White campions are common throughout lowland Britain, but rare in Ireland, Wales and the south-west. Where they meet, pink-flowered hybrid plants can often be found.

A or P   80cm   Summer

Ragged-Robin

Lychnis flos-cuculi

This, the only common *Lychnis*, is a familiar wildflower with a charmingly descriptive common name. The flower is unmistakable. The 5 **rose-red petals are deeply cut into 4 thin lobes**, giving the flower a 'ragged' look. The stems are slender and reddish, bearing several flowers. The **simple, narrow leaves** are arranged in opposite pairs on the stem. Like many marsh plants, ragged-Robin is much scarcer than in earlier times.

Throughout British Isles, but local in the arable lowlands.

P   80cm   Early summer

Bladder and Sea Campion

Silene vulgaris and *S. maritima*

Another familiar pair of campions. The flowers are easy to recognise: they have a **thin, inflated calyx** that persists round the capsule. The petals are **white and 2-lobed**. Unlike the red and white campions, the bladder campion flowers are mostly bisexual, though female flowers also occur. Both plants are perennials.

The bladder campion grows on roadside verges and other grassy places. Its **upright stems bear several flowers often held to one side**. The smaller sea campion, mostly on coastal rocks, is a much more handsome plant with

single large flowers held upright on the leaf mat.

Because bladder and sea campion will set seed freely if crossed, modern Floras tend to treat them as subspecies of a single species. In Britain, however, they rarely meet, and intermediate plants are not common. The bladder campion is common inland in most of England, Wales and S Scotland and local in Ireland, whilst the sea campion occurs all around our coasts, and rarely inland.

P   60cm and 20cm   Summer

Hypericum hirsutum

Hypericum montanum

Hypericum elodes

Silene alba

female flower with
father calyx on left

Silene dioica

Silene alba

Lychnis flos-cuculi

Silene vulgaris

Silene maritima

Moss Campion
Silene acaulis
Anyone would be forgiven for not recognising this **moss-like mountain plant** as a campion at all. The **tight mats or cushions** bear **small pink flowers which are almost stalkless**. The petals show the 2-lobed character of a campion, though the lobes are shallow. White-flowered plants sometimes occur.

This most attractive mountain flower can be found in all main mountain ranges; it also comes down to sea-level in Orkney, Shetland and the Outer Isles.
P   5cm   Summer

Nottingham Catchfly
Silene nutans
The Latin name of this attractive plant refers to the nodding flowers, while the common name recalls an early record on the walls of Nottingham Castle. The **evening-scented flowers** are borne on **sticky stalks** in a **loose, rather one-sided inflorescence**; they have **narrow, deeply 2-lobed, whitish petals which unroll at dusk** to attract the night-flying moths for pollination.

Truly wild on limestone rocks in several parts of England and Wales, and on coastal shingle in S England.
P   60cm   Summer

Night-flowering Catchfly
Silene noctiflora
The **unbranched, hairy stems** of this cornfield weed **bear 2 or 3 flowers** that are quite inconspicuous during the day. **Towards evening** the young flowers open, and the **deeply 2-lobed petals unroll, pale pink on top** and yellowish beneath. The **long, stickily hairy calyx** behind each flower provides an easily recognisable feature.

Like many annual weeds, much reduced by modern farming. It was always largely restricted to S and E England, and preferring lime-rich soils.
A   30cm   Late summer and autumn

Maiden Pink
Dianthus deltoides
Though related garden pinks and carnations are familiar, this is our only widespread native pink, a loosely-tufted, **shortly hairy plant with prostrate shoots bearing short leaves** and **(usually) single flowers** on erect stalks. The **pink petals are toothed, and have whitish spots**. As in all *Dianthus* the **calyx is surrounded by an epicalyx of bracts** (in this species 2 or 4) and there are **2 styles**.

A local and decreasing plant of lowland Britain; probably introduced in SE Ireland.
P   25cm   Summer

Soapwort
Saponaria officinalis
A robust plant with **thick, white, underground runners**. The **leaves are ovate with 2 parallel side veins almost as strong as the mid-vein**. The **flowers** (in the normal form) have **5 pale pink, entire petals and 2 styles**. The double-flowered form with extra 'petals' of varied size and shape is commonly seen.

An ancient medicinal herb, usually seen in or near old gardens, scattered through British Isles; perhaps native by streams in a few places in SW England and Wales.
P   80cm   Late summer

Chickweeds
The 3 genera, *Cerastium, Myosoton* and *Stellaria*, can be distinguished from other members of the Pink Family (Caryophyllaceae) by having 2-lobed petals (a character they share with *Silene* and *Lychnis*) and 5 free sepals, not a tubular calyx. They are all weak-stemmed, white-flowered herbs commonly called chickweeds. Most *Cerastium* species are obviously hairy (hence the name mouse-ear), whilst *Stellaria*, the true chickweeds, are often more or less hairless.

Field Mouse-ear
Cerastium arvense
A **hairy, mat-forming** plant with narrow leaves and relatively **large white flowers** on glandular-hairy stalks. The **deeply 2-lobed petals are twice as long as the sepals**. The only native lowland *Cerastium* with showy flowers, easily distinguished from the garden *C. tomentosum* (snow-in-summer), which quite often escapes from cultivation, by the greenish, not white-felted, leaves and stems.

On well-drained soils mainly in the east of Britain, and rare in W Scotland, Ireland, Wales and SW England.
P   20cm   Summer

Alpine Mouse-ear
Cerastium alpinum
Like field mouse-ear, but more handsome, with **white-woolly stems and broader leaves**, and **flowers up to 2.5cm across**.

A mountain plant, not uncommon in the Scottish Highlands where the rocks are basic, but rare in N Wales, the Lake District and S Scotland: absent from Ireland.
P   10cm   Summer

Silene acaulis

Silene nutans

Silene noctiflora

Dianthus deltoides

Saponaria officinalis

Cerastium arvense

Cerastium alpinum

Common Mouse-ear
Cerastium fontanum subsp.
triviale
A **more or less hairy short-lived
perennial** (sometimes annual)
with trailing non-flowering
shoots and weak, ascending
flowering ones; **leaves** more or
less **narrowly elliptical**, stalkless. Flowers in a loose inflorescence, with **petals usually equalling or slightly exceeding sepals**.
    One of the few truly ubiquitous
plants found throughout British
Isles in both cultivated and
uncultivated ground.
A or P   40cm   Spring to early
autumn

Sticky Mouse-ear
Cerastium glomeratum
A glandular-hairy annual with
yellowish-green leaves and **erect
flowering shoots**. The **flowers** are
**very short-stalked in compact
clusters with green bracts**, and
have **narrow, deeply 2-lobed
petals about equalling sepals**.
    A common weed of arable land
and waste places, also on sand-
dunes, throughout British Isles
except high on mountains.
A   30cm   Spring and summer

Little Mouse-ear
Cerastium semidecandrum
A very small glandular-hairy
**annual with erect stems branch-
ing at the base**. The flowers have
**bracts that are green below but
thin and whitish in upper half**
(see drawing). The **petals** are
only slightly notched, and
shorter than the sepals. The
**flower stalk turns sharply back
as the capsule develops**.
    On dry sandy or chalky soils
throughout British Isles, but only
common in S and E England.
It often behaves as a 'winter
annual', germinating in the
autumn and over-wintering.
A   5cm   Spring

Sea Mouse-ear
Cerastium diffusum
A small glandular-hairy annual
with **dark green leaves** and
prostrate or ascending flowering
shoots. **The flowers are** short-
stalked **in a loose inflorescence
with green bracts** and **narrow,
shallowly 2-lobed petals shorter
than sepals**. They usually have
4 sepals and petals, but not
infrequently (as in the plant
portrayed here) can have 5.
    Common around the coasts of
the British Isles especially on
sand-dunes and shingle; locally
inland, often on railway ballast.
A   10cm   Early summer

BRACTS

*Cerastium
semidecandrum*

C. diffusum

Water Chickweed
Myosoton aquaticum
A **weak, straggling plant** with
**fragile stems bearing thin, ovate
leaves** and large flowers in a
loose, wide-branching inflorescence. The **petals, much longer
than the sepals, are split nearly
to the base into 2 divergent
lobes**, so that the open flower
seems to have 10 narrow petals.
The capsule is egg-shaped on a
sharply turned-back stalk.
    Rather common in wet places
in most of lowland England and
Wales, but more or less absent
from Scotland and Ireland.
P (? always)   80cm   Summer

Common Chickweed
Stellaria media
An annual herb often over-
wintering, with **weak** stems and
a rather straggling habit. The
stems bear **a single line of hairs
down each internode** between
the pairs of more or less hairless,
ovate leaves. The flowers are
small, and the **petals are somewhat shorter than the sepals,
with 3–8 stamens** (sometimes the
petals are hardly developed). As
the capsules develop, their stalks
curve downwards.
    Like common mouse-ear, this
familiar weed is found throughout British Isles in cultivated and
disturbed ground.
A   30cm   All year

Greater Chickweed
Stellaria neglecta
An annual or short-lived perennial, like a large common
chickweed (up to 90cm), and
with **larger, quite showy flowers
with the petals usually somewhat longer than the sepals, and
10 stamens.**
    Grows in more natural com-
munities than its weed relative,
being found in hedgerows, wood
margins and other damp and
shady places. Rather local, and
mainly confined to England and
Wales, though present rarely in
Scotland and also in NW Ireland.
(A)P   90cm   Spring and early
summer

Wood Stitchwort
Stellaria nemorum
A woodland plant resembling
greater chickweed in general
appearance, but **truly perennial
and with stems more or less
hairy all round. The petals are
about twice as long as the sepals**.
    This is a rather local plant of
damp woods and stream sides in
northern Britain, not recorded
with certainty in Ireland.
P   60cm   Early summer

Cerastium fontanum

Cerastium semidecandrum

Cerastium glomeratum

Cerastium diffusum

Myosoton aquaticum

Stellaria media

Stellaria neglecta

Stellaria nemorum

Stitchworts

The remaining species of *Stellaria* differ from the chickweeds in having narrow, linear to oblong leaves, and more or less 4-angled, not round, stems. They are usually all called stitchworts.

Greater Stitchwort
Stellaria holostea
A familiar wildflower of our hedgerows. The leaves, up to 8cm long, are **rather stiff, often grey-green**, and **very narrow, tapering from the base to a long, fine point**. The **large white flowers** have **deeply 2-lobed petals, long stalks, and green, leaf-like bracts**. The **ripe capsule is almost spherical and equals the calyx**.

Common throughout much of the British Isles, but rare in W Ireland, and absent from the Outer Hebrides, Orkney and Shetland.
P   60cm   Spring and early summer

Lesser Stitchwort
Stellaria graminea
Like a smaller edition of greater stitchwort, with **leaves up to 4cm, not long-pointed or stiff**, and small flowers with petals hardly longer than the sepals. The petal-size varies, but the safest character is that of the **bracts**, which are **thin and papery, not green, and have marginal hairs**. The **ripe capsule is ovoid** and longer than the calyx.

Common on rather dry, acid, heathy ground throughout much of British Isles.
P   60cm   Late spring and summer

Marsh Stitchwort
Stellaria palustris
Like a very weak-stemmed greater stitchwort, often scrambling up other plants, and best distinguished from both greater and lesser stitchwort by the **bracts which have a narrow central green strip and wide membranous margins without hairs**. The plant is often blue-green in colour, but pure green variants also occur.

Local and declining in marshes and fens in England, Wales and lowland Scotland; in Ireland mostly in the Central Plain.
P   60cm   Summer

Bog Stitchwort
Stellaria alsine
The smallest of the stitchworts, hairless, with **elliptical leaves usually only 5–10mm long**, and **small flowers with petals shorter than the sepals**. The calyx is **funnel-shaped at the base** (well shown in photograph), and the **petals are cut almost to the base into 2 widely diverging lobes**.

Frequent in wet places, especially on neutral or acid soils, throughout British Isles.
P   40cm   Summer

Upright Chickweed
Moenchia erecta
With unlobed petals and 4 styles this interesting plant is intermediate between the chickweeds and the pearlworts.

A **neat, rigid, hairless, grey-blue annual** with an **erect stem**, short-stalked, strap-shaped, basal leaves and stalkless stem-leaves. The flowers have 4 or 5 sepals and petals, usually 4 stamens, and 4 short, recurved styles. The **sepals are narrow, acute, with broad white margins**.

A local and decreasing plant of gravelly pastures, sea-cliffs and sand-dunes in England and Wales only.
A   12cm   Late spring

Pearlworts

The genus *Sagina* is easy to recognise: they are small plants mostly found in open ground, in which the leaves are awl-shaped and more or less joined in pairs round the stem at their base. The petals are white and entire, if present, and there are 4 or 5 styles. The capsule splits to the base into 4 or 5 parts to set free the ripe seeds.

Knotted Pearlwort
Sagina nodosa
A tufted perennial with a short main non-flowering shoot, and several ascending flowering stems which arise from the basal rosette of leaves. On these stems the upper leaves are very short, and have tufts of similar leaves in their axils, giving the 'knotted' appearance. The **flowers** are larger than in other pearlworts, **up to 1cm across, with petals 2–3 times as long as sepals**.

Throughout British Isles on open, damp soils usually with base-rich ground water, but not very common.
P   15cm   Summer

Procumbent Pearlwort
Sagina procumbens
A tufted or mat-forming perennial with short non-flowering main stem and **prostrate flowering laterals freely rooting near their base**. Leaves up to 1.2cm, **with a very short terminal point**. Flower stalks slender, hairless. **Sepals 4, blunt, spreading in ripe fruit. Petals often absent**; but sometimes 4 minute white ones present.

Throughout British Isles, a common weed of paths, walls, lawns and cultivated ground, but also on open ground in mountains. A truly ubiquitous plant.
P   5cm   Spring to late summer

Stellaria holostea

Stellaria graminea

Stellaria palustris

Stellaria alsine

Moenchia erecta

Sagina nodosa

Sagina procumbens

Heath Pearlwort
Sagina subulata

Like common pearlwort, but with **leaves gradually narrowing to a long point, 5-partite flowers** with **petals almost equalling sepals**, and **sepals appressed to the ripe capsule**. The usual form of this plant is glandular-hairy, but this character cannot be reliably used to distinguish it from common pearlwort, as hairless variants occur.

A rather local and decreasing plant of heathy and rocky ground, especially near the sea, most common in Scotland and W Ireland; absent from much of central and eastern England.

P 5cm Summer

Sandworts

Our native sandworts can be easily divided into the narrow-leaved species (*Minuartia*) and the broad-leaved ones (*Arenaria, Honkenya* and *Moehringia*). Technically, the differences are not so simple, and in our gardens we may grow narrow-leaved *Arenaria* species, but that need not concern us here. All sandworts have entire petals (if these are developed).

Sea Pearlwort
Sagina maritima

Like a small, tufted common pearlwort, but **annual**, with **fleshy, usually blunt leaves**, and **sepals half-spreading around the ripe capsule**.

Local on rocks and sand-dunes all round the coasts of British Isles: also occurs on Scottish mountains.

Since common pearlwort is also usually common near the sea, one has to look carefully for this neat little plant. The photographs show well the difference in the way the fruiting sepals are held.

A 5cm Summer

Spring Sandwort
Minuartia verna

A **loosely tufted perennial** with **narrowly awl-shaped**, more or less pointed, **strongly 3-veined and rather rigid** leaves. **Flowers up to 1.2cm across** on slender stalks in a few-flowered inflorescence. **Petals 5, white, a little longer than the pointed sepals.** Styles 3.

Rocky ground, especially on limestone and around lead workings. Mainly in N England and N Wales, but also in W Ireland and (rarely) in Scotland.

P 15cm Spring and summer

Annual Pearlwort
Sagina apetala

A **delicate annual** with slender taproot, erect main stem, ascending laterals, and a basal leaf rosette usually withering early. **Leaves tapering to a long point.** Flowers **4-partite**, with **petals minute and falling early** (rarely absent), and ovate sepals which may be spreading or appressed in fruit.

Common throughout British Isles on bare ground, paths, walls etc. A variable species which has been subdivided, but there is little agreement on how to do this.

A 10cm Spring and summer

Fine-leaved Sandwort
Minuartia hybrida

A slender annual with delicate stems, thin, narrowly awl-shaped leaves and flowers on long stalks in a branched inflorescence. **Sepals 5, ovate-lanceolate, pointed, with a conspicuous white margin; petals 5, white, not quite as long as sepals.** Styles 3.

A local and decreasing weed of arable land and waste ground mainly in S and E England; absent from Scotland, but scattered in C Ireland.

A 10cm Early summer

Thyme-leaved Sandwort
Arenaria serpyllifolia

A **rather slender, usually annual** plant, **often much-branched** and bushy in growth, **with rough hairs, short, ovate, acute leaves** and numerous small flowers in a branched inflorescence. Petals are white and often shorter than the acute sepals; the **capsules are more or less flask-shaped**.

Common on bare ground, wall-tops, etc. throughout much of British Isles. The plant illustrated is subsp. *serpyllifolia*, common on chalky soils; plants on wall-tops and dry sandy soils are usually the slenderer subsp. *leptoclados*.

A(P) 20cm All year

Three-nerved Sandwort
Moehringia trinervia

A **weak, hairy, straggling**, usually annual plant with a general similarity to common chickweed, but easily distinguished by the **veins on the leaves which are 3** (sometimes 5), **with the 2 laterals curving towards the leaf-tip**. (In chickweed, the lateral veins run out to the leaf-margin in the usual way.) The flowers are solitary and long-stalked in the leaf axils, and the white **petals are entire and shorter than the sepals**.

Common in woodland throughout most of British Isles.

A(P) 30cm Summer

Sea Sandwort
Honkenya peploides

A **fleshy, mat-forming plant with long white runners** in sand and shingle, and short, stocky shoots. The **leaves** are **ovate, stalkless and very thick**, and the **greenish-white small-petalled flowers** are produced freely. Unmistakable in flower, though can be confused with sea-milkwort (see p.122) when no flowers are present. The leaves of the latter are more or less oblong, not ovate.

Common on sandy and shingly ground on coasts all round British Isles, and quite tolerant of short immersion in sea-water.

P 5cm Summer

Sagina subulata

Sagina maritima

Sagina apetala

Minuartia verna

Minuartia hybrida

Arenaria serpyllifolia

Moehringia trinervia

Honkenya peploides

Cyphel
Minuartia sedoides
A **moss-like cushion plant** with crowded, fleshy, blunt, awl-shaped leaves. The plants are **dioecious**, bearing either male or female **flowers**, which are borne **on very short stalks** on the cushion. The **sepals are ovate, blunt, and yellowish-green. Petals are absent from female flowers**, and usually developed, though **small, in male ones**.

A locally common plant on Scottish mountains from Perthshire northwards.

P 8cm Summer

Corn Spurrey
Spergula arvensis
A **straggling, stickily hairy weed** with **'whorls' of narrow, fleshy, linear leaves on weak stems** (actually the leaves are in pairs, but have tufts of similar leaves in their axils). The numerous white flowers on long stalks have petals somewhat longer than the sepals, and the **stalks of the young capsules are very sharply deflexed from the base** (see photograph).

An unmistakable weed of acid, sandy soils in gardens, fields and waste ground, locally common throughout British Isles.

A 50cm Summer

Sand and Sea-spurreys
A group of small, low-growing plants associated with sandy or rocky ground especially near the sea. All of them have **pale, thin, papery stipules joined round each stem-node**, and the **flowers are usually pink**, not white.

Sand Spurrey
Spergularia rubra
The only inland *Spergularia*, so often easily identified by habitat. The plants have straggling, often prostrate, glandular-hairy stems with **linear, long-pointed leaves and conspicuous silvery stipules**, and pink flowers with **petals slightly shorter than the sepals.**

Not uncommon on acid, sandy soils throughout most of Britain, rare in Ireland and much of NW Scotland.

A(B) 10cm Summer

Lesser Sea-spurrey
Spergularia marina
Like a sea-side version of the sand spurrey, but **with rather fleshy, not long-pointed leaves**, and **whitish, not silvery, stipules**.

Common in salt-marshes round most of the British and Irish coasts; inland records are mainly from sides of roads treated with salt in winter.

A 10cm Summer

Greater Sea-spurrey
Spergularia media
A more robust plant than either of the preceding, **usually hairless**, with a stouter taproot and somewhat flattened, ascending stems. The leaves are similar to the lesser sea-spurrey, but the flowers are often larger, **with whitish petals** exceeding the sepals. The **large, flattened seeds usually have an obvious, broad wing round them** (though this character is not entirely reliable).

Common in salt-marshes round most of the British and Irish coasts, but more restricted than lesser sea-spurrey.

P 25cm Summer

Rock Sea-spurrey
Spergularia rupicola
Most easily recognised by where it grows, on coastal rocks and walls. **A neat, usually tufted plant covered with glandular hairs**, and quite pretty in flower, **with deep pink petals usually slightly larger than the sepals.**

Locally common on the coasts of SW England, Wales and S and W Ireland, extending north to the Outer Hebrides, and quite absent from the east coast of Britain.

P 10cm Summer

Annual Knawel
Scleranthus annuus
The only common member of a small group of inconspicuous, low-growing plants belonging to the Caryophyllaceae. They are characterised by having stipules (like *Spergularia*), but their flowers are mostly without petals. The annual knawel has **short, stocky stems**, and condensed **clusters of small flowers**. The **calyx forms a persistent cup round the single-seeded fruit** and the **separate green calyx-teeth have a narrow, colourless margin.**

On dry sandy and gravelly ground throughout much of Britain; local in Ireland.

A 5cm Summer

Minuartia sedoides

Spergula arvensis

Spergularia rubra

Spergularia marina

Spergularia media

Spergularia rupicola

Scleranthus annuus

Blinks

Montia fontana

A small, inconspicuous plant with opposite pairs of leaves, very variable in growth habit from compact tufts (land forms) to long, loose rooting stems in water. The flowers are very small, with **2 sepals and a minute white corolla, quickly withered**. The plant is best identified by the **small round capsules, splitting into 3 valves and containing up to 3 seeds**.

Rather common in wet places throughout British Isles except in parts of lowland England where the soils are lime-rich.

A, P 5cm Spring and summer

Springbeauty

Montia perfoliata

This N American plant is very distinctive, and quite unlike its native relative. It is a hairless annual with long-stalked, rather fleshy basal leaves and erect flowering stems. Below the **group of small white flowers is an opposite pair of wide stem-leaves completely joined round the stem**. The seeds are quite large, black and shining, often only one in each capsule.

Introduced into Britain in the early 19th century, and now quite common on acid, sandy soils especially in south and east England. Very rare in Ireland.

A 20cm Spring

Pink Purslane

Montia sibirica

Another N American alien, this time from the Pacific coast. Like springbeauty it is a hairless, rather fleshy-leaved plant with a **pair of stem leaves but these are not joined round the stem**. The flowers are much larger and the petals are a **pretty pinkish colour with dark veins, and deeply notched**.

Locally common in damp hedgerows, stream sides, etc. mostly in SW England, NW England and S and C Scotland; very rare in Ireland. Introduced early in the 19th century.

A, P 30cm Late spring and early summer

Hottentot-fig

Carpobrotus edulis

One of the very few South African plants really naturalised anywhere in Britain, this **robust, fleshy, trailing** relative of the familiar 'ice-plants' of our gardens has **enormous (up to 10cm) magenta- or yellow-coloured flowers with large numbers of very thin petals**. The fruit is fleshy (and eaten in S Africa).

Locally common on sea-cliffs in SW England, the Scillies and the Channel Isles; also near Dublin and on the Mull of Kintyre.

P 15cm (tall) Summer

The Beet Family (Chenopodiaceae)

A familiar group of plants with soft, often rather fleshy leaves and small greenish flowers in which there are no separate sepals and petals. Beet and spinach are familiar vegetables, and many are common weeds, including goosefoots (*Chenopodium*) and oraches (*Atriplex*) which often grow in soils rich in animal manure. The goosefoots differ from the oraches in having ordinary hermaphrodite flowers and in having alternate lower branches.

Good-King-Henry

Chenopodium bonus-henricus

The only reasonably common goosefoot that is **perennial**, with the general appearance of garden spinach. The **leaves are broad and spear-shaped**, and the **many tiny flowers** are arranged **in a narrow spike**.

Naturalised from former cultivation as a pot-herb, not uncommon near farms and old cottages in England, Wales and S Scotland; absent from N Scotland and local in Ireland.

P 60cm Summer

Fat-hen

Chenopodium album

The commonest of all the goosefoots, **recognised by the whitish 'mealy' hair** on leaves and stems. The leaves vary in shape from narrowly lance-shaped to ovate and are usually toothed. The **inflorescence is usually rather branched and dense**.

A common weed throughout British Isles except parts of the N and W Highlands.

A 1m Summer and autumn

Many-seeded Goosefoot

Chenopodium polyspermum

A **hairless** plant with **thin, entire, more or less elliptical leaves** and an **inflorescence with rather wide branches**. The plant is often reddish in colour in autumn.

A not uncommon weed in low-land England south of the Humber-Severn line; rare in Wales, Scotland and Ireland.

A 80cm Late Summer and autumn

Red Goosefoot

Chenopodium rubrum

A **hairless** plant often with **almost prostrate, rather fleshy, reddish stems**. The **leaves** are variable in shape, **commonly ovate to triangular, with few large irregular teeth**.

In waste places, manure heaps and cultivated ground, often near the sea. Common in low-land England, but rare in the west, and almost absent from Scotland and Ireland.

A 50cm Summer and autumn

Montia fontana

Montia perfoliata

Montia sibirica

Carpobrotus edulis

Chenopodium bonus-henricus

Chenopodium album

Chenopodium polyspermum

Chenopodium rubrum

Sea Beet
Beta vulgaris subsp. *maritima*
This is the wild relative of the cultivated beetroot and sugar beet, lacking the swollen stem-base. The **thick, usually reddish stems** are often **prostrate**, and the **undivided, leathery leaves** are triangular to diamond-shaped. The small green flowers are massed into spike-like inflorescences, and the **one-seeded fruits hold together in small groups**.

Common on sea-shores of much of England, Wales and Ireland; rare on Scottish coasts north of the Forth and Clyde.
A to P   1m   Summer

Common Orache
Atriplex patula
The oraches, unlike beet and the goosefoots, have separate male flowers, and female flowers with a pair of green bracteoles, but otherwise show a general resemblance. Common orache is a **rather mealy, much-branched annual, with the lower branches opposite**, and rather variable **leaves, the lower usually roughly diamond-shaped and toothed, the upper narrow and entire**.

A common weed of heavily manured ground throughout most of British Isles.
A   1m   Late summer

Spear-leaved Orache
Atriplex prostrata
Like common orache, but **much less mealy** and with **broader, often spear-shaped leaves** and **bracteoles broadest at base** (see drawing).

A common weed in lowland England, but mainly coastal in N and W Britain and Ireland.
A   1m   Late summer

Babington's Orache
Atriplex glabriuscula
A **small, usually reddish plant** related to common orache and spear-leaved orache, and best distinguished by the **large, thickened pair of bracteoles surrounding the developing fruit** (see drawing).

Around the coasts of the British Isles, on sandy and gravelly shores.
A   20cm   Late summer

Frosted Orache
Atriplex laciniata
A **whitish, often silvery-mealy**, prostrate plant with much-branched reddish or yellowish stems. The leaves are similar in shape to the Babington's orache, but are thick and very mealy on both surfaces. In the fruiting stage, the **thickened, united bases of the bracteoles become hardened**.

Scattered round the coasts of the British Isles, especially on gravelly shores around high-tide mark.
A   30cm   Late summer

BRACTEOLES

Atriplex prostrata

A. glabriuscula

Grass-leaved Orache
Atriplex littoralis
An **erect** rather mealy **plant with very narrow leaves**. In **fruit the pair of bracteoles develop a strong warty cover**.

Scattered around the coasts of the British Isles, but commonest in eastern England, and avoiding sandy or rocky shores.
A   80cm   Late summer

Sea-purslane
Halimione portulacoides
This common mealy **perennial** of salt-marshes is **somewhat woody at the base**. It differs from the oraches in having 2, **3-lobed bracteoles nearly completely fused round the fruit**. The **lower leaves are more or less elliptical**, the upper linear.

Locally abundant in salt-marshes in most of England; rarer in Wales, S and E Ireland and S Scotland.
P (shrubby at base) 80cm Late summer to autumn

In coastal communities the sea-purslane is easily told from the oraches by the woody perennial habit and its elliptical leaves. Distinguishing the different kinds of annual orache, however, is sometimes very difficult, and even experts argue about them!

Beta vulgaris subsp. *maritima*

Atriplex patula

Atriplex prostrata

Atriplex laciniata

Atriplex littoralis

Halimione portulacoides

Annual Sea-blite
Suaeda maritima

A much-branched, hairless, often reddish annual of very varied habit, best distinguished by its **fleshy, more or less pointed, half-cylindrical leaves**. The **flowers are very small in groups at the base of the leaves**, and some are female only, with 2 minute bracteoles.

Rather common on sea-coasts round the British Isles, especially in salt-marshes below high-tides.

A 40cm Late summer and autumn

Shrubby Sea-blite
Suaeda vera

A much-branched shrubby relative of the annual sea-blite with **small, more or less cylindrical, evergreen leaves** densely covering the stems.

A local sea-side plant, often on shingle-banks, restricted to S and E England. Its occurrence on the nature reserve of Gibraltar Point, Lincolnshire is the furthest north record in Europe for this remarkable shrub.

P 1m Late summer and autumn

Prickly Saltwort
Salsola kali

A much-branched, usually prostrate annual, easily recognised on sandy sea-shores by its **narrow succulent leaves ending in sharp prickles**. The small, pale green flowers appear at the base of the leaves, each flower protected by a pair of prickly bracteoles.

On sandy shores round the British Isles; absent only from Shetland. Formerly gathered and burnt to make washing soda from the ash.

A 40cm Late summer

Glasswort
Salicornia species

Glassworts are very easily identifiable from all other coastal plants. The **much-branched succulent stems are jointed and appear leafless** because the fleshy leaves are completely joined in pairs. **The small flowers appear in paired groups of 3 arranged in a triangle at each segment** (see drawing).

They are found on salt-marshes around the British Isles. Like *Salsola*, glasswort was formerly collected and burnt as a source of soda for soap and glass-making. In eastern England the plant is sold as 'samphire' to eat with fish.

Distinguishing the different kinds of glasswort is a matter for the specialist. Two of the commonest species are *S. europaea*, which usually goes yellowish-green with a pink flush as it matures, and *S. ramosissima*, dark green turning deep purplish-red. Since they are annuals, differences in time of germination and growth conditions can make individual plants look very different indeed.

A 30cm Late summer

Perennial Glasswort
Sarcocornia perennis

Obviously a glasswort, but **perennial**, with a **slightly woody base, and rooting from the often creeping stems**. The **flowers differ** from *Salicornia* in that they **are all more or less equal, arranged in a row at each segment**.

Gravelly sea-shores and salt-marshes in S and E England; very rare in Wales and SE Ireland.

P (shrubby) 30cm Late summer and autumn

Mallows and Related Plants
(Malvaceae)

Members of the Mallow family wild in Britain are usually easy to recognise. They have showy 5-petalled flowers in the middle of which the many stamens are united below into a tube. In fruit there is a ring of one-seeded nutlets, inside a persistent calyx of 5 sepals and an outer epicalyx of 3–9 segments (see drawing).

Common Mallow
Malva sylvestris

One of the handsomest of our common wildflowers, with **robust, erect or spreading, hairy stems and lobed leaves, round in outline**. The large **flowers up to 4cm across** have pinkish-purple petals with dark veins.

Common on roadsides and waste places through most of England; less common in Wales, and in Scotland nearly confined to the south-east; widespread but not very common in Ireland.

P 80cm Summer

Suaeda maritima

Suaeda vera

Salsola kali

Salicornia europaea

Salicornia – plant

Sarcocornia perennis

Malva sylvestris

*fruit showing calyx
and epicalyx below*

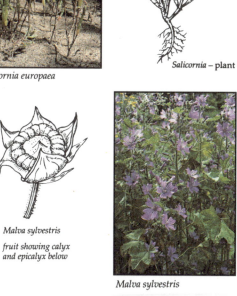

Malva sylvestris

Musk Mallow
Malva moschata

A neater, rather aristocratic relative of the common mallow, most easily distinguished by its **deeply-cut stem leaves**. The flowers are pink (more rarely white).

A widespread but rather local plant of hedgebanks and grassy places with a similar distribution to the common mallow.

P   60cm   Summer

Dwarf Mallow
Malva neglecta

Usually annual, with low, often prostrate, stellately-hairy stems. The leaves resemble the common mallow in shape, but the **flowers are smaller (up to 2.5cm)** and the **petals are very pale pink or whitish, with darker veins**.

A common weed in south and east England, often on roadsides or waste ground; rather rare in the west of Britain, Scotland and Ireland.

A(B – P?)   30cm   Summer

Tree Mallow
Lavatera arborea

The tree mallow is unmistakable. The **plants are biennial, with a woody 'trunk' and the tall flowering stems are covered with soft stellate hairs**. The large softly-hairy leaves are similar to the common mallow in shape, and the **large pinkish-purple flowers are arranged on long racemes**.

Coastal rocks and waste ground near the sea in SW England, Wales, the Isle of Man; mainly on the S and SW coast of Ireland: outside this region the plant is probably introduced.

B   3m   Late summer

Marsh Mallow
Althaea officinalis

A familiar old medicinal and culinary herb, easily recognised by its **tall, grey-velvety stems**, rather **sharply-lobed or toothed leaves**, and the **very pale pink flowers usually with a darker centre**.

Found wild near the sea, by brackish ditches and at the upper edge of salt-marshes, etc. Mainly on the south and east coasts of England, but scattered elsewhere and not uncommon in S Wales and SW Ireland. Because of its long cultivation, it is often found growing as an introduction in both inland and coastal localities.

P   1.2m   Late summer

Flax

In olden times, fields of flax and linseed, bright blue when the plants were in flower, were quite a familiar sight. The cultivated plant (still sometimes grown for 'linseed oil' in eastern England) is *Linum usitatissimum*; it is closely related to the wild pale flax described here.

Pale Flax
Linum bienne

A **hairless plant with rather slender stems and very narrow leaves**. The **pale blue flowers** (which tend to drop their petals quickly like most flaxes) **have 5 sepals, petals and stamens**, and the **fruit is a round capsule** which splits open along 10 lines to free 10 seeds.

Not uncommon in dry grassland especially near the sea, mainly in S and W England, and S and E Ireland: absent from Scotland and most of the east of England.

B (P)   50cm   Summer

Fairy Flax
Linum catharticum

This small **slender, hairless annual** does not look like other flaxes. It has **erect stems with opposite pairs of oblong leaves**, and **many small, white flowers** which are succeeded by round capsules.

Common in grassland (often but not always on limestone and chalk), heathland, sand-dunes etc. throughout British Isles, and ascending to near the tops of mountains.

A   20cm   Summer

Allseed
Radiola linoides

An even smaller annual than the fairy flax, allseed has **thin, hairless stems which are often widely branched so that the small plant has a bushy habit**. The **opposite leaves are ovate**. The **flowers** are very numerous on short stalks, **with tiny white petals**, and are followed by very small round capsules.

Recorded throughout most of the British Isles, on damp, bare sandy or peaty ground, but not easy to find; perhaps most common in the New Forest and on the west coast of Ireland.

A   5cm   Summer

Malva moschata

Malva neglecta

Lavatera arborea

Althaea officinalis

Linum bienne

Linum catharticum

Radiola linoides

Crane's-bills

Crane's-bills are amongst the commonest of our hedgerow and roadside plants. They have leaves that are round in outline (though variously dissected), and the flowers, usually in pairs, have 5 sepals, 5 usually pink or bluish petals, and 10 stamens. The common name refers to the fruit, which has a long central beak; the 5 large seeds are explosively shed by a remarkable mechanism in which 5 strips of fruit wall roll up and fling out the ripe seeds (see drawing p.54).

Pencilled Crane's-bill
Geranium versicolor
This pretty crane's-bill is a garden escape, easily recognised by its **pale pinkish, shallowly 2-lobed petals marked with darker veins**. Strictly speaking, many of the plants seen both in gardens and in the wild are of hybrid origin between the true pencilled crane's-bill, *G. versicolor* and the closely-allied French crane's-bill, *G. endressii*.

Not uncommon in SW England and S Wales, occasionally found elsewhere in England. Native of C and S Italy and the S Balkan Peninsula.

P   50cm   Summer

Meadow Crane's-bill
Geranium pratense
A showy wildflower easy to recognise. The **long-stalked basal leaves are very deeply cut**, and the hairy stems bear **large, bright violet-blue flowers** often as much as **4cm across.** The young fruits, in pairs, hang downwards.

Widespread on roadsides and meadows throughout much of England and S Scotland; rare or absent as a native plant in SW England, Wales, Ireland and the rest of Scotland, but sometimes introduced *via* gardens.

P   80cm   Summer

Wood Crane's-bill
Geranium sylvaticum
Rather similar to the meadow crane's-bill, and best distinguished by its **young fruits not pointing downwards** and the smaller, more **reddish-violet colour of the petals**. The leaves are generally less deeply and narrowly dissected.

A northern plant, very characteristic of the limestone uplands of N England, and very rare (mainly introduced) south of there; widespread in Scotland except the north, and very rare in Ireland.

P   80cm   Summer

Dusky Crane's-bill
Geranium phaeum
An extraordinary wildflower with a **unique blackish-purple petal colour**, further distinguished by the way the **petals stand out flat or even turn back** (well shown in photograph).

Long cultivated in gardens, and widely naturalised on roadsides, etc. throughout Britain except NW Scotland; rare in Ireland. The native home of this plant is the mountains of C and S Europe.

P   60cm   Summer

Bloody Crane's-bill
Geranium sanguineum
A lower-growing crane's-bill than the preceding ones, often with a rather bushy habit. The **leaves are very deeply dissected into narrow lobes**, and the **flowers are generally solitary (not in pairs)** on long stalks, and **up to 3cm across**. The **petals are bright purplish-crimson** (hence the name).

On fixed sand-dunes round the coast mainly in W and NE Britain, and also inland on limestone rocks and grassland, especially in N England; very local in Ireland, mainly on the Burren limestone.

P   30cm   Mid to late summer

Hedgerow Crane's-bill
Geranium pyrenaicum
Distinguished from the other perennial species by its very hairy, **5- to 9-lobed leaves** and flowers up to 2cm across, with **deeply-lobed, purplish-red (rarely white) petals**.

Rather common on roadsides and hedgebanks in much of England and Wales, extending north to Inverness in Scotland, and scattered in Ireland.

P   50cm   Summer

Long-stalked Crane's-bill
Geranium columbinum
A branched, rather slender and straggling plant, with deeply divided leaves, and **paired flowers up to 1.5cm across, on long, thin stalks up to 12cm long**. The **petals are purplish-pink and more or less rounded**. In **fruit the stalks spread and then curve upwards** (see photograph).

Scattered in dry grassland and edges of arable fields usually on chalk or limestone in much of Britain, but absent from W and N Scotland; mainly in the south of Ireland.

A   50cm   Summer

Cut-leaved Crane's-bill
Geranium dissectum
As its name implies, this common plant has **very deeply dissected leaves with many narrow segments**. The **deep pink flowers are paired, on short stalks**, and smaller than the preceding species, **not more than 1cm across**.

Common as a weed on cultivated and waste ground throughout most of British Isles, but rare in NE Scotland.

A   50cm   Spring to summer

Geranium versicolor

Geranium pratense

Geranium sylvaticum

Geranium phaeum

Geranium sanguineum

Geranium pyrenaicum

Geranium columbinum

Geranium dissectum

Dove's-foot Crane's-bill
Geranium molle
One of our commonest wild-flowers, with **densely hairy, branching stems**, and **5- to 9-lobed leaves**. The **small flowers**, often much less than 1cm across, have **pinkish-purple (sometimes white) petals that are quite deeply lobed**, and the **fruit-portions are hairless**.

Common throughout British Isles, in dry grassland, waste places and cultivated ground.

A 30cm Spring to summer

Small-flowered Crane's-bill
Geranium pusillum
Best distinguished from the dove's-foot crane's-bill by the **hairy fruit-portions** (an easy character, because the difference can be seen using a hand-lens even before the fruit is ripe). In addition the hairs on the stems are all one length, not both long and short as in *G. molle*. The deeply-lobed petals are usually **pale lilac** (see photograph).

Common in most of England, but rare in or absent from much of Wales, W Scotland and Ireland.

A 30cm Summer

Round-leaved Crane's-bill
Geranium rotundifolium
A badly-named plant! In fact, it is like the dove's-foot crane's-bill, but has **leaves kidney-shaped, not round in outline**. It is best told from both the preceding species by the **rounded, not lobed, petals that are pale pink in colour**. The fruit-portions are hairy.

Local in hedgebanks and waste ground in S and SW England and S Ireland: rare and uncertain further north.

A 30cm Summer

Shining Crane's-bill
Geranium lucidum
A pretty plant with an appro-priate name, easily distinguished by **its neat, almost hairless, bright green, shining, lobed leaves and flowers with pink, rounded petals**.

On shady rocks and walls, and damp hedgebanks, particularly on limestone and chalk, over much of the British Isles, but absent from N Scotland, and rare in N Ireland

A 40cm Summer

Herb-Robert
Geranium robertianum
One of our best-known wild-flowers. The **fragile reddish-tinged stems are branched from the base**, and the **leaves are deeply 5-lobed**. The **flowers are up to 2cm across, with rather narrowly wedge-shaped pink** (rarely white) petals. The **sepals are held lightly together in flower and young fruit**, and are usually deep red in colour.

Throughout British Isles, common except in the extreme north, in hedgerows, rocky ground, on shingle by the sea, etc.

A or B 50cm Summer

Geranium – fruit distributing seeds

Common Stork's-bill
Erodium cicutarium
A pretty plant, more or less hairy and sometimes glandular, often in rosette form, with **feathery-pinnate basal leaves and long-stalked groups of flowers**. The flowers are very similar to the crane's-bills with **pink, rounded petals**, but the fruits have **a very long beak up to 4cm**.

Common near the sea in dry grassland, sand-dunes and waste places all round the British Isles; less common inland but wide-spread in England, especially on sandy soils.

A 50cm Summer

Musk Stork's-bill
Erodium moschatum
Like the common stork's-bill, but **very strongly glandular-hairy and smelling of musk**, and with **less deeply divided leaflets** (see photograph).

Rather rare, mainly coastal, from Cornwall to Suffolk and S Lancashire: also occasionally seen inland: coastal round much of Ireland.

A 60cm Summer

Sea Stork's-bill
Erodium maritimum
An attractive little plant, easily recognised from other crane's-bills and stork's-bills by its **small oval leaves pinnately lobed to about half-way**, and the **flowers are solitary or paired on stalks about equalling the leaves**, and the **flowers are small**, with **pale pink, rounded petals (some-times the petals do not develop)**.

Mainly coastal, in dry grass-land and dunes, in the west and south from S Scotland to Cornwall and Hampshire; rare elsewhere in Britain and S and E Ireland.

A or B 10cm Summer

Geranium molle

Geranium pusillum

Geranium rotundifolium

Geranium lucidum

Geranium robertianum

Erodium cicutarium

Erodium moschatum

Erodium maritimum

Wood-sorrel
Oxalis acetosella

Oxalis species combine flower-type of *Geranium* with different capsular fruit and characteristic 'shamrock'-like leaves.

Wood-sorrel has slender, creeping rootstock, and **compound leaves each with 3 bright green, wedge-shaped leaflets**. The **delicate flowers have 5 white petals prettily veined on lilac** (sometimes the whole petal is lilac-coloured).

Common in woodlands, on shady rocks and in damp hedgerows throughout British Isles, though rare in parts of East Anglia. Our only native species.

P 15cm Spring and summer

Pink-sorrel
Oxalis articulata

A pretty garden plant occasionally found as an escape. The combination of **large, bright pink flowers with a dark 'eye' and 'shamrock' leaves** is unmistakable. The plant has a tufted habit and grows from a thick, fleshy rootstock.

Occasional on roadsides and waste places, especially in SW England. Native of temperate S America.

P 20cm Summer

Procumbent Yellow-sorrel
Oxalis corniculata

A creeping little plant, **freely rooting along the prostrate stems, with 'shamrock' leaves in which the 3 leaflets are bilobed**. The **flowers are borne in groups of 1–6 on long stalks**; they have **narrowly wedge-shaped yellow petals**, and **the individual flower stalks turn down after flowering**.

An introduced plant, whose native home is uncertain; now common on waste ground, paths, etc. as a persistent weed in much of England and Wales especially the south and southwest; rather rare in Scotland and Ireland.

P (A) 15cm Summer

Upright Yellow-sorrel
Oxalis europaea

This plant differs from the previous one in having **solitary erect stems and whorled or clustered leaves**. The yellow flowers are in groups of 2–5, and the petals are often smaller than in the procumbent yellow-sorrel.

An introduced weed of waste places and gardens, mainly in S and E England, and rare in N Wales, Scotland and Ireland. Native of N America.

P (A) 40cm Summer

Balsams
(Balsaminaceae)

Although classified near to the crane's-bill and wood-sorrel, our balsams, only one of which is native, have a very different-looking flower, in which sepals and petals combine to make an irregular, spurred flower. The capsular fruit 'explodes' when ripe, scattering seeds. All balsams are hairless annuals with simple leaves.

The first 3 balsams produce, in addition to the normal open flowers, smaller flowers which do not open and set seed by self-pollination in the bud.

Touch-me-not Balsam
Impatiens noli-tangere

Our single native balsam is an erect plant with swollen nodes, **alternate, more or less ovate leaves** with 10–15 coarse teeth on each side, and **few yellow, brown-spotted flowers**. The **spur behind the flower gradually curves through 90°**.

Thought to be a native plant only in the Lake District and N Wales, but recorded widely outside these areas, by stream sides and in wet woodland.

A 50cm Summer and early autumn

Small Balsam
Impatiens parviflora

This increasingly common plant resembles the touch-me-not balsam, but has **small, pale yellow, unspotted flowers**, and a **nearly straight spur to the flower**. The leaves differ in that they have **more numerous small teeth (more than 20 on each side)**.

Locally common in woodland and shady places mainly in S and E England, but still spreading and recorded as far north as Inverness. Native of Central Asia, now widely naturalised in Europe.

A 80cm Late summer and autumn

Orange Balsam
Impatiens capensis

Differs from the touch-me-not balsam in its **smaller leaves with fewer teeth (not more than 10 to a side), and much larger, orange flowers spotted with brown**. The **spur is suddenly bent through 180°**.

Naturalised on river banks and damp waste places mainly in S and C England, and apparently still spreading. In spite of its Latin name, a native of eastern N America.

A 50cm Summer

Indian Balsam
Impatiens glandulifera

A very handsome plant, **standing up to 2m high**, with **thick, hollow, reddish stems**, and **opposite or whorled leaves**. The **large, hooded, purplish-pink flowers can be as much as 4cm long**.

A native of the Himalayas, now completely naturalised on river banks and in wet waste places especially in N and C England, where it can sometimes be the dominant vegetation by industrially polluted streams. Widespread in Wales, Ireland and parts of Scotland.

A 2m Late summer and autumn

Oxalis acetosella

Oxalis articulata

Oxalis corniculata

Oxalis europaea

Impatiens noli-tangere

Impatiens parviflora

Impatiens capensis

Impatiens glandulifera

Pea Family (Leguminosae)

Sweet-peas and broad and runner beans are widely grown in gardens: clovers invade our lawns. They all have flowers with a large upper petal – the **standard**, 2 side petals – **wings**, and a lower petal which is usually 2 joined together by their lower margins to form the **keel** (see drawing).

Most members of the pea family found growing wild in Britain are herbs but a few, in the genera *Genista, Ulex, Cytisus* and *Ononis,* are shrubs which, even if low-growing, are woody at the base.

Common Gorse
Ulex europaeus

A spiny shrub over 1m high with yellow, pea-like **flowers in late winter or early spring**. It may overlap with late-flowering western gorse. Where the two grow together common gorse is recognised by its **deeply-furrowed, normally straight**, spines, **bracteoles** at the base of the sepals 2–**4mm wide, much wider than the flower stalk** (see drawing), and ripe **pods 11–20mm long**.

Heaths, rough grassland and hedges, usually on lime-free soils, throughout British Isles; to 600m in Wales.
P 2m Late winter and early spring

Broom
Cytisus scoparius

Spineless, golden wands of flowering stems waving in the spring wind must surely be broom. The identification can be confirmed at close quarters by **trifoliate leaves covered in clinging hairs** and the long spirally-coiled style. The **pods** are explosive and the 2 halves **coil up after splitting**.

Sandy heaths, woods and waste ground except Orkney and Shetland, to 600m in Scotland. A prostrate form with densely hairy leaves and young twigs occurs on coastal cliffs in Cornwall and the Channel Isles.
P 2m Spring and early summer

Dyer's Greenweed
Genista tinctoria

This small shrub has green, smooth, **spineless twigs** which branch near the ground, and simple, **oval leaves with long, wavy hairs along the margin**. The flowers, with almost hairless petals, are clustered towards the tip of the main stems, each in the axil of its own small leaf. The **pods** which develop are **obtuse at both ends**.

Occurs in masses in rough, lightly-grazed grassland on poor soils throughout lowland England, Wales and southern Scotland.
P 70cm Mid-summer to early autumn

Western Gorse
Ulex gallii

Distinguished from common gorse by its deep, golden-yellow flowers, only **faintly furrowed, usually curved**, spines, **bracteoles** at the base of the sepals **less than 1mm wide**, only a little wider than the flower stalks (see drawing), and ripe pods c.1cm long. Differs from dwarf gorse in flowers having **wings**, usually **longer than the keel** and 2.5–3.5mm longer than the sepals.

Heaths and acid grassland. Common throughout Wales, W England and S Ireland; rare and coastal elsewhere.
P 2m Late summer and autumn

Common Restharrow
Ononis repens

The true 'restharrow', distinguished from spiny restharrow by having tough, **creeping underground stems** which are so strong that they used to hold up the harrow when horse-drawn. Also recognised by having **stems hairy all round**, obtuse leaflets, **wings** of the flowers **equalling the keel**, and ripe **pods shorter than the sepals**.

Common in rough grassland and sand-dunes throughout lowland British Isles but rare and mainly coastal in the north and extreme west.
P 30cm Summer and early autumn

Petty Whin
Genista anglica

A small, normally **prickly**, shrub with many creeping, smooth **twigs** branching near the ground, and simple, narrowly **oval, hairless leaves**. The hairless flowers are at the top of short branches of the main stem. The **pods** which develop **have acute points at both ends**.

Widespread but decreasing in poor acid soils of heaths and moors throughout Britain to 750m in Central Scotland.
P 70cm Late spring and early summer

Dwarf Gorse
Ulex minor

Shorter than the other 2 species with many prostrate branches. As the diagram shows the **faintly-furrowed spines** are usually **curved** and **c.1cm long**, and the **bracteoles** at the base of the sepals are **less than 1mm wide** and **narrower than the flower stalks**. The ripe **pods** are only **c.7mm long** but persist for nearly a year. Distinguished from western gorse by the **wings, keel and sepals** being almost **equal in length**.

Lowland heaths in SE England, East Anglia and, rarely, in Nottinghamshire and Cumbria.
P 1m Late summer and autumn

Spiny Restharrow
Ononis spinosa

An erect or ascending species **lacking underground stems** and with aerial **stems** usually clothed **with spines and 2 rows of hairs**. The **leaflets** are **acute** and narrower than those of common restharrow, the **wings** of the flowers are **shorter than the keel** whilst the ripe **pods** are **longer than the sepals**.

Abundant in rough grassland, especially on heavy clay soils, in lowland England and Wales; rare and coastal in S Scotland.
P 60cm Summer and early autumn

standard wings

keel

Pea family – flower

Genista tinctoria

Genista anglica

Ulex europaeus

Ulex gallii

sepal

bracteole

Ulex minor

U. europaeus

U. gallii

Cytisus scoparius

Ononis repens

Ononis spinosa

Medicks, Melilots and Clovers

Medicks, melilots and clovers all have leaves divided into 3 similar leaflets, with stipules at the base of the leaf-stalk, where it joins the stem, which are a different shape. In bird's-foot trefoil (p.68), which also appears to be trifoliate, there are 2 further leaflets of the same shape, replacing the minute stipules, at the base of the leaf-stalk.

In **medicks** the heads of flowers have petals which **soon fall** to reveal **pods** which are **curved, often into tight spirals,** and **frequently spiny.**

A hybrid between lucerne and sickle medick with flowers varying between mauve-yellow, metallic blue, cream, green and black is frequent on road verges where the two parents occur together and may occasionally be found elsewhere.

Lucerne
Medicago sativa
Readily recognised by the **blue to violet flowers on stalks shorter than the calyx tube** (the undivided part), which develop into **smooth, 10–20 seeded, pods with a spiral of 1½–3 turns.** Its very deep roots make it drought resistant and particularly valuable as a crop on light, lime-rich, soils.

An introduction from the Mediterranean which is now widespread as an escape on roadside verges and in waste places in the lowlands of Britain, rarely in Ireland.

P   90cm   Summer

Bur Medick
Medicago minima
This is the rarest and smallest of the 3 medicks with **spiny fruits,** instantly recognised by the **shaggy hairiness of the whole plant,** the **pods densely hairy beneath the spines and less than 5mm across,** whilst the **stipules** at the base of the leaf are **shallowly and bluntly,** never deeply and acutely, **toothed.**

Very rare or local on lowland, sandy heaths in East Anglia and along the coast from E Sussex to Norfolk.

A   20cm   Late spring and early summer

Toothed Medick
Medicago polymorpha
The English name refers not to the leaflets but to the **stipules** at the base of the leaf-stalk which are **divided like a comb into c.20 acute teeth** on either side. Distinguished from bur medick by the larger **hairless pods up to 8mm across** and from spotted medick by the **absence of a blotch on the leaflets.**

A local native of sandy or gravelly open ground near the sea from Cornwall to Norfolk: rare and introduced elsewhere.
A   60cm   Late spring and summer

Spotted Medick
Medicago arabica
Immediately recognised by the black spot **(blotch) on each of the 3 leaflets.** Differs from toothed medick by having **globe-shaped,** not flattened, **pods** and by the **stipules** being **jaggedly toothed** not comb-like. The spiral coils of its prickly pod earned it the name of 'cogweed' in Somerset.

Grassland and waste places in the southern half of England, especially in the south-east, and on the coast of Wales.

A   50cm   Spring and summer

Sickle Medick
Medicago falcata
Distinguished from other yellow-flowered medicks by the **flowers over 7mm long** and from lucerne, after the petals have withered, by **sickle-shaped, never spirally-coiled, 2–5 seeded, pods on stalks longer than the calyx tube.**

Rough grassland on slightly acid or lime-rich coarse sand in East Anglia: otherwise a rare casual.

P   60cm   Summer

Black Medick
Medicago lupulina
A **deep yellow** flowered medick with heads of 10–50 **flowers** only up to **3mm long** which develop into **kidney-shaped, heavily-veined, one-seeded pods** which are **black when ripe.** Before the pods appear it may be confused with lesser trefoil (p.66) but distinguished by the **protrusion of the central nerve of the leaflets into a mucro** (see drawing).

Widespread in grassland and on roadsides of the lowlands to 400m in the N Pennines. Pale yellow forms sown with grass and clover occasionally escape.
A or P   50cm   Spring and summer

LEAFLETS

Medicago lupulina

Trifolium dubium

Medicago sativa

Medicago falcata

Medicago minima

Medicago lupulina

Medicago polymorpha

Medicago arabica

Melilots

Melilots have small **yellow or white flowers on short stalks in spikes** which lengthen after flowering and have **short, straight, thick pods**. Many smell strongly of new-mown hay, especially when drying, because of the coumarin in their leaves. Once much-valued as herbs to make a melilot plaster or poultice.

White Melilot
Melilotus alba

The only **white-flowered** melilot found wild in Europe outside Russia, but not so easily **distinguished from ribbed melilot in fruit** though the **pods are flatter**, more **greyish-brown**, and **reticulately veined** rather than ribbed.

A widespread weed of waste places in the lowlands . of England; rare elsewhere and never persistent in Scotland and Ireland.

A or B   1.5m   Summer

Tall Melilot
Melilotus altissima

Separated from ribbed melilot by having **all the golden-yellow petals** (wings, standard and keel) **the same length** (*N.B. altissima* = all). In fruit it is the only species with **hairy pods** which **are black when ripe with persistent styles** (see drawing).

Widespread on roadsides and in waste places in lowland England; rare and mainly near the coast elsewhere.

B or P   1.5m   Summer

Clovers

Clovers usually **have dense heads of flowers** on short stalks though 1 or 2, including bird's-foot clover, have only 6 or fewer flowers. All are recognised by having a petal, the **standard**, which **persists** so that **the small 1–10 seeded pod is often hidden until it sheds its seeds** from the top. The flowers have nectar attractive to bumble-bees which are essential for pollination, their weight on landing forces the pollen on to the bees' undersides on which it is carried to another plant.

Ribbed Melilot
Melilotus officinalis

Separated from tall melilot in flower by having **wings and standard longer than the keel** — a little off being equal (*N.B. officinalis = off* equal). In fruit readily recognised by the strongly **transversely ribbed, hairless, brown pods** with styles which usually fall **off** (see drawing). The annual *M. indica*, small melilot, with both yellow flowers and pods less than 3mm long, may also be found.

Scattered in fields and waste places throughout the lowlands of England; rare elsewhere.
B   1.5m   Summer and early autumn

Bird's-foot Clover
Trifolium ornithopodioides

This creeping species is recognisable as a clover by its trifoliate leaves and large linear (untoothed) stipules, but is unusual in that the clusters of **pinky-white flowers** along the stem normally have only **1–3 flowers per cluster** and that the **slightly curved, 5–8 seeded pods**, up to **7mm long**, are **not hidden by the petals**.

A local plant, almost confined to sand-dunes and gravelly places near the coast in the southern half of the British Isles.
A   20cm   Summer

Red Clover
Trifolium pratense

Red clover is one of a group of species which have prominent heads of flowers at the top of their stems and do not spread by creeping along the ground and rooting at intervals. It often has **whitish, crescent-shaped spots near the base of its elliptical leaflets** and has **stipules** of which the free part is triangular **with an abrupt point up to 3mm long**. The globe-shaped heads, made of flowers up to 1.5cm long, develop pods which open near the top by splitting transversely.

Grassland throughout British Isles to 825m in Scotland.
P   60cm   Late spring to autumn

Zigzag Clover
Trifolium medium

Superficially like red clover but separated by the longer, **narrow leaflets with only a faint spot** and the **stipules** in which the **free part is narrow** and **at least 5mm long**. The terminal **heads of flowers**, up to 1.5cm long, are round but **flattened from above** and they are a more reddish-purple than red clover.

Grassy banks throughout the lowlands to 450m in the Pennines but infrequent in East Anglia and Ireland.
P   50cm   Summer and early autumn

Sulphur Clover
Trifolium ochroleucon

Readily distinguished from all the other native clovers by its large, **upright, terminal heads of creamy-yellow flowers**, up to 1.5cm long, and the overall hairiness of its leaves and stems. The **stipules** resemble those of zigzag clover in shape, with the free part **ending in an acute tip up to 1cm long**.

Grassland and roadside banks on the boulder-clay of eastern England west to Northamptonshire.
P   50cm   Summer

Leguminosae   Melilotus 63

Pods

Melilotus altissima

M. officinalis

Melilotus altissima

Melilotus officinalis

Melilotus alba

Trifolium ornithopodioides

Trifolium pratense

Trifolium medium

Trifolium ochroleucon

Sea Clover
Trifolium squamosum
This hairy annual has leaflets, normally oval, with **stipules** having the **free part narrow** and **as long as the part attached to the leaf-stalk**. The terminal heads are made of **pink flowers up to 7mm long** which **scarcely exceed the calyx** and are less than half the length of other species in this group. **After** flowering the **petals fall**, the **calyx grows** and the **uneven-lengthed teeth spread outwards** giving a star-like appearance.

In short grassland near the coast or beside estuaries from S Wales round to Lincolnshire.
A   40cm   Summer

Hare's-foot Clover
Trifolium arvense
Perhaps the easiest to identify of all clovers with terminal **heads** because they are **long, narrow and fluffy** looking like hares' or rabbits' feet. The 'fluff' is made of **long ciliate hairs on narrow calyx teeth which are twice as long as the tube**. The pink or white flowers are only half the length of the calyx.

Widespread in sandy fields and meadows, and in sand-dunes especially along the west coast of Britain and round Ireland.
A   40cm   Summer and early autumn

Knotted Clover
Trifolium striatum
A prostrate to erect, softly-hairy, annual with stalkless, **pink-flowered heads** along the stems which become **enfolded by the stipules** of the adjacent leaf **as they mature**. The leaves are distinctly hairy and the **side veins of the leaflets are thin and straight** not backwardly curved near the margin. The **calyx** enlarges in fruit but the **teeth remain more or less erect**.

Bare patches in short grassland on sand or gravel, scattered throughout the lowlands to 300m in the southern Pennines.
A   40cm   Late spring and summer

Rough Clover
Trifolium scabrum
Another, usually prostrate, softly-hairy annual clover with stalkless heads, distinguished from knotted clover by the **white flowers** and the **leaflets** in which the **side veins** are **thickened and curved backwards** near the margin. As the calyx ripens the **teeth** become very rigid and **turn back** giving the whole head a starry look.

Thinly scattered on dry, sandy soils in the lowlands; less frequent than knotted clover and mainly coastal except in East Anglia.
A   20cm   Late spring and summer

Clustered Clover
Trifolium glomeratum
A normally prostrate but **hairless annual** with **globe-shaped, stalkless heads of purplish flowers**, longer than the calyx, in the axils of **leaves, with thin, straight side veins**, which embrace the stem and end in a long point. The **calyx** is strongly ribbed and the tri-angular **teeth narrow abruptly to a spiny point less than half the length of the tube**: the teeth turn back when mature.

Rare in open, grassy places on sand and gravel, mainly near the sea, from Cornwall to Norfolk.
A   25cm   Summer

Suffocated Clover
Trifolium suffocatum
A prostrate, **hairy annual** readily recognised by the **crowded, stalkless heads of white flowers**, shorter than their calyx, **often touching each other**. The **calyx** is weakly ribbed, with narrow **teeth, tapering gradually to a narrow point, as long as the tube** which do not turn back at maturity.

Rare in open grassy places on sand and gravel near the coast from Cornwall to Yorkshire, and on Anglesey in Wales.
A   10cm   Spring and summer

Alsike Clover
Trifolium hybridum
Distinguished from most other clovers by the **large heads of whitish flowers** on long stalks, up to 15cm, and from white clover by its **non-creeping habit**, the absence of a white band on the leaflets, the **stipules narrowing gradually to a long point**, and the faintly ribbed **calyx** with **teeth nearly twice as long as the tube**. The flowers are erect at first but later curve down and become rose-red so that the heads appear red with a white centre.

Naturalised on roadsides and field margins of the lowlands.
P   60cm   Summer and early autumn

Trifolium squamosum

Trifolium arvense

Trifolium striatum

Trifolium scabrum

Trifolium glomeratum

Trifolium suffocatum

Trifolium hybridum

White Clover
Trifolium repens
Our commonest clover and a widespread constituent of all except the most acid of our native grasslands. Distinguished from alsike clover by its **creeping habit**, rooting at the nodes, the leaflets usually with a white band towards the base, the **stipules ending abruptly in a short point**, and the **calyx** with green veins and **teeth over half as long as the tube**.

Throughout British Isles to 900m in the Scottish Highlands.
P   50cm   Summer and early autumn

Strawberry Clover
Trifolium fragiferum
Though superficially like white clover in flower there can be no mistaking it in fruit: the **upper part of the hairy calyx** in strawberry clover **swells and encloses the pod**. The **side veins of the leaflets** are also different: those of strawberry are **thickened and curved back** at the margin whereas, in white clover, they are thin and almost straight.

Grassy places on heavy soils in southern and eastern England; near the coast, often on saline soils, elsewhere.
P   30cm   Summer and early autumn

Subterranean Clover
Trifolium subterraneum
A hairy, prostrate annual with **cream flowers in heads** made up **of a few fertile flowers, up to 1.2cm**, and **numerous sterile, petalless flowers** in the centre. The calyces enlarge when in fruit and turn back forming a base to the inflorescence, which is then buried in the soil by the growth downwards of its stalk.

Sandy and gravelly grassland in the southern half of England, on the coast of Wales and in one place on the E coast of Ireland.
A   20cm   Late spring and early summer.

Lesser Trefoil
Trifolium dubium
A yellow clover separated from hop trefoil by the **flower-heads up to 7mm across, of 10–25 flowers, each one c.3mm long** with a narrow **standard** which is **folded over the pod** in fruit and turns dark brown when dead. Sometimes confused with black medick (p.60) but distinguished by the **leaflets lacking the protruding central vein**, or mucro (see drawing p.61), and by the persistent, not soon falling, petals.

Grassland throughout British Isles to 450m in the Welsh hills.
A   25cm   Late spring to autumn

Hop Trefoil
Trifolium campestre
This is the largest of the yellow-flowered wild clovers: recognised by **flower-heads up to 1.5cm across with about 40 flowers**, each **flower 5–7mm long** with a **standard** which is **not folded over the pod** in fruit. The ripe seeds are yellow and rather shiny. The heads resemble, in miniature, the cones of the hop, especially when they have withered to a light brown.

In grassland, especially lime-rich, throughout the lowlands of the British Isles, to 350m in the Peak District.
A   35cm   Summer and early autumn

Slender Trefoil
Trifolium micranthum
This, the rarest of the 3 yellow clovers, has **heads of only 2–6 flowers**, each **on a slender stalk as long as its calyx tube**.

Dry grassland, often on sand or gravel, thinly scattered throughout the southern half of England and Wales and near the coast of southern Ireland; almost absent from Scotland.
A   10cm   Summer

Trifolium repens

Trifolium fragiferum

Trifolium subterraneum

Trifolium dubium

Trifolium campestre

Trifolium micranthum

Bird's-foot-trefoils

The genus *Lotus*, bird's-foot-trefoil, **is recognised by having 5**, not 3, **leaflets**. However the **lower pair** are **attached to the stem** taking the place of the stipules of clover. Bird's-foot-trefoil is a reference to the way the 4 or 5 ripe pods are spread like the claws of a foot.

Common Bird's-foot-trefoil
Lotus corniculatus

One of the 2 largest flowered of our 5 native species, in each up to 1.6cm long, and separated from the other, greater bird's-foot-trefoil, by the almost complete **absence of hairs**, the **solid**, not hollow, **stems**, the **flowers rarely more than 6 in a head**, and the **calyx teeth erect** in bud, the 2 upper with an obtuse angle between them (see drawing).

Common and widespread in grassland throughout British Isles to 900m in the Scottish Highlands.

P   40cm   Summer and early autumn

Greater Bird's-foot-trefoil
Lotus uliginosus

An often hairy perennial, creeping and rooting at the base, with a **hollow stem, flowers** up to 1.6cm long, **in heads of** usually **8 or more**, with **calyx teeth** very obviously **turned back** in bud, the 2 upper with an acute angle between them (see drawing).

Common in damp grassland throughout most of the British Isles to 500m on Dartmoor, but rare in N Scotland and central Ireland.

P   60cm   Summer

Narrow-leaved Bird's-foot-trefoil
Lotus tenuis

Similar to common bird's-foot-trefoil but with much more wiry stems and often taller and more branched, with **leaflets about 4 times as long as broad. Flowers** only about **1cm long, rarely more than 4 in a head**, with very narrow calyx teeth.

Local in dry grassland in England and Wales mainly south and east of a line from R Humber to R Severn; rare and coastal elsewhere.

P   90cm   Summer

Hairy Bird's-foot-trefoil
Lotus subbiflorus

One of the 2 very **hairy annual** species recognised by their small **flowers less than 1cm long**. Hairy bird's-foot-trefoil is distinguished by having a lower petal (the keel) which turns through a right-angle when viewed from the side, and a ripe **pod** which is **less than 3 times as long as the calyx** and has **fewer than 12 seeds**. Slender bird's-foot-trefoil, *L. angustissimus*, has **pods over 3 times as long as the calyx** and with **more than 12 seeds.**

Dry grassland in England near the sea from Hampshire westwards, SW Wales and SW Ireland.

A   30cm   Summer

Kidney Vetch
Anthyllis vulneraria

This pretty, but very variable, perennial has **2 heads of** yellow, cream, white or crimson **flowers close together at the top of a long stalk**. The bluish, often **hairy, leaves** are made up **of 3–9 leaflets**, the largest at the tip. After flowering the **hairy calyx enlarges to form a persistent, woolly head.**

Widespread throughout British Isles on dry, usually lime-rich, soils and in cliff-top grassland; to 825m in the Scottish Highlands.

P   60cm   Summer and early autumn

Purple Milk-vetch
Astragalus danicus

A creeping perennial with leaves of **6–13 pairs of leaflets**, lacking tendrils, the leaflets **broadest near the base** and **having long, soft, white, shining hairs**. The **purple flowers**, up to 1.5cm long, are erect **in clusters of c.15** and have calyces covered in a mixture of black and white hairs.

Short grassland on lime-rich soils and sand-dunes, mainly on the east side of England and Scotland but also on cliffs in SW Scotland, Man and W Ireland.

Supposed to increase the milk production of goats.

P   35cm   Late spring and summer

Wild Liquorice
Astragalus glycyphyllos

A stout, prostrate, yellowish-green, hairless herb with leaves without tendrils and **4–6 pairs of oval leaflets, broadest in the middle.** The heads of large, up to 1.5cm, **greenish-white flowers** are arranged **in a short spike up to 5cm long** which **develops into** an unmistakable **cluster of many-seeded, slightly curved, ridged pods with persistent beaks.**

In rough grassland and scrub on lime-rich, often clayey, soils scattered through lowland England and eastern Scotland.

P   1m   Summer

FLOWERS

Lotus uliginosus

L. corniculatus

Lotus corniculatus

Lotus uliginosus

Lotus tenuis

Lotus subbiflorus

Anthyllis vulneraria

Astragalus danicus

Astragalus glycyphyllos

Bird's-foot
Ornithopus perpusillus
A finely hairy, prostrate annual recognised by its **leaves with 4–7 pairs of leaflets**, its **white flowers** veined with crimson in solitary, 3–6 flowered heads, and by its **pods** up to 2cm curved and **divided into one-seeded joints** which, when clustered together, resemble a bird's foot. This is the origin of the scientific name *Ornithopus* (see drawing).

Dry, acid, sandy and gravelly soils throughout England and Wales to 300m in Powys; rare in southern Scotland and eastern Ireland.
A 45cm Late spring and summer

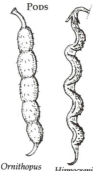

PODS

Ornithopus perpusillus

Hippocrepis comosa

Horseshoe Vetch
Hippocrepis comosa
Recognised in summer by its peculiar, snake-like **pods of many one-seeded joints**, each curved **in a horseshoe shape** from which the plant takes its English and scientific names (see drawing). Earlier in the year the flattened heads of **bright yellow flowers** might be confused with bird's-foot-trefoil but the **leaves of 3–8 pairs of leaflets** are quite distinctive.

Short chalk and limestone grassland in lowland England and Wales to 550m in the northern Pennines.
P 40cm Late spring and summer

Crown Vetch
Coronilla varia
This hairless, perennial herb is superficially like a clover with its **prominent heads of 10–12 flowers**, up to 1.2cm, which **vary in colour** from white and pink to purple, but the **leaves** are not trifoliate, having **7–12 pairs of elliptical leaflets**. The **pods** which develop are **slender and jointed**, up to 6cm, like bird's-foot, but **end in a long curved beak**.

Once cultivated for forage and now established in rough grassland in scattered localities in lowland Britain.
P 60cm Summer

Sainfoin
Onobrychis viciifolia
Recognised from a distance by its **long spikes of deep pink** or pink-striped **flowers** held well above the leaves. Each leaf is of **6–12 pairs of narrow, shortly-stalked leaflets** with hairy undersides. The **stipules** at the base of the leaf-stalk are **pale, not green**. The ripe **pods** are unmistakable being **short, flattened and with a rough, strongly-veined surface.**

Long grown as a forage crop and now widely established on roadside verges and in waste places in lowland England, especially on lime-rich soils, but also a native of old downland.
P 60cm Summer

Tares and Vetches

Tares and vetches (*Vicia* species) are climbing or scrambling herbs with pea-like flowers and leaves of 2–many pairs of variously-shaped **leaflets** usually **ending in a simple or branched tendril** which it twines round neighbouring plants or fences. The **stems** are **not winged** as in some species of *Lathyrus* (p.75).

Hairy Tare
Vicia hirsuta
Tares are slender annuals with flowers less than 8mm long. Hairy tare has **4–8 pairs of leaflets** less than 1.2cm long, spikes of **dirty-white** or purplish **flowers up to 5mm long** with almost **equal calyx teeth** the upper as long as the tube, which develop into **hairy pods** up to 1cm long **with 2 seeds**, easy to see without opening the pod.

Widespread on dry banks, roadside verges and disturbed grassland throughout the lowlands to 350m in Devon; often abundant on old railway lines.
A 30cm Late spring and summer

Smooth Tare
Vicia tetrasperma
A hairless tare with **4–6 pairs of leaflets** up to 2cm long, stalks of only 1 or 2 **pale blue** or mauve **flowers up to 4mm long** with very **unequal calyx teeth**, the upper 2 shorter than the tube. The **flower stalk** is **about as long as the leaves** and carries **hairless pods**, up to 1.5cm long **with 4 seeds**, which can be counted even when the pod is young, and have an oblong scar (hilum).

Grassland and bushy places in lowland England, the coasts of Wales and, very rarely, in southern Scotland.
A 60cm Late spring and summer

Slender Tare
Vicia tenuissima
Similar to smooth tare but with only 3–4 pairs of leaflets which are up to 2.5cm long, and stalks of 1–4 **flowers** which **have blue wings and standards and a greenish-white keel with a blue tip**. The **flower-stalk** is **longer than the leaves** and develops **hairless pods** up to 1.7cm long **with 5–8 seeds** which have a circular scar.

Local in hedgebanks and field borders in the southern half of England.
A 60cm Summer

Ornithopus perpusillus

Hippocrepis comosa

Coronilla varia

Onobrychis viciifolia

Vicia hirsuta

Vicia tetrasperma

Vicia tenuissima

Tufted Vetch
Vicia cracca
Our commonest perennial vetch with a **many-flowered spike on a stalk up to 10cm long**. There are **up to 40 blue-purple flowers**, each **1–1.2cm long**, arranged on one side of the stalk with unevenlengthed calyx teeth, the upper minute. Each leaf ends in a **branched tendril** and has **6–15 pairs of narrow, somewhat hairy, leaflets** often ending in a short point or mucro.

Rough grassland, hedgerows and other bushy places throughout British Isles to about 350m.
P   2m   Summer

Wood Bitter-vetch
Vicia orobus
An erect plant recognised by its **6–20 flowered spikes on stalks** which are about **as long as the leaves**, and by the **white flowers tinged with purple up to 1.5cm long**. The leaves have **6–12 pairs of elliptical, hairy leaflets** ending in short points but **lack a tendril at the tip**. The stipules at the base are large, toothed, and half-arrow shaped.

A very local plant found in rocky, wooded places and on coastal cliffs. Mainly in W Britain, especially in the Welsh hills and the Southern Uplands.
P   60cm   Summer and early autumn

Wood Vetch
Vicia sylvatica
A beautiful, trailing, hairless perennial with **flowers up to 2cm long** which are **white with blue or purple veins, in spikes of 6–20** on a stalk longer than the inflorescence. The leaves have **5–12 pairs of oblong leaflets** which end in a short point, and **long, much-branched tendrils**. The stipules are semi-circular with many teeth at the base.

Thinly scattered throughout British Isles in a range of habitats from woods and rocky places inland, to coastal cliffs and shingle beaches where it forms round, prostrate patches.
P   1.3m   Summer

Bush Vetch
Vicia sepium
An almost hairless, trailing or climbing perennial with **short spikes of** only **2–6 flowers up to 1.5cm long** which are **pale purple** and on very short stalks appearing **clustered at the base of the leaf**. The calyx teeth are unequal, the smaller ones shorter than the tube. Each leaf of **5–9 pairs of elliptical leaflets** with a short point at the tip, ends in a **branched tendril**.

Rough grassland, hedges and woodland to 800m in the Scottish Highlands. With strongly-growing underground stems it can be a troublesome garden weed.
P   1m   Late spring and summer

Common Vetch
Vicia sativa
A variable, slightly hairy species distinguished from other vetches by the **black spot**, *c.* 1mm across, in the centre of the **underside of the stipule**. The **flowers** are usually only **1 or 2 together at the base of the leaf** which is of **3–8 pairs of leaflets**. Two forms are recognised: the native narrow-leaved vetch, *V. sativa* subsp. *nigra*, with leaflets *c.* 3mm wide, flowers 1–1.8cm long and pods less than 4cm, and the widely sown vetch or tare grown for fodder, *V. sativa* subsp. *sativa*, with broader leaflets up to 1.5cm wide, with flowers 2–2.5cm long and pods of 4–5cm.

Roadsides, waste places and as an escape from cultivation throughout lowlands of British Isles.
A   1.2m   Late spring and summer

Spring Vetch
Vicia lathyroides
As the name implies this is an early flowering annual which is like a small common vetch but **lacks the spotted stipule**. It has tiny, **solitary flowers, less than 7mm long**, at the base of the leaf which is **of 2–3 pairs of leaflets** and ends in an **unbranched tendril or has none**.

Scattered in dry, sandy, often open, grassland throughout lowland Britain but mainly coastal in the west; N and E coasts of Ireland.
A   20cm   Spring and early summer

Bithynian Vetch
Vicia bithynica
Distinguished from other vetches by the large **flowers up to 2cm long** which are **solitary or in pairs** and have a **purple standard and white wings and keel**. They are carried **on a short, stout, hairy stalk up to 5cm**. The leaves have only **1 or 2 pairs of leaflets, branched tendrils** and very large **stipules, over 1cm long, with prominent teeth**.

Rare and local in bushy places and on sea-cliffs, mainly in the southern half of England with isolated coastal localities in N England, N Wales and S Scotland.
P   60cm   Late spring and early summer

Vicia cracca

Vicia orobus

Vicia sylvatica

Vicia sepium

Vicia sativa

Vicia lathyroides

Vicia bithynica

Peas and Vetchlings

Peas and vetchlings belong to the genus *Lathyrus* and may be separated from other plants with pea-like flowers by the presence of tendrils, the usually few pairs of leaflets with parallel veins and the winged stems. Not easily separated from *Vicia:* the only certain character is **the style** which, in *Lathyrus*, **is hairy on the upper side only** (see drawing).

Yellow Vetchling
Lathyrus aphaca

In mature plants the **leaves** are **reduced to a single tendril** and are **replaced**, functionally, by a **large pair of spear-shaped stipules as long as the internodes**. Seedlings have 1 or 2 leaves with a single pair of elliptical leaflets. The **flowers** are **solitary** on stalks up to 5cm long, and develop into pods up to 3.5cm long with 6–8 **smooth seeds**.

Rare in dry places in rough grassland and old hedgerows. Native only in southern England, introduced elsewhere.

A 1m Summer

Grass Vetchling
Lathyrus nissolia

Takes its English name from its resemblance to grass in which it grows which makes it difficult to find. There is a total absence of **leaflets** which are **replaced by** alternate, **long and narrow phyllodes** (flattened leaf-stalks) just **like leaves of grass**. It only becomes easy to recognise when it produces 1–2 crimson flowers on stalks 3–4cm long which develop pods up to 6cm long with 15–20 **rough seeds**.

Rough grassland in lowlands south of a line from R Humber to R Severn; casual further north.

A 90cm Late spring and summer

Meadow Vetchling
Lathyrus pratensis

This is the commonest vetchling and, apart from the rare yellow vetchling, is the only one with **yellow flowers**. Differs from that species in having a distinct pair of leaflets as well as **spear-shaped stipules** which are **shorter than the internodes**, branched, not simple, tendrils, and **flowers in clusters of 5–12** on a stout stalk up to 8cm long.

Hedgerows and rough grassland throughout British Isles to 500m in the northern Pennines.

P 1.2m Late spring and summer

Narrow-leaved Everlasting-pea
Lathyrus sylvestris

A vigorous, scrambling plant up to 2m long with a bluish-green bloom, recognised by its single pair of **leaflets** up to 15cm long about **8 times as long as broad**, the narrow sword-shaped **stipules only half as wide as the** markedly **winged stem**, and the cluster of 3–12 handsome pink **flowers** about **2cm across** which develop into long brown **pods** up to **7cm long**.

Thickets and hedgebanks in lowland Wales and the southern half of England, also rarely on the Scottish coast.

P 2m Summer

Broad-leaved Everlasting-pea
Lathyrus latifolius

Similar to narrow-leaved everlasting-pea but with **leaflets** only about **3 times as long as broad**, the **stipules more than half the width of the winged stem**, and much larger **flowers** up to **3cm across** which develop into brown **pods** as much as **11cm long**.

A native of central and southern Europe, often cultivated for its handsome flowers and escaping on to railway banks and roadsides.

P 3m Summer

Marsh Pea
Lathyrus palustris

A rare and rapidly declining species of lowland fens and damp, bushy places which are being drained. Difficult to distinguish from vetches, *Vicia* spp, because it has **2–5 pairs of leaflets** and branched tendrils. However the stem is strongly winged and the style has a row of hairs on the side towards the **calyx**, which **has very unequal teeth**, the lowest 3–4 times as long as the upper.

Mainly confined to eastern England north of R Thames, to central Ireland and the L Neagh region of Ulster.

P 1.2m Late spring and summer

Sea Pea
Lathyrus japonicus

Sea pea grows in **patches on** seashore **shingle** where it may be instantly recognised by the **bluish-green leaflets in 2–5 pairs**, and the clusters of 2–12 flowers on a stout stalk shorter than the leaves, which develop into fat pods with up to 11 edible seeds. It is said that in 1551 the people of Orford and Aldeburgh in Suffolk were kept alive by eating these seeds: they must have been hungry as the seeds are very bitter.

Coastal shingle banks from Norfolk to Glamorgan and, rarely, in W Ireland.

P 90cm Summer

Bitter-vetch
Lathyrus montanus

Though the Latin name, *montanus*, is a little misleading because the plant may be found in the lowlands of much of Britain, it is absent from a large area between the R Thames and the Wash, whilst ascending to 800m in the Highlands of Scotland. Another *Lathyrus* which may be mistaken for a *Vicia* with **2–4 pairs of leaflets** and the tendrils reduced to a short point: it does, however, have a winged stem and hairs on the calyx side of the style. The **calyx teeth** are **unequal**, the **lower** about **as long as the tube**.

P 50cm Spring and early summer

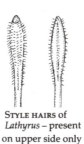

STYLE HAIRS of
Lathyrus – present
on upper side only

Lathyrus aphaca

Lathyrus nissolia

Lathyrus pratensis

Lathyrus sylvestris

Lathyrus latifolius

Lathyrus palustris

Lathyrus japonicus

Lathyrus montanus

Rose Family (Rosaceae) Rubus

A very familiar genus because we enjoy its edible fruits – blackberries and raspberries in particular. The large flowers have 5 sepals, 5 usually showy petals and numerous stamens, and the familiar 'berry' develops from a group of carpels which become fleshy around a small 'stone' containing a seed (drupelet).

Cloudberry
Rubus chamaemorus

The aristocrat of the genus, the cloudberry is a small northern plant **with a creeping rhizome and annual, leafy flowering shoots**. There are **separate male and female plants**, which differ in leaf shape, those of the female having shallower lobes (our photograph shows this well). When finally ripe, the **fruit turns from red to orange.**

Locally abundant on mountain moorland and peat bogs, from N Wales and the Pennines northwards; very rare in Ireland.

P 20cm Summer

Stone Bramble
Rubus saxatilis

Like the cloudberry, another northern plant which is also herbaceous. Easily distinguished by its **long non-flowering runners which root at the tips**. The leaves are compound, of 3 broad, toothed leaflets; the leaf-stalks and stems sometimes bear weak prickles. The **rather small white flowers are in groups of 2–8** on erect stems, and the **fruit has a few scarlet drupelets.**

Shady rocks and open woodland in hilly regions, especially on limestone, from SW England northwards; widespread but not common in Ireland.

P 40cm Summer

Raspberry
Rubus idaeus

A very familiar garden fruit, with tall, **erect, prickly woody stems, spreading freely by root suckers.** The **leaves have 3–7 leaflets which are white beneath**, and the **fruits have numerous, reddish, dull and softly hairy drupelets which separate from the receptacle when picked.**

Recorded throughout British Isles, but commonest in the north.

P 1.5m Summer

Dewberry
Rubus caesius

Dewberries are familiar in lowland England; they have **weakly prickly, spreading or trailing stems which are hairless and have a strong waxy bloom**. The leaves have 3 leaflets, and the flowers are relatively large with white or pinkish petals. The **dewberry has few, large, wide-spaced drupelets with a strong bluish 'bloom'.**

Common, mainly on basic soils, in C and E England; more local in SW England, Wales, Scotland and Ireland, and absent from N and NW Scotland.

P 20cm Summer

Bramble
Rubus fruticosus

Brambles are confusingly variable, and some 300 different kinds have been recognised in Britain. Typically, they have **long woody arching stems which root readily**, and the familiar **blackberry contains many drupelets, black when ripe** and remaining attached to the receptacle when picked. They can all be called *Rubus fruticosus*.

Common throughout British Isles except in N Scotland and parts of the Highlands; absent from Shetland.

P 1.5m Summer

Dropwort
Filipendula vulgaris

An **erect, nearly hairless plant** with a **basal rosette of compound leaves**, each with 8–20 pairs of closely-packed leaflets which are themselves deeply cut, and few, small stem leaves. The **flowers are in an irregular branched inflorescence**; each has (usually) **6 creamy-white petals, numerous stamens** and a group of carpels which develop into small one-seeded dry fruits (achenes).

Widespread in England in chalk or limestone grassland, but rare in the south-west, local in Wales and Scotland, and on the limestone of the west of Ireland.

P 40cm Summer

Meadowsweet
Filipendula ulmaria

One of our really familiar wildflowers, **with a very characteristic aroma** (crush the leaves!) **of oil of wintergreen**. The basal rosette **leaves are large, with 2–5 pairs of toothed, ovate leaflets**; the stem-leaves are similar. The **small flowers are very numerous in a large irregular branched inflorescence**; each flower is like the dropwort but has (usually) 5 smaller, creamy-white petals.

Common in wet places throughout British Isles.

P 1m Summer

Marsh Cinquefoil
Potentilla palustris

This cinquefoil has a **long, woody, creeping rhizome** and more or less erect stems. The lower leaves have 5 or 7 roughly oblong leaflets, the upper ones have 3 only. **The large flowers have 5 sepals and an extra 'epicalyx' of small, narrow segments between the sepals**. The petals are shorter than the sepals, and there are numerous stamens and carpels. **All parts of the flower are purplish.**

Rather common in marshes, wet moorland and bogs throughout British Isles except parts of S and C England.

P 40cm Summer

Rubus chamaemorus

Rubus saxatilis

Rubus idaeus

Rubus caesius

Rubus fruticosus

Filipendula vulgaris

Filipendula ulmaria

Potentilla palustris

Silverweed and Cinquefoils

All the species of *Potentilla* described on this page are low-growing perennial plants with yellow or white flowers. They all share the character of the epicalyx (already described for the marsh cinquefoil on p.76): this is well shown in the picture of trailing tormentil (bud to right of middle).

Silverweed
Potentilla anserina
Easily recognised by its **long, creeping, rooting and flowering runners** and its **feathery, compound leaves with 7–12 pairs of main leaflets interspersed with smaller ones**. The silvery hairiness which gives the plant its common name is normally shown on both sides of the leaves. The flowers are large, often more than 2cm across.
Found throughout British Isles. Its native habits are damp sand-dunes, but found on roadsides, waste ground and especially round duck-ponds.
P 15cm Summer

Hoary Cinquefoil
Potentilla argentea
Most easily recognised among the cinquefoils that follow, all of which have palmate leaves with 3, 5 or 7 leaflets radiating from a central point, **by the whitish woolly under-surface of the leaflets** (well shown in the photograph). The pale yellow flowers are 1–1.5cm across.
A rather local plant of dry, sandy grassland, mainly in E England, but extending to E Wales and SE Scotland; absent from Ireland.
P 20cm Summer

Spring Cinquefoil
Potentilla tabernaemontani
A **mat-forming** plant **somewhat woody at base, with many prostrate branches**, often rooting along their length. The leaves are rather variable, some forms having 5 leaflets, others regularly 7. The yellow **flowers, produced early in the season, are 1–1.5cm across**.
A very local plant of rather dry chalk or limestone grassland from Hampshire and Suffolk to C Scotland; absent from Ireland.
P 15cm Spring

Alpine Cinquefoil
Potentilla crantzii
A handsome mountain plant related to the spring cinquefoil, and best distinguished by its habit of growth, as the photograph shows. The **plants do not form a mat**, and the flowering stems rise up from the rootstock. The **flower is larger, up to 2cm across**, and the **petal is a deeper yellow, often with a darker orange spot near its base**.
Rather rare on rock ledges and in upland grassland, usually on basic rock, from N Wales and the Yorkshire Dales to N Scotland; absent from Ireland.
P 25cm Summer

Tormentil
Potentilla erecta
A common cinquefoil, easily distinguished by its **small, regularly 4-petalled flowers** and **most of its leaves with 3 leaflets**. The plant has a thick, woody stock, from which the flowering stems arise; these never root, so the plants do not spread vegetatively.
Found throughout British Isles in both dry and wet places, but commonest on light acid soils such as sandy heaths.
P 30cm Summer

Creeping Cinquefoil
Potentilla reptans
In this species **long creeping runners root freely at the nodes**, and bear the **solitary flowers on long slender flower stalks** along their length. The **leaves have 5 leaflets** (on vigorous plants there may be 7). The large, 5-petalled **flowers** may be **2.5cm across**.
Common on roadsides, hedgebanks etc. throughout England, Wales and Ireland, but rare in the Highlands and N Scotland, and unknown in Orkney and Shetland.
P 20cm Summer

Trailing Tormentil
Potentilla anglica
An interesting plant, with characters intermediate between the tormentil and the creeping cinquefoil, and best told by its **flowers which regularly on the same plant show both 4 and 5 petals**. The **flowering stems usually trail on the ground**, and may root late in the season.
Scattered throughout much of the British Isles, often in open heathy woodland, but absent from N Scotland, Orkney and Shetland.
P 30cm Summer

Barren Strawberry
Potentilla sterilis
This 'odd man out' among the cinquefoils, with **small white flowers**, has a general resemblance to the true wild strawberry (p.80) and is **one of the very early spring flowers of woodland**. The **leaves, with 3 ovate leaflets**, are like those of the strawberry, but can be distinguished by **the spreading (not silky) hairs on the underside**. Short runners may be produced, but these do not root readily at the nodes.
Common in open woodland throughout most of the British Isles except N Scotland; absent from Shetland.
P 15cm Spring

Potentilla anserina

Potentilla argentea

Potentilla tabernaemontani

Potentilla crantzii

Potentilla erecta

Potentilla reptans

Potentilla anglica

Potentilla sterilis

Sibbaldia
Sibbaldia procumbens

This small mountain relative of the cinquefoils is a **compact, tufted plant** with a short woody rootstock. The **leaves have 3 bluish-green, obovate leaflets**, and the flowers are small, few together in dense groups. They have the structure of a cinquefoil flower, but the **petals are very small, narrow, and yellowish (sometimes absent).**

On mountains from Westmorland and Peebles northwards, locally common in the Scottish Highlands; absent from Ireland.
P 10cm Summer

Wild Strawberry
Fragaria vesca

The wild relative of garden strawberry, related to *Potentilla*. In that genus the fruiting head of achenes remains small and dry, whereas the strawberry is a large, swollen, fleshy head. Wild strawberry resembles the barren strawberry in flower but is distinguished by its longer, rooting runners, its larger petals which touch or slightly overlap, and by the back of the leaves which have a flat silky sheen of hairs.

Open woodland throughout British Isles, but rarer in N Scotland, Orkney and Shetland.
P 20cm Spring and early summer

Garden Strawberry
Fragaria x ananassa

The garden strawberry has **much larger flowers (and fruits)** than the wild strawberry, and the whole plant is indeed a 'larger edition' of that species.

Not uncommon as a garden escape on waste ground, railway banks etc., mostly in lowland England.
P 35cm Early summer

Wood Avens
Geum urbanum

Wood avens, sometimes called herb-Bennet, is related to the cinquefoils (note the epicalyx!). The hairy stems arise from a rosette of **large, pinnate leaves in which the end leaflet is much larger than the others**, and there are several stem-leaves with fewer leaflets. The **yellow flowers are held erect on long stalks**. In fruit there is a **compact head of achenes each with a stiff hook at the tip.**

Common in hedgebanks, etc. throughout most of the British Isles, but rare in N Scotland and absent from Shetland.
P 60cm Early summer

Where the 2 *Geum* species meet, remarkable 'hybrid swarms' may be found; in such populations many plants show flowers intermediate in shape and colour.

Water Avens
Geum rivale

Our only other wild *Geum* looks very different in flower from wood avens, though it is closely related. The much larger **flowers are nodding on long stalks**, and the **petals are** a dull **orange-pink** colour, **largely concealed by the purple calyx**. The fruiting heads are similar to those of wood avens, but larger.

In marshes, wet woods and damp rock ledges, mostly on limestone, over much of Britain, but rare in the south-east of England; widespread but not common in Ireland.
P 60cm Summer

Mountain Avens
Dryas octopetala

A much-branched **prostrate dwarf shrub** with **numerous small, stalked, oblong leaves with blunt shallow teeth, the upper surface dark green, the underside covered in whitish hairs**. The large **white flowers** are stalked and the **petals are usually 8 in number**. In fruit there is a **large silvery head of achenes with long feathery styles**.

On limestone and other basic rock mainly on mountains, from N Wales and Yorkshire to N Scotland. Locally common on the Burren in W Ireland; otherwise rare in Ireland and only in the north.
P 10cm Summer

Agrimony
Agrimonia

Agrimony is a familiar hedgerow plant, with large pinnate leaves rather like those of meadowsweet (p.76) and **long narrow spikes of yellow flowers**, succeeded by many **hard fruits crowned by a ring of small spines**. This remarkable 'burr' fruit develops from the base of the flower, and encloses 1 or 2 seeds.

There are 2 kinds of agrimony, best separated by the appearance of the ripe fruit. In the common species, *A. eupatoria*, the conical part of the **fruit is deeply ridged**, whilst in the more local fragrant agrimony, *A. procera*, the fruit is

somewhat wider and the **ridges are poorly developed** (see photograph). The fragrant agrimony is a more robust plant with many aromatic glands on the stems and leaves.

Common agrimony occurs in hedgebanks and on roadsides throughout British Isles except N Scotland, Orkney and Shetland. Fragrant agrimony is widespread, but generally much less common, and frequent only in S England.
P 80cm Summer

Sibbaldia procumbens

Fragaria vesca

Fragaria x *ananassa*

Geum urbanum

Geum rivale

Dryas octopetala

Agrimonia eupatoria

Agrimonia A. eupatoria (left)
& *A. procera*

Lady's-mantle
Alchemilla vulgaris
This familiar plant has **lobed basal leaves round in outline** (not unlike the common mallow, p.48), and **heads of small greenish flowers**. Each flower has 4 sepals, with 4 narrower epicalyx segments (like *Potentilla*, p.78); there are no petals, and only 4 stamens. The simple ovary develops into a single-seeded nutlet.

The seed is set without fertilisation, and all plants raised from seed resemble accurately their mother plant. This so-called apomictic reproduction is responsible for the existence of distinct 'microspecies', of which only 3 are common. Our photograph shows one: *A. xanthochlora*. A single leaf can tell you which of the 3 you have. In *A. xanthochlora* the upper leaf surface is hairless and the leaf-stalk is densely spreading-hairy. In *A. glabra*, which also has a hairless upper leaf surface, the leaf-stalk has few, inconspicuous, appressed hairs. In *A. filicaulis* both leaf surfaces and the leaf-stalk have obvious spreading hairs.

In meadows, pastures, roadsides, etc. throughout much of the British Isles, ascending to over 1000m, but not common in S and SE England and S Ireland.
P 50cm Summer

Alpine Lady's-mantle
Alchemilla alpina
A smaller, neater, mountain relative of the ordinary lady's-mantle, easily distinguished by its pretty leaves with 5–7 narrow leaflets, green on top and silvery-hairy beneath. The small yellowish-green flowers closely resemble those of the lady's-mantle, and the seed develops apomictically.

Common on mountains in the Scottish Highlands, especially where snow lies late and where the rock is basic; locally common in the W of the Lake District, but absent from Snowdonia, and very rare in the Irish mountains.
P 15cm Summer

Parsley-piert
Aphanes arvensis
This small annual plant looks very different from the lady's-mantle, but is related by its floral structure. The stems bear **leaves with deep lobes** and there are **well-developed lobed stipules where the leaf-stalks join the stem**. The tiny greenish flowers are flask-shaped, with a small calyx and epicalyx at the top; there is only one stamen, and a small nutlet develops inside the 'flask'. The plants, like many weeds of arable and open ground, are very variable in size. In winter-wet sandy ground a different but closely-related species can be found: *A. microcarpa*, a more slender plant most easily distinguished from *A. arvensis* by the shape of the stipule-lobes. In *A. arvensis* these are triangular, whilst in *A. microcarpa* they are blunt and finger-like (see drawing).

Formerly widespread as a weed of arable land; also on limestone or sandy ground where the soil is thin. Apparently much rarer as a weed since the use of herbicides in agriculture.
A 10cm Spring and summer

Salad Burnet
Sanguisorba minor
A deep-rooted herb with **pinnate basal leaves** and **wiry, often reddish stems bearing dense round heads of small flowers**. In each head the flowers have 4 green sepals, no epicalyx and no petals, and the **uppermost flowers are female only with bright red, feathery stigmas**. In the lower flowers there are numerous stamens shedding pollen into the wind.

In chalk and limestone grassland, common in much of England; rare in Scotland and much of Wales and local in Ireland.
P 30cm Summer

Great Burnet
Sanguisorba officinalis
A handsome larger relative of the salad burnet, with **large, deep red, oblong heads of flowers** in which the sepals contribute the colour. The pinnate basal leaves resemble those of the salad burnet, but can be 2 or 3 times as large.

In damp grassland, wood margins, etc., locally common from the S Midlands to the Scottish border, but absent from most of Scotland, and rare in N and C Wales and Ireland.
P 1m Summer

Roseroot
Sedum rosea
Members of the stonecrop family are succulent plants with simple, fleshy leaves, and flowers with a group of separate 'pods' (follicles) for an ovary.

The hairless flowering stems of roseroot arise from a very **thick, scaly, woody rootstock**. The numerous **stem-leaves are blue-green and rather fleshy**. Male and female flowers are on separate plants.

Mountain rocks in N England, N Wales, Scotland and Ireland, and on sea-cliffs in the northwest.
P 30cm Summer

Orpine
Sedum telephium
A **rather fleshy, hairless plant** with the general appearance of roseroot, but growing in the lowlands. The **heads of flowers are looser and reddish-purple in** colour. The **flowers are hermaphrodite**, each with 5 green sepals and 5 reddish petals.

In woodlands and hedgerows, scattered over much of lowland England, Wales and Scotland, but probably an escape from cultivation in many places and doubtfully native in Ireland.
P 50cm Late summer

Alchemilla vulgaris

Alchemilla alpina

Aphanes arvensis

Stipules

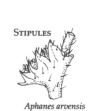

Aphanes arvensis

A. microcarpa

Sanguisorba minor

Sanguisorba officinalis

Sedum rosea

Sedum telephium

English Stonecrop
Sedum anglicum
A small, evergreen, **hairless, glaucous, often reddish** and **very fleshy** plant **with creeping and rooting stems** and short, fat, rounded overlapping leaves clasping the stems. The **white flowers, tinged with pink**, are on short, slightly branched, erect stems; when open, they are more than 1cm across and starlike with 5 pointed petals.

Rocky ground, especially in W Britain and W Ireland, avoiding lime-rich soils, and especially common along the W coast.
P   5cm   Summer

White Stonecrop
Sedum album
Like the English stonecrop, but larger, with longer **cylindrical leaves** and much larger, **more branched inflorescences**.

On rocks and walls, perhaps native in a few places (N Somerset, Devon), but commonly escaped from gardens and growing wild.
P   15cm   Summer

Biting Stonecrop
Sedum acre
This plant has the general appearance of the English stonecrop, but is easily recognised by the **bitter, peppery taste** when a small piece is (cautiously!) chewed. When in flower, there is no difficulty, for the **petals are bright yellow**.

Dry places, including walls, sand-dunes and rocks, especially chalk and limestone; common throughout British Isles, except NW Scotland, and absent from Shetland.
P   8cm   Summer

Rock Stonecrop
Sedum forsteranum
An **evergreen, fleshy plant** with **numerous creeping stems forming large mats**, from which the flowering branches ascend. The numerous **more or less cylindrical leaves** tend to be crowded at the erect tips of the creeping stems. The flat-topped **inflorescence has 4 or 5 main branches** and contains **many yellow flowers with blunt petals**.

As a native confined to Wales, the bordering counties, and SW England, where it is locally common on rocky ground. In other places it is almost certainly a garden escape.
P   25cm   Summer

Reflexed Stonecrop
Sedum reflexum
Resembles the rock stonecrop, but is **more robust**, and **the leaves on the flowering stems are often bent outwards and downwards** (hence the name). The flowers are somewhat larger, and the **petals are pointed**.

A commonly cultivated plant, often naturalised on old walls and rocks in Britain and Ireland, but not recorded north of Kincardine in Scotland.
P   30cm   Summer

Hairy Stonecrop
Sedum villosum
A remarkable little plant **growing**, unlike its relatives, **in wet places**. It has the general appearance of the other smaller species described here but **its erect shoots and leaves are covered with glandular hairs. The few flowers are on long stalks**, and the **petals are pink**.

By stream sides and on wet, stony ground in the mountains, from Yorkshire and Lancashire northwards to E Scotland. Absent from the mountains of N and W Scotland, Ireland and Wales.
P (? B)   15cm   Summer

Mossy Stonecrop
Crassula tillaea
The smallest land flowering plant in Britain! This extraordinary diminutive plant **looks just like a reddish moss on the ground**. Looked at with a hand-lens, the **tiny succulent shoots are seen to have thick, concave leaves in pairs** along the stems, and in nearly every leaf-axil there is a **very small flower with 3(4) sepals and petals**.

Locally common on sandy or gravelly soil in a few places in S and E England, particularly in the Breckland, where it often marks out winter-wet depressions on tracks in the sandy soil.
A   3cm   Spring and summer

Navelwort
Umbilicus rupestris
A hairless, fleshy plant with basal **leaves circular in outline and attached to the long leaf-stalk in the middle, making a navel-like depression**. The **long, showy inflorescence** bears many **pendulous greenish-white flowers** in which the **corolla is tubular**.

On rocks and walls, common in west of England, Wales, SW Scotland and much of Ireland, but rare in the east and absent from E and N Scotland.
P   40cm   Summer

Sedum anglicum

Sedum album

Sedum acre

Sedum forsteranum

Sedum reflexum

Sedum villosum

Crassula tillaea

Umbilicus rupestris

Saxifrage Family

Saxifrages are very popular rock-garden plants, and our native species include a few attractive mountain flowers. They are all characterised by having regular flowers with 1 or 2 whorls of stamens and **a capsular fruit on which the 2 thick styles persist at the top**. Golden-saxifrages (*Chrysosplenium*) differ from true saxifrages mainly in the absence of petals in the small, rather densely-packed yellow-green flowers.

Rue-leaved Saxifrage
Saxifraga tridactylites

This tiny annual has **erect, glandular-hairy, often reddish stems** arising from **a rosette of small 3- or 5-lobed leaves**. The few small **flowers**, on slender stalks, **have a bell-shaped receptacle** on top of which the 5 small sepals and **5 white petals** are attached.

Rather common on old walls, dry grassland, limestone rocks, etc. through much of lowland England and Wales; local in Scotland, but extending to the Hebrides and Caithness; throughout Ireland, but rare in the south-west and north-east.

A   8cm   Spring

Starry Saxifrage
Saxifraga stellaris

A **neat, pretty rosette plant** with **rather thick, slightly toothed leaves** more or less wedge-shaped in outline. The **thin, leafless, glandular-hairy flowering stems have up to 12 flowers on slender stalks**. In flower the 5 sepals are turned back, and the **5 petals, c.5mm long, spread like a star; they are white with 2 yellow spots at the base**.

Rather common in wet, stony places on all our mountains, including the Irish; found on the summit of Ben Nevis, the highest mountain, at 1343m.

P   15cm   Summer

Meadow Saxifrage
Saxifraga granulata

An unusual plant that **overwinters entirely as bulbils** formed the previous summer in the axils of **rosette leaves**. The **glandular-hairy flowering shoots arise from the rosette leaves which are long-stalked** and **kidney-shaped with coarse teeth**. The **open flowers with 5 white, rounded petals are quite large, up to 2cm across**.

Widespread in old grassland, especially on basic soils, mainly in eastern Britain from NE Scotland southwards; rare and probably introduced in Ireland and much of W Britain

P   50cm   Late spring

Mossy Saxifrage
Saxifraga hypnoides

A pretty, almost hairless plant forming **large mats of prostrate non-flowering leafy shoots often with bulbils in the leaf-axils**. On the flowering rosettes the **leaves are 3- to 5-lobed** with long stalks; those of the non-flowering shoots are often unlobed. The flowers are solitary or in groups of 2–5, on slender glandular stalks, and the **narrowly-oblong petals are pure white**.

Local on rocks in hilly areas from N Somerset to Caithness; in Ireland mainly in the mountains.

P   15cm   Summer

Yellow Saxifrage
Saxifraga aizoides

Unmistakable in flower by a mountain stream, the yellow saxifrage has a **creeping habit, with numerous small, narrowly oblong, stalkless bright green leaves** and short inflorescences bearing 1–10 flowers. The sepals can be seen between **the narrow, bright yellow petals in the open flowers, which can be 1.5cm across**. Sometimes the petals are strongly red-spotted.

By streamsides and on wet rocks mainly in mountains, locally common, from Yorkshire and Westmorland to Orkney; only in N and NW Ireland.

P   10cm   Summer

Purple Saxifrage
Saxifraga oppositifolia

Many people would claim this is our most beautiful mountain flower. The **purple flowers are borne on short, densely leafy stalks** and often cover the mat of foliage. On the long **prostrate non-flowering shoots the short, thick, shining blue-green leaves are tightly packed in opposite pairs, and have curious depressions near the apex which secrete lime, appearing as white dots**.

Local on mountains, especially on basic rocks, from the Brecon Beacons northwards in Britain; NW Ireland only.

P   2cm   Spring

Opposite-leaved Golden-saxifrage
Chrysosplenium oppositifolium

A loosely mat-forming plant with **many spreading, leafy, rooting stems which have opposite pairs of leaves circular in outline**. The flowering shoots bear 1–3 pairs **of smaller leaves**, and the inflorescence is a **flattened, yellow-green head of numerous small flowers**, each with 4 or 5 sepals and **no petals**.

Common on wet rocks, in shady woodland, and by streams in most of British Isles, though absent from Cambridgeshire and Huntingdonshire; uncommon in EC England and C Ireland.

P   15cm   Spring and summer

Alternate-leaved Golden-saxifrage
Chrysosplenium alternifolium

A more local plant than the preceding, spreading by **leafless runners** and with more robust flowering stems. Best known by its **alternate**, not opposite, **kidney-shaped leaves which on the flowering stems are usually single**.

Local, in similar places to the much commoner opposite-leaved golden-saxifrage, but absent from Ireland and the extreme west of Britain.

P   20cm   Spring and summer

Saxifraga tridactylites

Saxifraga stellaris

Saxifraga granulata

Saxifraga hypnoides

Saxifraga aizoides

Saxifraga oppositifolia

Chrysosplenium oppositifolium

Chrysosplenium alternifolium

Grass-of-Parnassus
Parnassia palustris
A beautiful wildflower. The **large, white, 5-petalled flowers, about the size of daisies, are on stalks with a single, heart-shaped leaf** near the base. The other leaves are similar and all basal. In detail the flower is unique; between each of the 5 normal stamens are **5 fan-shaped 'staminodes' with glistening glands that attract insects.**
Widespread but rather local in marshy and boggy ground; commoner in N England, N Wales and Scotland. Local in Ireland, absent from the SW.
P   25cm   Late summer and autumn

Round-leaved Sundew
Drosera rotundifolia
A single **'pin-cushion' leaf** is enough to identify this, the commonest of our 3 sundews. The leaves are **circular on long stalks in a spreading rosette** (see drawing). Like the other 2 British species this is a carnivorous plant of boggy ground which catches its prey (mainly small insects and spiders) on the sticky hairs of the 'pin-cushion'. All our sundews have **small white flowers** which **rarely open** and are self-pollinated in bud.
Throughout British Isles in acid bogs; now rare or extinct in much of lowland England.
P   8cm   Summer

Great Sundew
Drosera anglica
The most handsome of our sundews, especially when, as in our photograph, we are lucky enough to find it with wide-open flowers. The **leaves are long and tapering into the stalk**, quite different in shape from the round-leafed sundew (see drawing).
In similar places to the common species, but only really common in NW Scotland and NW Ireland; elsewhere rare and local, and extinct over much of England.
P   25cm   Summer

Oblong-leaved Sundew
Drosera intermedia
As its scientific name implies, our third sundew has **leaves intermediate** in shape between the other two (see drawing). It is usually a small plant, to be looked for in more open peaty places where the round-leafed sundew is growing (the 2 species often grow together, but round-leaved sundew can grow better in competition with bog-moss).
Locally abundant in W Scotland and W Ireland; elsewhere very local and extinct in many places in England.
P   10cm   Summer

Purple-Loosestrife
Lythrum salicaria
A familiar, handsome wildflower of wet places, with **narrow, many-flowered reddish-purple spikes** of flowers, and **narrow, hairy leaves in opposite pairs (or commonly in whorls of three)**. The flowers have 6 petals and 12 stamens. Different plants show 3 possible arrangements of the simple style in the centre of the flower: they may be short, mid, or long-styled.
Locally abundant in marshes, river-sides, etc. throughout England, Wales and Ireland; in Scotland mainly in the west, absent from much of the north.
P   1.2m   Summer

Water-purslane
Lythrum portula
Quite unlike the purple loosestrife to which it is related, this is a **small, hairless, almost fleshy annual with stems creeping and rooting at the nodes**. The leaves are broadly spoon-shaped and in pairs. The tiny flowers betray their relationship by having **6 calyx-teeth and 6 or 12 stamens**, but the petals are often, as in our photograph, minute or absent.
Scattered throughout the British Isles on bare muddy or peaty ground around pools and in heath and moorland, locally common but absent from N Scotland and Shetland.
A   5cm   Late summer

Willowherbs (Onagraceae)
The true willowherbs of the genus *Epilobium* differ from *Chamaenerion* (p.90) in having **leaves in pairs**, not spirally arranged, and in the **flowers which are regular and not held horizontally**. The long, thin capsular fruit with white plumed seed is the same in both. They are dealt with on this and the following page.

Great Willowherb
Epilobium hirsutum
Great willowherb is a hairy plant easily told by its **large 4-petalled pinkish-purple flowers**. The **leaves are strap-shaped, unstalked and (usually) in pairs** along the stems. Each **flower has** 8 stamens and **a single prominent style divided at the tip into 4 stigmas**.
Common in wet places throughout most of England, Wales and Ireland, but less common in Scotland, and absent from much of the Highlands, W Scotland and the islands.
P   1.5m   Summer

Hoary Willowherb
Epilobium parviflorum
Like a small edition of the great willowherb, with **smaller, pale pink, deeply-notched petals** and stems **covered with short, dense glandular hairs** (and therefore looking grey-green). The **style**, as in the great willowherb, is **obviously divided into 4 stigmas** (see drawing p.91).
Common in wet places throughout much of the British Isles, but rarer in N Scotland and absent from Shetland.
P   60cm   Summer

Parnassia palustris

Drosera rotundifolia

Drosera anglica

LEAVES

Drosera rotundifolia

D. angelica

D. intermedia

Lythrum salicaria

Lythrum portula

Epilobium hirsutum

Epilobium parviflorum

Broad-leaved Willowherb
Epilobium montanum
Most readily distinguished from all other willowherbs by its **almost hairless, ovate leaves with distinct stalks**. The pink flowers are relatively large and the **style** (as in the 2 species on p.88) **is obviously divided into 4 stigmas**.

Common on the less acid soils, often as a garden or roadside weed, throughout the British Isles; rather sparse in N Scotland and parts of Ireland.

P   50cm   Summer

Spear-leaved Willowherb
Epilobium lanceolatum
Amongst narrow-leaved willowherbs, this species is easily distinguished by **being only sparsely hairy** except in the inflorescence, and in having **a 4-cleft style** in the flower. The stems are simple or slightly branched, and bear **narrowly elliptical or spearshaped leaves wedge-shaped at the base and clearly stalked**. The pink petals are 6–8mm.

On roadsides, waste places and disturbed ground mainly in S England and S Wales northwards to N Wales and Norfolk, apparently increasing.
P   60cm   Summer
[Not illustrated]

American Willowherb
Epilobium ciliatum
This plant, first recorded in Britain in 1891, and now the commonest willowherb in many parts of England, is best distinguished by the following combination of characters: **narrow, short-stalked leaves, dense glandular hairiness in the inflorescence, and small pink flowers with undivided stigma**. The stems are often reddish.

An American alien, common in lowland England on waste and disturbed ground. Still spreading, and recently recorded from several parts of Ireland and from 2 Hebridean islands.
P   1m   Summer

Pale Willowherb
Epilobium roseum
This native willowherb is most easily confused with the American species, but differs in the following ways. Its **leaves have long stalks** (5–10mm: less than 3mm in *E. ciliatum*), and the **shortly 2-lobed petals are at first almost white**, later streaked with pink. Both species have glandular hairs in the upper part of the stem, and undivided stigmas.

Throughout lowland Britain northwards to Perthshire, often on disturbed ground, nowhere very common; in Ireland only in the north-east.
P   60cm   Summer

Square-stalked Willowherb
Epilobium tetragonum
Easily distinguished from the 2 preceding willowherbs by **the absence of glandular hairs on the stem and inflorescence branches** and by the **stalkless leaves**. The flowers are larger, with pale pinkish petals up to 7mm.
Common in lowland England, rare in Scotland and Ireland.

Rather variable in leaf-shape; the locally common plant in much of SE England has shiny, narrowly strap-shaped leaves by which it can usually readily be distinguished.
P   60cm   Summer
[Not illustrated]

Short-fruited Willowherb
Epilobium obscurum
Like the square-stalked willowherb, but with **narrowly ovate leaves** and **much shorter capsules (not more than 6cm**, compared with 7–10cm). In flower the presence of a **few glandular hairs on the calyx-tube** is diagnostic.

Locally common in wet places throughout British Isles, especially in the north and west. In W Ireland the commonest species.
P   60cm   Summer

Marsh Willowherb
Epilobium palustre
A **rather delicate narrow-leaved** willowherb, **with very thin runners at the base**. The **slender stems have no raised lines or angles** (though often 2 lines of hairs), and bear several **small flowers drooping in late bud, but held horizontally when open**.

In marshes and acid fens throughout the British Isles, avoiding lime and therefore rather rare in parts of lowland England.
P   40cm   Summer

New Zealand Willowherb
Epilobium brunnescens
(*E. nerterioides, E. pedunculare*)
This attractive, mat-forming 'alpine' is very easily recognised by its **slender creeping stems rooting at the nodes** and **small, almost circular, hairless leaves**. The **flowers are borne singly on slender stalks** and the small petals are white or pink. The long, thin capsules are freely produced.

Introduced as a garden plant around 1900, this successful alien from the New Zealand mountains is now locally common by streams and on wet rocks in all upland areas in the British Isles, and is still spreading.
P   7cm   Summer

Rose-bay Willowherb
Chamaenerion angustifolium
Unmistakable with its **tall stems with many large, bright pinkishpurple flowers**. The **leaves are narrow, numerous and spirally arranged**. The numerous flowers are borne horizontally in the narrow inflorescences: each has 4 purple sepals, and 4 rose-purple petals of which the 2 upper are larger than the lower pair. In **fruit, the long thin capsules split to release the white-plumed seeds** in abundance.

Common throughout much of Britain to 1000m, but rare in NW Scotland, and much of Ireland.
P   1.2m   Late summer

Epilobium montanum

STIGMAS

Epilobium montanum (divided)

E. roseum (undivided)

Epilobium ciliatum

Epilobium roseum

Epilobium obscurum

Epilobium palustre

Epilobium brunnescens

Chamaenerion angustifolium

Evening-primroses

The evening-primroses are not native plants, but are often seen in waste places and sand-dunes. They are annuals or biennials, with large, usually yellow, flowers which open towards evening and are more or less fragrant. The 4 sepals and petals, and the long capsule developing below the flower, indicate their relationship to the willowherbs in the family Onagraceae, but the seeds have no plume of hairs.

Common Evening-primrose
Oenothera biennis

An **erect, robust, hairy plant**, with leafy stems, more or less oblong leaves in a basal rosette, and **large yellow flowers** in the axils of the upper stem-leaves. The 4 sepals turn back when the petals unfold, and drop off quickly. The **broad, yellow petals are up to 3cm**. The sepals and capsules are covered with stiff bulbous-based hairs.

Apparently native in continental Europe, and early introduced into Britain. Waste ground, roadsides, etc. mainly in England; rare in Scotland and Wales and absent from Ireland.

B 1m Summer

Large-flowered Evening-primrose
Oenothera erythrosepala

Like the common evening-primrose, but flowers even larger, with **petals up to 5cm**; best told by the **red colour of the sepals** and the **red bulbous bases of the stiff hairs** on many parts of the plant. (In *O. biennis* the sepals are entirely green, and many bulbous hairs are also green.)

Introduced into Britain from N America in the early 19th century, and now the commonest evening-primrose, on sand-dunes, roadsides and waste places in England and Wales: local in Scotland and N Ireland.

B 1.5m Summer

Fragrant Evening-primrose
Oenothera stricta

A **rather slender** plant, with **narrow leaves** and **very fragrant flowers** with large **petals originally deep yellow with a basal red spot**, becoming reddish throughout as they fade.

Locally common on sand-dunes and coastal waste places, mainly in S and SW England and Wales; very rare in Scotland and Ireland. Native of Chile.

A or B 90cm Summer and early autumn

Enchanter's-nightshade
Circaea lutetiana

A familiar woodland plant with erect hairy stems from **long-creeping rhizomes**, and **opposite, ovate, stalked leaves thin in texture and almost hairless**. The **flowers are small and white, with parts in twos, on slender stalks in a long, bractless raceme. The fruit is short, 1–2-seeded, with hook-tipped bristles.**

Common in woods and shady places throughout England, Wales, Ireland and S Scotland to 400m; rare in N Scotland and absent from the Outer Hebrides, Orkney and Shetland.

P 60cm Summer

Upland Enchanter's-nightshade
Circaea x intermedia

Like the preceding, but much smaller and more delicate, with **runners in the lower leaf-axils** and **distinctly heart-shaped leaves. Best told later in the season by its inability** as a species-hybrid **to set any seed**.

A remarkable example of a not uncommon sterile hybrid of which one parent (the true alpine enchanter's-nightshade, *Circaea alpina*) is rare in Britain. In shady, rocky places in upland W and N Britain from S Wales northwards; very local in Ireland.

P 40cm Summer

Bastard-toadflax
Thesium humifusum

A small, hairless, **yellowish-green plant** parasitic on roots of other plants, with a woody stock, and spreading or **prostrate stems with very narrow one-veined leaves**. The small, yellowish-white flowers have a single perianth of 5 triangular parts, and the **small ovoid fruit is crowned by the persistent perianth** (well shown in photograph).

A local plant of chalk and limestone grassland in England northwards to Gloucester and Lincolnshire.

P 15cm Summer

Mistletoe
Viscum album

Unique in our flora, the mistletoe is a somewhat **woody evergreen parasitic on trees**, with **thick, leathery leaves in opposite pairs** on the wide-branching stems. The **small, yellow-green male and female flowers** are usually produced on separate plants, and the **familiar white berry**, ripe around Christmas-time, **contains a single seed**.

Native on a variety of trees, most commonly on apple (where it is often cultivated) in much of England and Wales, but rare in the north and absent from Scotland and Ireland.

P 1m Winter and spring

Dwarf Cornel
Cornus suecica

A charming and entirely unmistakable northern plant, with **annual erect stems** arising from long rhizomes, and **ovate 3–5-veined leaves in opposite pairs**. The large white terminal 'flowers', up to 2cm across, are made up of **a central cluster of small purplish flowers surrounded by 4 white ovate bracts looking like petals**. The fruit is a red 'berry' (actually a stone fruit).

On mountain moorlands, rare in N England and S Scotland, but rather common in the Highlands of Scotland; absent from the Hebrides and Ireland.

P 20cm Summer

Oenothera biennis

Oenothera erythrosepala

Oenothera stricta

Circaea lutetiana

Circaea x *intermedia*

Thesium humifusum

Viscum album

Cornus suecica

Ivy
Hedera helix
This unmistakable woody climber retains its hold on walls, rocks and trees by means of little rootlets. It is not a parasite, gaining neither food nor water from the plants it clings to: it does no harm to healthy trees. The **leaves vary in shape**: the lower, on climbing or running shoots, are **5-angled** whilst those **higher up** may be simple. Ivy **flowers in autumn** when many insects are attracted to the nectar of its greenish-yellow umbels.

Throughout the British Isles ascending to over 600m in N Ireland.

P   30m   Autumn

Umbellifers
Members of the *Umbelliferae* are easily recognised by the arrangement of the **flowers** of the majority of the species **on spreading stalks from a central point** like the ribs of an umbrella. **There are 2 layers**: the **leaf-like appendages below the lower ribs are called bracts**, whilst **those below the upper ribs are bracteoles**. Plants may have both bracts and bracteoles, neither, or bracteoles alone, but never bracts without bracteoles. The fruit is often the most distinctive feature: **each 5-petalled flower develops 2 one-seeded carpels** (see drawing).

Marsh Pennywort
Hydrocotyle vulgaris
Instantly recognised by the carpet of **round, wavy-margined leaves** up to 3.5cm across **with central stalks**, which cover the surface of marshy places. The **flowers are inconspicuous, tiny and green**, hidden by the leaves. The **umbels** are not arranged like other members of the family, but **in irregular clusters of 3–6 flowers**, some terminal, some lower, on a single stalk arising at ground level from the base of a leaf-stalk.

Throughout British Isles to 400m in Wales.

P   25cm   Summer

Sanicle
Sanicula europaea
Recognised by the **dark green, glossy, hairless leaves divided into 5 toothed lobes**, forming a rosette on the floor of shady woods. Lower layer of umbel of few, often 3, stalks: the upper layer is of small clusters of stalkless or short-stalked pink or white flowers – these develop **burr-like fruits** which cling to fur and clothing.

Scrub and woods, especially of beech and oak, throughout the British Isles, except the outer islands, to 450m in N Ireland.

P   60cm   Late spring to early autumn

Sea-holly
Eryngium maritimum
Easily recognised by its **large, prickly, waxy-looking leaves** and its compact, thistle-like heads of misty-blue flowers **growing on sea-shore** sand or shingle. More difficult to recognise it is an umbellifer. The toothed 'leaves' surrounding the heads of flowers are the bracts: the purplish-blue bracteoles encircle small, stalkless clusters of flowers, often exceeding them in length.

Around our coasts but scarcely, if ever, on the east side north of Yorkshire.

P   60cm   Summer

Rough Chervil
Chaerophyllum temulentum
Distinguished from all other umbellifers by the **purple-spotted, hairy,** solid (not hollow) **stems** and, later, by the **fruits** which are **c.5mm long**, narrowing upwards, and **dark brown with lighter ridges**. The **third common roadside umbellifer to flower** (after cow parsley and hogweed) and usually **at the back of the verge**, especially where wooded.

Hedgebanks throughout the lowlands to 350m in southern Pennines: absent from NW Scotland and western Ireland.

B   1m   Summer

Bur Chervil
Anthriscus caucalis
The only umbellifer with **hollow stems and narrow fruits covered in hooked spines**: it is usually bractless (occasionally 1), but has 4–5 oval, pointed bracteoles with long hairs on the margins.

Hedgebanks and sandy places, especially near the sea, mainly south and east of line from R Humber to R Severn; often casual elsewhere.

A   80cm   Early summer

Cow Parsley
Anthriscus sylvestris
The **most abundant roadside umbellifer and the first to flower**, turning thousands of miles of verges white from late April through May. Later recognised by the **hollow stems**, which make cheap pea-shooters, and the **smooth blackish fruits, over 6mm long**, 6 times as long as broad, tapering towards the top.

Throughout the British Isles to 750m in SW Ireland.

P   1m   Late spring and early summer

Shepherd's-needle
Scandix pecten-veneris
When in fruit one of the easiest umbellifers to identify. Each upper layer of the umbel has *c*.5 **tiny flowers**, often **with unequal petals**, which **develop into erect 'needles' up to 7cm in length**. The 2 styles persist at the top of the beak, the 2 fruits develop at the bottom surrounded by a ring of bifid, or further divided, bracteoles.

Once a widespread arable weed in lowland S and E England: now almost eliminated by herbicides.

A   50cm   Late spring and early summer

UMBELLIFERS

flower
bracteole
ray
bract

Umbel

Fruit – *Heracleum*

Hedera helix

Hydrocotyle vulgaris

Sanicula europaea

Eryngium maritimum

Chaerophyllum temulentum

Anthriscus caucalis

Anthriscus sylvestris

Scandix pecten-veneris

Sweet Cicely
Myrrhis odorata

Often replaces cow parsley as the common roadside umbellifer in the hillier areas of England and in much of Scotland but differs in having a solid stem. Recognised from a distance by the **white blotched leaves**: close up has a strong **smell** of aniseed when rubbed including the **long, narrow fruits** which start green but are **black when ripe and reach 2.5cm**.

Cultivated as a pot-herb and frequent near houses throughout Scotland, N England, Wales and Ireland; to 500m in the Pennines.
P 1m Late spring and early summer

Hedge-parsleys

Hedge-parsleys are distinguished from all other umbellifers **by their spiny fruits and solid stems**, and by not having a strong carrot-like smell.

Upright Hedge-parsley
Torilis japonica

The fourth of the common roadside umbellifers to flower, coming in July just after rough chervil, and recognised by its **rough, bristly stems** with the bristles turned downwards. Easily separated from other hedge-parsleys by having **4 or more bracts**, the upper layers of the umbel with 5 or more stalks and **small fruits, less than 3.5mm, widest near the base**.

Hedgerows and rough grassland throughout British Isles except for the far north, reaching nearly 400m in the Pennines.
A or B 1.25m Summer

Spreading Hedge-parsley
Torilis arvensis

A usually bushy annual distinguished from other hedge-parsleys by the **absence of bracts** (or only 1), the upper layer of the umbel with 5 or fewer stalks, and by the **fruits** which are **parallel-sided**, not tapering noticeably from bottom to top.

A rapidly declining weed of arable fields, mainly in the southern half of England.
A 40cm Summer

Knotted Hedge-parsley
Torilis nodosa

'Knotted' refers to the way in which the **umbels** of this species are so **shortly stalked** that the **fruits** are **crowded together** in a bundle at the base of a leaf-stalk on the other side of the stem – there is no other umbellifer like it. If a single **fruit** is removed it will be seen that the **outer half has long spines** but **the inner** has **only tubercles**.

Scattered in dry places in England, Wales, S Scotland and the southern half of Ireland; mainly coastal in the west.
A 35cm Late spring and

Alexanders
Smyrnium olusatrum

Driving round most of Britain in the spring you can tell when you are near the sea by the sight of hedgerows lined by this striking plant with **dark green, shining leaves** and **yellowish-green flowers**. Later in the season, when the leaves have withered, the ridged stem and the **laterally compressed, rounded and ridged black fruits, up to 8mm long**, make it still recognisable.

Formerly grown as a pot-herb, now widely naturalised, but rare inland and in Scotland generally.
B 1.5m Spring and early summer

Hemlock
Conium maculatum

This umbellifer with much-divided fern-like leaves is the only one with **spotted, hairless stems** which usually also have a **waxy bloom**. Later it is easy to distinguish from other wayside species because the **fruits** are small, **c.3mm long, round and have wavy ridges**. Angelica is the only other species with wavy ridges but its fruits are over 5mm long. Extremely poisonous and said to smell of mice.

Roadsides in damp places, canal and river banks throughout the lowlands.
B 2m Summer

Slender Hare's-ear
Bupleurum tenuissimum

Hare's-ears are unusual for umbellifers **in having undivided leaves, bracts and bracteoles**. Slender hare's-ear must be one of the most overlooked British plants: with wiry stems and long, **narrow grass-like leaves** it is often extremely difficult to see in the maritime grassland where it grows. The **yellow flowers** develop into small, **c.2mm, rounded, narrowly winged fruits** covered in rough, short tubercles.

Salt-marshes and tidal river banks south of a line from R Humber to R Severn.
A 50cm Summer and autumn

False Thorow-wax
Bupleurum subovatum

Instantly recognised by the **leaves, about 3 times as long as broad**, through which the stems appear to grow – hence the name 'thorow-wax' because 'the stalk waxeth throw the leaves': they may also look like hare's-ears to some.

This seed contaminant commonly turns up in gardens and waste places: the true thorow-wax, which has leaves only about twice as long as broad and 4–8 **rays to the lower layer of the umbel** (not **2–3** as in **false thorow-wax**) was once widespread in arable fields but is now extinct.
A 30cm Summer and autumn

Myrrhis odorata

Torilis japonica

Torilis arvensis

Torilis nodosa

Smyrnium olusatrum

Conium maculatum

Bupleurum tenuissimum

Bupleurum subovatum

Wild Celery
Apium graveolens
Apium species are hairless marsh or water plants recognised by having their **umbels on very short stalks** (sometimes almost absent) and **arising on the opposite side of the stem from the leaves.** *Apium graveolens* has **upper leaves divided into 3 segments, lacks bracts and bracteoles** and has a strong **smell of celery**. The fruits are round and only *c*.1.5mm long.

In damp and often brackish places near the coasts of England, Wales and Ireland, and occasionally inland in areas formerly inundated by the sea.
B 60cm Summer

Fool's Water-cress
Apium nodiflorum
The English name suggests possible confusion with the real thing and derives from the lower **pinnate leaves, with 2–4 pairs of toothed leaflets**, and its aquatic habit. Distinguished from wild celery by the **upper leaves having at least 5** (not 3) **segments**, the presence of **4–7 conspicuous bracteoles** beneath the upper layer of the umbels, and the larger, *c*.2.5mm long, egg-shaped fruits.

Ditches and shallow water throughout the lowlands to 300m in Wales. Rare, mainly W coast, in Scotland.
P 1m Summer

Lesser Marshwort
Apium inundatum
As the scientific name indicates this plant often grows submerged in water, where its **leaves are finely divided into linear lobes**, however upper leaves of terrestrial plants may have *c*.7 flattened, toothed lobes. Like *A. nodiflorum* there are **conspicuous bracteoles** (usually 4–6) but the 2.5–3.0mm long fruits are elliptic rather than egg-shaped.

Lakes, ponds and ditches throughout the British Isles to 500m in the Pennines, but declining due to drainage.
P 75cm Summer

Garden Parsley
Petroselinum crispum
Instantly recognisable by its **yellow flowers in flat-topped umbels**, the shiny, **hairless, much-divided leaves and the familiar smell**. Specimens which have escaped from gardens and become established on cliffs and on waste ground often do not have the crisped (or curled) leaves of the cultivated form shown in the picture. The **smooth egg-shaped fruits** are *c*.2.5mm long with turned back styles.

Scattered throughout the British Isles but rarely established in Scotland.
B 75cm Summer

Corn Parsley
Petroselinum segetum
Apart from the **smell of parsley** given by the stem and fruit when crushed, not much like our garden parsley. The, mainly **basal, leaves are divided into 4–12 pairs of up to 3.5cm leaflets** which have **obtuse teeth** with a cartilage-like margin and a **tiny point at the tip**. The white flowers are in **umbels with both bracts and bracteoles and** have **very unequal stalks**. The **egg-shaped fruits**, *c*.2.5mm long, are **prominently ridged**.

Arable fields and dry banks south and east of a line from R Humber to R Severn
A or B 1m Late summer

Stone parsley
Sison amomum
Similar to corn parsley but readily distinguished by the nauseous **smell of petrol**, not parsley, given off by the stems and fruits when crushed. The **basal leaves have fewer, 2–5, pairs of larger, up to 6cm, leaflets**, whilst the **stalks of the umbels are more nearly equal**, with often only one much shorter than the rest. The **globose fruits**, *c*.3mm long, are **less prominently ridged** than corn parsley.

Hedge bottoms, mainly south and east of a line from R Humber to R Severn and on Welsh coast.
B 1m Summer

Cowbane
Cicuta virosa
Distinguished from other **aquatic** umbellifers by its tall, **hairless, hollow stems, the leaves much-divided into narrow, saw-toothed segments** and the **absence of bracts** below the lower level of umbel stalks. The **fruits** are **small**, up to 2mm, and **globose**. Very poisonous, producing convulsions which can kill humans but, more frequently, cattle.

Shallow water in lakes and fens now confined to E Anglia, the Cheshire Plain, the Borders and S Scotland and the northern half of Ireland.
P 1.5m Summer

Whorled Caraway
Carum verticillatum
Distinguished by the **yarrow-like leaves** growing **in acid marshes** and on stream banks in the west of Britain and in SW and NE Ireland. These leaves with their whorled, finely-divided segments, **arise from the fibrous base** of the stem. The slender, hairless, hollow stems carry very few, short leaves and umbels of white flowers, with **conspicuous deflexed bracts** but **upright bracteoles**. The **elliptic fruits**, up to 3mm, **have conspicuous ridges**.
P 60cm Summer

Pignut
Conopodium majus
Recognised by the **leaves** much divided into **linear segments**. The **lower**, triangular in outline, soon **wither and are yellow when the plant flowers** in acid, usually dry, woods and hedges. The **stem**, hollow after flowering, is **connected by a tapering, white, wavy, underground part, to the** dark brown **tuber** which is edible with a nutty flavour. The **fruits** are also brown, **oblong, up to 4mm long**.

Throughout British Isles.
P 60cm Late spring and early summer

Apium graveolens

Apium nodiflorum

Apium inundatum

Petroselinum crispum

Petroselinum segetum

Sison amomum

Cicuta virosa

Carum verticillatum

Conopodium majus

Burnet-saxifrage
Pimpinella saxifraga

One of the few umbels with white flowers which **lack both bracts and bracteoles**, but most readily recognised by having **2 kinds of leaves**: the lowest and uppermost simply pinnate with **4–6 pairs of oval, toothed leaflets, the intermediate much divided into linear segments.** Identifiable from a distance by the **drooping young flower-heads**, clearly shown in the picture.

Dry grassland throughout most of British Isles. Often seen flowering in short grass on roadsides in late summer.

P 1m Summer

Greater Burnet-saxifrage
Pimpinella major

Like *P. saxifraga* **lacking bracts and bracteoles** but with only one kind of leaf – simply pinnate with **2–4** (not up to 6) **pairs of leaflets** which are **up to 6cm** (not 2.5cm) **long**. The **stems** are **hairless and hollow** (solid except for a small hole in fruit in *P. saxifraga*) and the fruits are egg-shaped up to 4mm (not globose, up to 2.5mm long).

Woodland margins and roadsides mainly in the eastern half of England from Kent to Northumberland, but rare in East Anglia and curiously abundant in SW Ireland.

P 1.2m Summer

Ground-elder
Aegopodium podagraria

A troublesome garden weed recognised by its **slender underground stems** which are almost impossible to eradicate. Above ground similar to *Pimpinella major* with **hollow stems and neither bracts nor bracteoles** but the **toothed leaflets** are usually **in threes** (not 2–4 pairs) and many of these are futher **divided into unequal lobes.** The ridged, egg-shaped fruit is *c.*4mm long.

Throughout British Isles on roadsides and in waste places, almost always an escape from cultivation.

P 1m Late spring and early summer

Lesser Water-parsnip
Berula erecta

May be confused with fool's water-cress, *Apium nodiflorum,* but distinguished by the lower **leaves with 5–9 pairs of yellowish-green leaflets** (not 2–4) which are **held horizontally** and by the presence of **a purple ring near the base of the leaf stalk.** In flower it has **4–7** conspicuous, **toothed or segmented bracts** below the lower umbel stalks (lacking or only 1–2 in *Apium*).

Marshes and shallow water throughout lowland British Isles, rare in W and N.

P 1m Summer and early autumn

Greater Water-parsnip
Sium latifolium

This tall, **hairless, hollow-stemmed perennial** growing in shallow water is recognised by its erect **leaves divided into 3–6 pairs of toothed leaflets** up to 12cm long. The lower level of the umbel has 20–30 branches with **2–6 bracts** at the base which are often **large and leaf-like.** The egg-shaped fruits, up to 4mm long, have thick, prominent ridges.

Ditches and pond-sides in S and E England and central Ireland. Declining with drainage.

P 2m Summer

Rock Samphire
Crithmum maritimum

A plant of coastal rocks and sea-cliffs and easily distinguished as the **only umbel with succulent leaves divided into many narrow segments** which taper at both ends. Even at a distance the **greenish-yellow flowers** in tight clusters are readily recognised. The fruit is egg-shaped up to 6mm long with thick, prominent ridges. Leaves formerly gathered in May and eaten as a pickle.

Coasts of Britain from Hebrides to Suffolk and all round Ireland.

P 45cm Summer

Hemlock Water-dropwort
Oenanthe crocata

The most widespread of our *Oenanthe* species, all of which are white-flowered marsh or water plants, usually with tuberous roots. *O. crocata* is much the tallest often growing in colonies along river banks and ditches. All parts are poisonous: the leaves may be mistaken for **wild celery** but that **has neither bracts nor bracteoles** – *O. crocata* **has both. Fruits** recognisable by their **cylindrical** shape **up to 5.5mm long**

Throughout S and W Britain, and Ireland except the centre: rare east of a line from London to Inverness.

P 2m Summer

Corky-fruited Water-dropwort
Oenanthe pimpinelloides

A local plant common only in S Hampshire, Somerset and E Devon and nowhere north of Gloucester. Recognised by having **upper leaves divided into long narrow segments,** the presence of **bracts below the lower umbels** and the **flat upper umbels with 12–20 bracteoles** beneath them. The **ripe fruits** are **cylindrical,** have broad ridges, are **up to 3.5mm long** with the **styles about the same length,** and stand **on thickened stalks.**

Meadows and other grassy places. Recently found in W Ireland.

P 1m Summer

Parsley Water-dropwort
Oenanthe lachenalii

Like *O. pimpinelloides* has upper leaves divided into long, narrow segments, and bracts beneath the lower umbels, but separated from that species by the **dome-shaped upper umbels with** only **5–9 bracteoles** below them. The ripe **fruits** are smaller, **up to 2.5mm,** with slender ridges and **styles only half their length, on unthickened stalks.**

In brackish and lime-rich freshwater marshes scattered throughout British Isles north to the Hebrides.

P 1m Summer

Pimpinella saxifraga

Pimpinella major

Aegopodium podagraria

Berula erecta

Sium latifolium

Crithmum maritimum

Oenanthe crocata

Oenanthe pimpinelloides

Oenanthe lachenalii

Tubular Water-dropwort
Oenanthe fistulosa
Readily recognised by the **very hollow stems** easily squashed between the fingers, by the **leaves** divided into long, narrow segments **with the hollow stalk much longer than the leafy part**, and by the **few (2–4) stalks to** the **lower layer of the umbel** without bracts below. Spotted from a distance by the tight flat-topped clusters of flowers which become dome-shaped in fruit.

Marshes and shallow water in lowland England and Ireland: very rare near the coasts of Wales and Scotland.

P 60cm Summer and early autumn

Fine-leaved Water-dropwort
Oenanthe aquatica
An erect plant, usually **growing in shallow standing water**, with **very finely divided leaves** which have linear segments. The hollow stems change direction in a characteristic way as the picture clearly shows. The **lower layer of the umbel has 4–10 stalks and** there are usually **no bracts below**. The upper layer is dome-shaped in flower and in fruit.

Lowlands of England and Ireland just reaching S Scotland and E Wales.

A or B 1.5m Spring and early summer

River-dropwort
Oenanthe fluviatilis
As the name implies a **plant of flowing water** with many **sub-merged leaves deeply cut into long narrow segments** and aerial leaves with egg-shaped to round-ish segments. May be confused with *O. crocata* but distinguished in flower by the **absence of bracts**, the **lower layer of the umbel with only 5–15** (not 12–40) **stalks**, and in fruit by their oval shape and length – up to 6.5mm.

Lowland rivers in SE England and central Ireland.

P 1m Summer and early autumn

Fool's Parsley
Aethusa cynapium
This annual is like no other umbel because, though it has **no bracts** below the layer of the umbel, the **bracteoles** above are **large and conspicuous** – up to 1cm long hanging vertically. The **leaves** are **parsley-like** but poisonous – only a fool would eat them. The **fruits** are **small and round** up to 3.5mm long with prominent keeled ridges.

In arable fields and on river banks throughout lowland British Isles but mainly coastal in Scotland.

A 80cm Summer and autumn

Fennel
Foeniculum vulgare
A tall, hairless, **yellow-flowered** umbel with **leaves divided into** very narrow **hair-like segments** which smell of 'cough-mixture' when rubbed. The stems are solid and there are **neither bracts nor bracteoles**. The fruits are oval and long – up to 6mm.

Cliffs, roadsides and waste places mainly in the southern half of British Isles and especially near the coast.

B or P 2.5m Summer and autumn

Pepper-saxifrage
Silaum silaus
A hairless, **yellow-flowered** perennial, with **leaves much-divided into very finely-toothed linear segments** ending in a short point or mucro, and with a **narrow** or almost non-existent **transparent margin to the sheath** at the base of the leaf-stalk. Similar to corn parsley but that has white flowers and a broad transparent margin to the sheath.

Damp meadows and grassy banks in lowland England, with a few localities in E Wales and S Scotland.

P 1m Summer

Spignel
Meum athamanticum
Our only umbel which could be described as a mountain plant. Recognised by the very **finely divided leaves** which are **nearly all basal** and **give off a strong aroma when crushed**. At ground level there are **abundant fibrous remains of old leaf-sheaths**. Stem leaves are small, bracts few and the white or pinkish flowers produce large fruits *c*.7mm long with thick, prominent ridges.

Grassland in the mountains of N Wales, N England and Scotland north to Inverness – rarely below 200m.

P 60cm Summer

Scots Lovage
Ligusticum scoticum
A bright, shining-green plant **found only on coastal cliffs and rocks** in Scotland and the northern half of Ireland. The **leaves** are mainly **divided into 3 segments each again divided into 3** which are **toothed only in the upper half**. The umbels have numerous narrow bracts and bracteoles and greenish-white, sometimes pinkish, flowers. The fruits are a narrow egg-shape, up to 7mm long, with prominent narrow wings.

P 90cm Summer

Wild Angelica
Angelica sylvestris
A large perennial with hairless stems perhaps most easily recognised by the generally **purplish** colour and by the very **prominent, inflated leaf-stalks often with only a minute leaf at the tip**. The umbels have densely hairy stalks, no bracts and white flowers which develop into egg-shaped, flattened fruits with broad wings at the margin.

Damp grassland, marshes and wet, open woods throughout British Isles to 900m in Scotland.

P 2m Summer and early autumn

Oenanthe fistulosa

Oenanthe aquatica

Oenanthe fluviatilis

Aethusa cynapium

Foeniculum vulgare

Silaum silaus

Meum athamanticum

Ligusticum scoticum

Angelica sylvestris

Milk-parsley
Peucedanum palustre
A very local plant of **fens and marshes** mainly in East Anglia and Yorkshire. Recognised by the often **purplish hollow stems**, the **leaves much-divided** into oval, finely-toothed segments and the **deflexed bracts and bracteoles** with up to **40 branches to the** lower layer of the **umbel**. The fruits are elliptical, up to 5mm, with prominent ridges and wings at the margin.

The food-plant of the caterpillars of the swallow-tail butterfly.
B 1.5m Summer and early autumn

Masterwort
Peucedanum ostruthium
Like Scots lovage, a shining, bright green perennial with hollow stems and **leaves divided into 3 segments each again divided into 3**, but in masterwort the **segments** are **toothed all round and the teeth** are **sharply pointed** and variable in depth. In flower the usually **bractless lower layer of the umbel** and the very numerous, **up to 60, slender branches**, are distinctive.

An escape from cultivation established in grassy places and by rivers in N England and lowland Scotland.
P 1m Summer

Wild Parsnip
Pastinaca sativa
A hairy, **yellow-flowered** umbel with **yellowish-green leaves only once divided into lobed and toothed segments** which give a **strong smell of parsnip** when crushed. The **hollow stem** and absence of both bracts and bracteoles confirm the identification. Closely related to the cultivated parsnip but with longer and denser hairs and broader leaf segments.

Widespread throughout S and E England, often dominant on road verges in summer: rare elsewhere.
B 1.5m Summer

Hogweed
Heracleum sphondylium
The coarse, tall, hairy umbel which **replaces cow parsley on road verges** as it starts flowering **at the beginning of summer**. Recognised from afar by the **flat plates of white flowers** held at different levels and, close to, by the **leaves once divided into lobed and toothed segments** the terminal one often with 3 more or less equal lobes. After flowering the **large, round flattened fruits, up to 8mm long**, are unmistakable.

Throughout British Isles to 1000m in Scotland.
B 2m Summer and autumn

Giant Hogweed
Heracleum mantegazzianum
This amazing 'giant' which can grow **over 5m tall** in a single season cannot be mistaken: the basal leaves alone may be 2.5m long and the **umbels have 50–150 branches**. The **fruit is elliptical up to 11mm long**. A dangerous plant to touch: the skin can become blistered if exposed to strong sunlight afterwards.

Introduced from SW Asia for ornament and now escaped and established in scattered localities throughout British Isles.
B or P 5m Summer

Wild Carrot
Daucus carota
Distinguished from all other umbels by having a **single purple or red flower in the centre of the inflorescence** and by the way the outer branches of the lower umbel grow upwards and inwards to enclose the fruits in a kind of nest. Also distinguished by the **carroty smell** given off by the leaves when crushed, the **bracts** at the base of the umbel **large** and **much-divided** and the **extremely hairy fruits**.

Throughout lowland British Isles, mainly coastal in Scotland.
B 1m Summer

White Bryony
Bryonia dioica
A hedgerow plant with **lobed yellowish-green leaves climbing with** the aid of **tendrils** which develop spiral coils to draw the plant to the hedge by changing direction in the middle. Plants are either male or female (the picture is of a male): flowers of the female produce **bright-red, poisonous berries in autumn**. Our only wild plant which belongs to the cucumber family, it has a massive, yellowish root formerly sold as a substitute for mandrake, *Mandragora officinalis*, prized as a medicine.

Lowland England and Wales.
P 6m Spring to autumn

Dog's Mercury
Mercurialis perennis
The commonest **woodland herb** in Britain forming **carpets of elliptical flat-green leaves** about 30cm above ground. The **hairy, unbranched plants are either male or female**: patches entirely of one sex are normal. The male in the picture is quite conspicuous – the long spikes of flowers have a mass of yellowish-green stamens: the female flower is hidden among the upper leaves. A poisonous plant but so unattractive it is unlikely to be eaten.

Hedges and woods throughout Great Britain to 1000m in Scotland: very rare in Ireland.
P 40cm Spring

Annual Mercury
Mercurialis annua
Very like dog's mercury in structure but a **hairless**, yellowish-green weed of gardens and waste places **with stems branching from near the base**. It also has **separate male and female plants** with the male flowering stems much more conspicuous than the female's which are hidden amongst the elliptical leaves.

Abundant in some parts of S England; rare and often not persistent elsewhere and almost unknown in Scotland.
A 50cm Summer and autumn

Peucedanum palustre

Peucedanum ostruthium

Pastinaca sativa

Heracleum sphondylium

Heracleum mantegazzianum

Daucus carota

Bryonia dioica

Mercurialis perennis

Mercurialis annua

Spurges

Spurges are usually easy to recognise. What looks like a single flower is actually a group of flowers with a female in the centre and several males (each represented by one stamen only) around it, the whole surrounded by 4 or 5 conspicuous 'glands' (see drawing). The fruit is a capsule with 3 cells, each with a single large seed. Spurges have poisonous milky juice in stems and leaves.

Caper Spurge
Euphorbia lathyris
A **stiffly erect, hairless** plant with **narrow, rigid, blue-green leaves** and small groups of flowers enclosed by (usually) 2 large, narrowly triangular bracts. The **fruit is quite large (up to 2cm across)** and the plant was formerly cultivated for the production of 'capers'. (The true caper, *Capparis*, is not found in Britain.)

Perhaps native in some woods from Somerset to Northamptonshire, but often grown in gardens and bird-sown in waste places north to C Scotland.
B   1.2m   Summer

Sun Spurge
Euphorbia helioscopia
An **erect, hairless annual with few or no branches**, and **very broad, blunt leaves** tapering to a narrow base. The yellow-green 'flowers' are arranged in a **terminal 5-rayed umbel**, and **the glands are rounded**.

A common weed of gardens and fields throughout the British Isles, though rather less frequent in N and W Scotland and Ireland.
A   50cm   Summer

Petty Spurge
Euphorbia peplus
Like the sun spurge, but smaller, and usually more branched, with **more numerous and less regular 3-rayed umbels**, and **glands with long slender 'horns'**.

One of the commonest garden and field weeds in England, found, like the sun spurge, throughout the British Isles.
A   30cm   Spring and summer

Dwarf Spurge
Euphorbia exigua
The smallest of the common annual weed spurges, easily recognised by its **very narrow leaves and bracts**. Like the petty spurge, the **glands have long slender 'horns'**.

A weed of cultivated ground in S and E England, but less common in N and W Britain. Frequent in C and E Ireland, rather rare elsewhere.
A   20cm   Summer

Portland Spurge
Euphorbia portlandica
A **stocky, hairless, blue-green plant with thick stems from a central root**, and thick, stalkless, **more or less obovate leaves terminating in a sudden point**. The 'flowers' are in 3- to 6-rayed umbels, and **the glands have long 'horns'**.

Local on sand-dunes around the S and W coast of Britain: all round the Irish coast, but rare in the south and west.
B or P   40cm   Summer

Sea Spurge
Euphorbia paralias
Like the Portland spurge in colour and habit, but **truly perennial, with a woody rootstock** and **very numerous, much narrower leaves without a terminal point**. **The glands have short 'horns'**.

Confined to coastal sands and shingle, but more widespread on the English coast than the Portland spurge, occurring in the west and south and from Norfolk to Kent in the east. In Ireland, rarer on the N and W coasts.
P   40cm   Summer and autumn

Cypress Spurge
Euphorbia cyparissias
A **hairless plant with many much-branched stems from a long, creeping rhizome, often forming dense patches**. The **numerous leaves are very narrow** (less than 2mm wide). The **often reddish umbels have 9 – 15 rays** and there are often side-branches below.

Grown in gardens and not thought to be a native plant, though it grows wild on the light sandy soils of the Breckland and in several other places in S and E England. It is recorded from several parts of Scotland, though not from Ireland.
P   30cm   Summer

Wood Spurge
Euphorbia amygdaloides
The only common spurge in English woods, easily recognised by its **hairy stems** and **large, yellowish, branched inflorescence** produced in the second year from erect stems growing from a thick rootstock.

Damp woodland, often very conspicuous in spring when flowering in recently coppiced areas. Common in S England and S Wales, occurring north to Cardigan and Norfolk. Not recorded (except as a rare introduction) in Scotland, and very rare in S Ireland.
P   80cm   Spring

gland

male flower

female flower

EUPHORBIA –
group of flowers

Euphorbia lathyris

Euphorbia helioscopia

Euphorbia peplus

Euphorbia exigua

Euphorbia portlandica

Euphorbia paralias

Euphorbia cyparissias

Euphorbia amygdaloides

Knotgrasses and Bistorts

Polygonum species are recognised by the stipules at the base of the leaf forming a sheath round the stem which is often transparent and fringed with hairs, and by the flowers with a single whorl of 5 'petals' which produce a single 3-sided fruit.

Polygonum – sheathing stipule

Knotgrass
Polygonum aviculare
One of our commonest and most variable annual weeds. Recognised by the **small oval leaves** which have silvery stipules and are **often larger on the main stem than on the flowering stem**, by the **clusters of 1–6 pink or white flowers** which give the knotted effect. Equal-leaved knotgrass (*P. arenastrum*) differs by being always prostrate, and by having leaves on the main stem and flowering stems about the same size.

Absent from Northern Isles.
A   1m   Spring to autumn

Alpine Bistort
Polygonum viviparum
This hairless plant of mountain grassland and wet rocks is recognised by the **long leaves, tapering at both ends** and with their **margins turned down**, which are held upright, and by the **spike-like inflorescence** which has **white flowers** (sometimes very few) **in the upper part** and many **purple bulbils below**.

Common in N England and Scotland rarely below 200m but at sea-level in the far north: isolated localities in N Wales and W Ireland.
P   30cm   Summer

Common Bistort
Polygonum bistorta
Recognised by the large patches of **broad, but pointed, leaves** from which arise numerous straight, **long-stalked spikes densely packed with pink or white flowers**. The parts below ground are not straight but twisted and the name *bistorta* is derived from the Latin *bis*, twice, and *tortus*, twisted, to describe the contorted underground stems.

Scattered in meadows and on roadsides throughout British Isles but most abundant in NW England: very rare in Ireland.
P   60cm   Summer

Amphibious Bistort
Polygonum amphibium
A plant with distinct land and water forms, the latter instantly **recognised by the** large patches of **floating, hairless leaves with a** more or less **square base** from amongst which arise masses of pink spikes of flowers. **On land the leaves are hairy with a tapered or rounded base.** At the water's edge both forms can occur on one plant.

Throughout the lowlands of British Isles.
P   60cm   Summer and early autumn

Redshank
Polygonum persicaria
An almost hairless annual weed recognised by the large **black blotch in the centre of the lance-shaped leaves** and the dense spikes of **pink flowers**. Separated from pale persicaria by the **absence of glands amongst the flowers** or on the stem beneath the heads.

Arable fields, waste places round the farm and on the margin of ponds and lakes throughout lowland British Isles to 450m in Shropshire.
A   75cm   Summer and autumn

Pale Persicaria
Polygonum lapathifolium
Closely related to, and often growing with, redshank. Distinguished by its **greenish-yellow**, not pink, **flowers**, with a large number of **short yellowish glands amongst them** and on the stalks below, and by the **absence of a black spot on the leaves**. In older plants the stems are much swollen above the stipules where the leaf-stalk is attached.

Arable fields, waste places and beside ponds throughout lowland British Isles to 450m in Shropshire but rare in Scotland.
A   1m   Summer and autumn

Water-pepper
Polygonum hydropiper
A slender, **yellow-green plant** recognised by its long **spike of well-separated flowers**, often **drooping at the tip**: under the lens the greenish flowers are seen to be **covered in yellow glandular dots**. The leaves have a peppery taste and contain an acrid juice which can irritate the skin especially between the fingers or on the back of the hand.

Marshes and water-sides mainly on acid soils throughout British Isles to 400m in Ireland: absent from N Scotland.
A   75cm   Summer and early autumn

Black Bindweed
Polygonum convolvulus
This clockwise turning bindweed is an annual with a twining stem and **leaves shaped like arrow-heads** similar to those of the field bindweed. However the **flowers** are very different being relatively inconspicuous though looking attractive **with the alternating green and white of their 'petals'**. The shining black triangular fruits are not attractive; they can be harmful to farm animals if fed grain containing any quantity.

Arable fields and waste places throughout lowland British Isles to 400m in Shropshire.
A   1.25m   Summer and autumn

Polygonum aviculare

Polygonum viviparum

Polygonum bistorta

Polygonum amphibium

Polygonum persicaria

Polygonum lapathifolium

Polygonum hydropiper

Polygonum convolvulus

Japanese Knotweed
Reynoutria japonica

Recognised from a distance as a tall jungle of hairless, cane-like stems up to 2m high with **heart-shaped, abruptly pointed leaves** up to 12cm long and developing **sprays of tiny white flowers** in late summer. Introduced from Japan as a garden plant in 1825 it has become an aggressive weed spreading by extensive underground stems. It is now illegal to introduce this species into the countryside.

Road verges, stream banks, railway lines and waste places throughout British Isles.

P 2m Late summer and autumn

Mountain Sorrel
Oxyria digyna

A cluster of **hairless, kidney-shaped**, somewhat **fleshy leaves** on rocks **beside a mountain stream** is sure to be this species. In late summer it produces a **branched, leafless spike of flowers** each with 4 'sepals' in 2 pairs, the inner enlarging in fruit but lacking any tubercles or swellings. The single-seeded fruits are broadly winged.

Mountain areas of Britain from N Wales northwards, rarely below 300m.

P 30cm Late summer

Docks and Sorrels

Docks and sorrels of the genus *Rumex* are distinguished by having 6 'sepals' in 2 whorls of 3: in docks the inner ones usually have tubercles (swellings) developing on the outside as the 3-sided fruit grows inside.

Common Sorrel
Rumex acetosa

A common grassland plant recognised by the **lance-shaped lower leaves** which have the lobes at the base pointing downwards and **upper leaves** which **clasp the stem**. The edges of the leaves are often turned under and they become a brilliant crimson in autumn. Male and female flowers on this and sheep's sorrel are on separate plants. Ripe female flowers do not produce tubercles.

Throughout British Isles to 1250m in Scotland.

P 1m Spring and summer

Sheep's Sorrel
Rumex acetosella

Similar to common sorrel but with **arrow-shaped leaves** which have the lobes at the base pointing outwards whilst the upper leaves do not clasp the stem and are generally stalked. Very variable: some forms on dry, sandy soils have extremely narrow leaves with the edges rolled under.

Heaths and acid grassland throughout British Isles to 1000m in Wales.

P 30cm Spring and summer

Water Dock
Rumex hydrolapathum

Recognised by its water-side habit and the enormous **lance-shaped leaves 1m or more in length** held vertically when young. In flower it is our tallest dock and distinguished by the 3 **triangular, untoothed inner 'sepals'** each **with a narrow tubercle extending over half their length**.

River, stream and canal banks in lowland England and Ireland; local and mainly coastal in Wales, rare in Scotland.

P 2m Summer and autumn

Monk's-rhubarb
Rumex alpinus

Recognised at speed along upland roads as **large patches of shining green, heart-shaped leaves** up to 40cm across with wavy margins. Puts up short, **dense inflorescence with** long-stalked flowers which develop **rounded, not heart-shaped, inner 'sepals' lacking tubercles**.

Introduced from the mountains of Europe for medicinal purposes and now established by farms, streams and roadsides in upland areas of Britain from the Peak District northwards.

P 70cm Summer

Northern Dock
Rumex longifolius

The tall dock **without tubercles on the inner 'sepals'**. Differs from monk's-rhubarb in having **inner 'sepals' heart-shaped not square at base, leaves much longer than broad**, and in **never forming large extensive patches**. May be confused with curled dock in upland areas where it replaces it but the absence of tubercles is diagnostic.

Uplands of Britain from Lancashire and Yorkshire northwards to 500m in Scotland: absent from Wales and Ireland.

P 1.2m Summer

Curled Dock
Rumex crispus

Our tallest common dock with **pointed, wavy-margined leaves 5–6 times as long as broad**, recognised in fruit by the truncate, **toothless inner 'sepals'**, 1, 2 or 3 of them **with** well-developed **smooth, oblong tubercles**, one often larger than any others. Coastal forms have 3 tubercles all the same size.

Waste places, rough grassland, pond margins and coastal shingle throughout British Isles to 600m in N England.

P 1m Summer and autumn

Reynoutria japonica

Oxyria digyna

Rumex acetosa

Rumex acetosella

Rumex hydrolapathum

Rumex alpinus

Rumex longifolius

Rumex crispus

Broad-leaved Dock
Rumex obtusifolius
The commonest tall roadside dock, distinguished from curled dock by the **flat bluntly-pointed leaves** only about **twice as long as broad** and the **strongly toothed inner 'sepals'** with a single **rounded tubercle**. These are the leaves normally used to rub on nettle stings (the plants grow together) and, in former times, to wrap round butter. Hybrids between broad-leaved and curled docks are frequent but much less fertile than the parents.

Roadside verges and waste places throughout British Isles to 550m in N England.

P   1m   Summer and autumn

Fiddle Dock
Rumex pulcher
Like broad-leaved dock this plant has **strongly-toothed inner 'sepals'** with 1 larger and 2 smaller tubercles but it is more easily recognised at a distance by the short habit and the **wiry branches**, the majority of which are **at right-angles to the main stem**. The **leaves have a narrow waist near the base** described as 'fiddle-shaped'.

Rough, dry grassland: remarkably frequent on village greens and in churchyards but only in the southern half of England and on the Welsh coast.

P   40cm   Summer

Clustered Dock
Rumex conglomeratus
This species might be confused with fiddle dock but, though its **branches** make a wide **angle with the main stem**, the majority are at **about 60°**, and the leaves are scarcely fiddle-shaped. The flowers are most distinctive with **all 3 inner sepals carrying a** large, oval **tubercle**. The **upper branches** of the inflorescence **have** numerous small **leaves** (bracts) **for ⅔ of their length**.

Marshy meadows and watersides throughout lowland British Isles.

P   50cm   Summer and autumn

Wood Dock
Rumex sanguineus
Similar to clustered dock but readily distinguished by the **angle of the branches to the main stem** being **about 30°**, the presence of **a tubercle on only one of the inner sepals** and the general **lack of** small **leaves** (bracts) **on** the flowering **branches** except perhaps near the base. An unusual variety, var. *sanguineus*, with blood-red veins may be found, usually near houses – normally the veins are green.

Woods, copses, roadsides and waste places throughout lowland England, to 350m in Yorkshire.

P   60cm   Summer

Marsh Dock
Rumex palustris
There are 2 rather rare waterside docks which have **golden inner sepals with long, narrow teeth**. In marsh dock the **teeth** are **shorter than** or only just equal to the **width of the sepals** and the tips of the sepals have acute points. In flower the anthers are 1mm long.

A local plant of river banks and pond margins on the east side of England from Sussex to Yorkshire with a few outliers near the Severn estuary.

B or P   60cm   Summer

Golden Dock
Rumex maritimus
Despite its Latin name, no more frequent near the sea than the similar marsh dock. Separated from that species by the **very long teeth on the inner sepals** which are **2 to 3 times longer than the width of the sepals** and by the obtuse tips to the sepals. Anthers are only *c*.0.5mm long.

Most frequently on the margins of muddy ponds, but also on river banks and dyke sides. An infrequent plant of lowland England and Wales north to Yorkshire and the Isle of Man. Probably spread by birds.

A, B or P   40cm   Summer and autumn

Pellitory-of-the-wall
Parietaria judaica
This member of the nettle family is instantly recognised by its reddish **branches carrying dull green leaves which spread** across the surface of walls and ruins **from a central point**. The flowers too are dull green but interesting: they may be male, female or hermaphrodite with females at the top of the cluster. Young stamens of male flowers spring outwards scattering a pollen cloud if touched when ripe.

Walls and, occasionally in the west, on hedge banks, throughout lowland British Isles north to Banff.

P   40cm   Summer and autumn

Common Nettle
Urtica dioica
A perennial which **grows in large colonies** spreading by its tough, yellow roots and easily distinguished from small nettle by the **blades of the lower leaves being longer than their stalks**. Like all nettles there are separate male and female flowers but here they are usually on separate plants, the male with 4 stamens, the female with a club-shaped much-divided stigma. Most plants sting but a form on fens and river banks (var. *inermis*) is harmless.

Throughout British Isles in hedge banks, woods and waste places to 800m in Scotland.

P   1.5m   Summer

Small Nettle
Urtica urens
An annual species, **not growing in large colonies**, and with the **blades of the lower leaves shorter than their stalks**. There are separate male and female flowers in short spikes on the same plant. All plants sting.

Cultivated ground, especially in gardens, throughout lowland British Isles to 500m in the Pennines.

A   60cm   Summer and early autumn

Rumex obtusifolius

Rumex pulcher

Rumex conglomeratus

Rumex sanguineus

Rumex palustris

Rumex maritimus

Parietaria judaica

Urtica dioica

Urtica urens

Hop
Humulus lupulus

This perennial is the only native member of the hemp family, which includes *Cannabis*. Each year it develops the **clockwise-spiralling hop bines** which can climb over **6m** in a season **carrying the characteristic vine-like, lobed leaves**. There are separate male and female plants. Only the latter produce the cones which are used to give the flavour to bitter beer.

Widely cultivated and escaping but also a native of wet woods by streams in the southern half of England and Wales.
P   6m   Summer

Heath Family (Ericaceae)

Members of the heath family, *Ericaceae*, have been included because, though they are all woody plants, several are familiar and beautiful wildflowers of heath, moorland and mountain. They have small simple leaves and flowers with joined petals and free stamens.

Trailing Azalea
Loiseleuria procumbens

This attractive mountain plant is related to our garden rhododendrons and azaleas. It has **small, opposite, ovate leaves, evergreen and thick in texture, on trailing stems**. The small pink flowers are in clusters; the **petals are joined at the base but spread widely**.

Mountain tops and upland moors in Scotland from Dumbarton northwards; absent from the Outer Hebrides and Ireland.
P   5cm   Summer

Bog-rosemary
Andromeda polifolia

A low-growing hairless shrub with a creeping rhizome, scattered, erect stems and **narrow, alternate leaves with turned-back margins, dark green above and grey beneath**. The **pretty flowers, nodding on long stalks, have an almost spherical pinkish-white corolla 5–7mm long**.

Bogs and wet heaths, from mid-Wales and Staffordshire to Perthshire; common in the central plain of Ireland. Much decreased in England because of the drainage of bogs.
P   30cm   Summer

Bearberry
Arctostaphylos uva-ursi

A prostrate evergreen shrub with long, rooting branches, often mat-forming, and **thick, obovate leaves**, dark green above and pale beneath. The small, white or pinkish flowers are in short racemes, and are succeeded by **red, glossy berries**, inedible to humans (hence the name!).

Dry moorland, often on rocks or slopes. Common in the Highlands of Scotland, to *c.*900m; extending south to Derbyshire, and in Ireland only in the north and west.
P   5cm (tall)   Summer

Heather
Calluna vulgaris

This very familiar plant of moor and heath has **small, opposite leaves** closely packed on the twiggy stems. The **numerous small flowers in the leaf-axils** have a **pinkish-purple persistent 4-lobed calyx larger than the corolla**, and beneath each flower are 4 ovate bracteoles. The fruit is a small, dry capsule with few seeds.

On acid soils throughout British Isles, ascending to over 700m and dominant on much 'heather moor' in the north.
P   60cm   Summer

Cross-leaved Heath
Erica tetralix

A **softly hairy small shrub** with numerous branched stems and **small, linear, glandular leaves 4 in a whorl** with turned-back margins hiding the under-surface. **The relatively large pink flowers are in terminal clusters which nod in the flowering stage.**

Bogs and wet heaths, common throughout much of the British Isles but local in midland England and SE Ireland.
P   60cm   Summer

Bell Heather
Erica cinerea

Rather like the cross-leaved heath, but **hairless, with leaves 3 in a whorl** and a **longer inflorescence with many (usually) reddish-purple flowers**.

On dry heaths and moors throughout much of the British Isles, but local in midland England and the central plain of Ireland.
P   60cm   Summer

Humulus lupulus

Loiseleuria procumbens

Andromeda polifolia

Arctostaphylos uva-ursi

Calluna vulgaris

Erica tetralix

Erica cinerea

Cowberry
Vaccinium vitis-idaea
A low evergreen shrub with the general appearance of the bearberry, but the **much-branched stems are not prostrate**, and the **thick, more or less elliptical leaves are very glossy on the upper surface. The pinkish flowers have more open corollas with turned-out lobes**. The bright red fruits are edible.

On moorland and open woodland on acid soils mainly in N Britain from Somerset, Leicestershire and Yorkshire northwards; in Ireland mainly in the north.
P   30cm   Summer

Bilberry
Vaccinium myrtillus
A **hairless deciduous shrub** with a creeping rhizome and **numerous erect branches bearing green, strongly-angled twigs**. The thin, green leaves have toothed margins, and the **greenish-red flowers** are succeeded by **succulent black berries with a waxy 'bloom'**.

Common throughout much of the British Isles on heather moorland and open woodland on acid soils, ascending in Scotland to near the top of the highest mountains; absent or rare in E Anglia and midland England.
P   60cm   Early summer

Bog Bilberry
Vaccinium uliginosum
Like the common bilberry, **but with brownish twigs that are round** (not angled) **and entire** (not toothed) **blue-green leaves**. The whitish flowers are succeeded by black, edible berries.

Locally abundant on mountain moorland from Shetland south to Kintyre and Selkirk in Scotland; also in Cumbria and Northumberland; absent from Ireland and the Outer Hebrides.
P   50cm   Early summer

Cranberry
Vaccinium oxycoccos
The cranberry is a **delicate, trailing plant with small ovate leaves**, and pretty **pink flowers on slender stalks. The 4 petals, joined only near their base, turn backwards**. The reddish edible fruit is spherical or pear-shaped.

In acid bogs, often growing in bog-moss (*Sphagnum*), common in N England and S and C Scotland; scattered throughout Ireland, but rather rare in the south-west.
P   5cm (tall)   Summer

Serrated Wintergreen
Orthilia secunda
This wintergreen is easily distinguished by its **light green, rather pointed leaves with toothed margins** and the **greenish-white flowers all bent to one side**.

A northern plant of upland woods and rock-ledges, ascending to over 700m in central Scotland where it is not uncommon. Absent from the Outer Hebrides, N Scotland, Orkney and Shetland; very rare in Ireland and Wales, and in England only in Cumbria.
P   10cm   Summer

Common Wintergreen
Pyrola minor
Wintergreens are evergreen herbs with creeping rhizomes and regular white flowers. They are partially saprophytic, feeding on decaying humus. The common wintergreen has **a rosette of broadly elliptical leaves** from which arises the **leafless flower-stalk bearing several more or less spherical flowers hanging downwards**. The **short, straight style does not protrude beyond the corolla**.

Scattered throughout much of the British Isles, but nowhere common. Ascends to over 500m in Scotland.
P   25cm   Summer

Intermediate Wintergreen
Pyrola media
Differs from common wintergreen in the **broader, almost circular leaves**, larger flowers and most clearly in the **longer style which protrudes from the flower**.

Not uncommon in the native pine-woods of the Scottish Highlands; otherwise rare, and extinct over much of lowland England; absent from Wales, and in Ireland only in the north and west.
P   30cm   Summer

Round-leaved Wintergreen
Pyrola rotundifolia
The most handsome of our wintergreens, with **glossy green, almost circular leaves**, and **large, open, pure-white flowers up to 1.2cm across**. Best distinguished by the **conspicuous bent style, much longer than the petals**.

Two subspecies are found, one in bogs, fens and damp woodland, scattered throughout eastern Britain, absent from Wales, and very rare in C Ireland, the other confined to slacks behind sand-dunes in Norfolk, Wales and Lancashire.
P   40cm   Late summer

Vaccinium vitis-idaea

Vaccinium myrtillus

Vaccinium uliginosum

Vaccinium oxycoccos

Orthilia secunda

Pyrola minor

Pyrola media

Pyrola rotundifolia

Yellow Bird's-nest
Monotropa hypopitys

This extraordinary plant **lacks any green colouring** and feeds totally on decaying humus in the soil. The whole **plant is a waxy, pale yellow colour**, and the **thick, simple stems** bear scale-like leaves. **The inflorescence is at first pendulous**, but straightens up in fruit. (The photograph shows a young flowering stage.)

In woods and on sand-dunes, scattered throughout much of the British Isles, but nowhere common; absent from W Scotland, E and S Ireland, much of Wales, and the SW peninsula.

P   30cm   Summer

Crowberry
Empetrum nigrum

A small, **evergreen, heath-like shrub**, with shiny, **alternate, oblong, densely-packed leaves with turned-back margins**. Usually the plants are dioecious, **males bearing small flowers with bright red stamens** (as in the photograph), and females, later in the season, with **black, inedible berries**. Hermaphrodite plants are found on some mountains, especially in Scotland; these can be treated as a distinct subspecies.

Locally abundant on mountain and moorland in N Britain, ascending to more than 1000m; absent south of a line from Somerset to Leicestershire, extinct in Sussex, and scattered throughout Ireland but mainly in the north.

P   20cm   Spring and early summer

Common Sea-lavender
Limonium vulgare

The sea-lavenders are familiar wildflowers around our coasts, where they often colour the salt-marshes in late summer with their **pale purple flowers**. Common sea-lavender is a **robust, rather fleshy plant** with **large, thick, pinnately-veined, elliptical leaves** arising from a woody stock; the **flowering stems branch freely, usually from above the middle, and the numerous small flowers are massed into flattened heads**. The flowers have a short corolla-tube with 5 lobes, and the 5 stamens are joined to the tube.

Coasts of Britain north to Dumfries and Fife, often abundant in the middle zone of salt-marshes. Absent from Ireland.

P   30cm   Late summer

Lax-flowered Sea-lavender
Limonium humile

Like the common sea-lavender, but with **the branches from well below the middle of the flowering stem, forming a loose, twiggy, not flat-topped, inflorescence**.

In muddy salt-marshes, with a similar distribution in Britain to the common sea-lavender, but somewhat rarer; in Ireland, all round the coast but rare in the north.

P   30cm   Late summer

Rock Sea-lavender
Limonium binervosum group

The rock sea-lavenders are a group of closely-related plants that differ from the two species already described. They are **smaller, neater plants** and have **leaves with 3 sub-parallel veins below. The individual flowers are usually rather larger and more brightly pinkish-purple coloured**.

On coastal rocks and shingle in England, Wales, Ireland and SW Scotland. The plant illustrated is the rare *L. recurvum* which grows only at Portland, Dorset.

P   25cm   Summer

Thrift
Armeria maritima

Thrift or sea-pink is an unmistakable wildflower of our coasts. The **numerous, long, very narrow, rather fleshy leaves** surround the woody stock, **often making a dense cushion**, and the **leafless flower-stalks bear a dense hemispherical head of pink (or sometimes white) flowers surrounded by a ring of chaffy bracts**.

Throughout British Isles on coastal rocks, in salt-marshes and pastures near the sea; also on mountains up to more than 1250m.

P   25cm   Spring to early autumn

Bird's-eye Primrose
Primula farinosa

A neat, pretty plant with a **rosette of broadly spoon-shaped leaves green on top and covered underneath by a grey-white meal**. From the rosette arises the **leafless flower-stalk** bearing a **small terminal group of pinkish-purple flowers**. The corolla has a short tube and 5 bifid lobes spreading widely.

One of the specialities of N England and S Scotland, where it grows, sometimes quite abundantly, in damp pastures on lime-rich soils. It is totally absent from the British Isles outside this restricted area.

P   15cm   Late spring

Monotropa hypopitys

Empetrum nigrum

Limonium vulgare

Limonium humile

Limonium recurvum

Armeria maritima

Primula farinosa

Primrose
Primula vulgaris
The primrose is so familiar in spring, both in the wild and in gardens, that it needs no detailed description. The **blunt, wrinkled and irregular toothed leaves** surround the base of the plant, from which arise the large **solitary, regular flowers, pale yellow with a darker 'eye'**.

Common in woods, hedgebanks and (in the west) in grassland throughout most of the British Isles, but local in S and W Ireland.

P 10cm Spring and summer

INFLORESCENCES

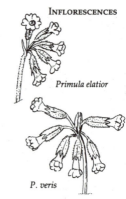

Primula elatior

P. veris

Cowslip
Primula veris
The cowslip is closely related to the primrose, and the leaves have to be distinguished with care. (They narrow more abruptly into the leaf-stalk.) The **familiar head of nodding, deep yellow flowers is borne on a long, shortly hairy, leafless stalk**. The corolla lobes are much smaller than those of the primrose and are strongly curved inwards.

Formerly abundant in meadows and pastures on lime-rich soils throughout much of the British Isles, but much reduced in recent years by the disappearance of permanent grassland.

P 20cm Spring

Oxlip
Primula elatior
The true oxlip resembles the cowslip (and the 'false oxlip' hybrid) in having **several yellow flowers on a single leafless stalk**, but is easily recognised by **paler-coloured more 'open' flowers which all bend over on the same side** (see drawing). (In the 'false oxlip' the flowers spread on all sides.) The leaves are longer and narrower than either the primrose or cowslip.

In wet woods on chalky boulder-clay in E Anglia, locally abundant in a small area in which primroses are rare or absent.

P 25cm Spring

Water-violet
Hottonia palustris
A **water plant with submerged, pinnately-dissected leaves in whorls** and erect **flowering stems emerging above the water surface**. The **pale lilac flowers**, with a yellow 'eye', **are up to 2.5cm across** and **arranged in whorls** along the stem.

In ponds and ditches, locally common in parts of E England, and extending to N Somerset, N Wales and NE Yorkshire; also rare in NE Scotland and NE Ireland.

P 40cm Early summer

Yellow Loosestrife
Lysimachia vulgaris
Very different in general appearance from the other 2 species, this is a **robust, hairy, rhizomatous plant** with erect flowering stems bearing **whorls of lance-shaped leaves, 2–4 in a whorl**, and many **yellow flowers in a long, narrow, branched inflorescence**. Individually the flowers resemble those of yellow pimpernel.

Locally common by rivers and lakes and in fens in much of the British Isles; absent from N Scotland, the Hebrides and the northern isles.

P 1.2m Summer

Yellow Pimpernel
Lysimachia nemorum
A **neat, hairless, prostrate plant with opposite, ovate, acute leaves** and **solitary flowers up to 1.2cm diameter on slender stalks** arising from the leaf axils. The **corolla-lobes spread out flat; they are pale yellow, with a darker yellow 'eye'**.

In damp woodlands, hedgebanks, etc. throughout most of the British Isles, but rare in parts of E Anglia.

P 5cm (tall) Summer

Creeping-Jenny
Lysimachia nummularia
This creeping plant is familiar in gardens, and differs from yellow pimpernel most obviously in the **leaves, which are blunt and almost circular in outline**, and in the **flowers which have a cup-shaped corolla of a much deeper yellow colour**.

In grassy places, hedgebanks, etc. often as an escape from gardens, throughout much of England, Wales, and S Scotland; absent from C and N Scotland and the islands; in Ireland mainly in the north.

P 5cm(tall) Summer

Primula vulgaris

Primula veris

Primula elatior

Hottonia palustris

Lysimachia vulgaris

Lysimachia nemorum

Lysimachia nummularia

Chickweed Wintergreen
Trientalis europaea

A **charming, delicate plant with slender, hairless, erect stems** bearing a **single whorl of 5 or 6 narrowly obovate leaves and a terminal flower**. The **white corolla has a variable number, most commonly 7, of ovate, pointed corolla-lobes**.

In the mossy, humus-rich ground layer of woodland, especially pine forest, from E Suffolk and Derbyshire northwards, becoming locally common in the Scottish Highlands; absent from Wales, Ireland and the Hebrides.
P   25cm   Summer

Bog Pimpernel
Anagallis tenella

A **slender, prostrate, freely-rooting, hairless little plant with pairs of small, almost circular leaves**. The single flowers are borne on very slender stalks standing above the leaves; they have a **funnel-shaped corolla with 5 or more deep lobes, pale pink with darker veins**.

In bogs and damp grassy places throughout much of the British Isles, but much commoner in the west, and locally rare or extinct through drainage in midland England.
P   3cm(tall)   Summer

Scarlet Pimpernel
Anagallis arvensis

One of our prettiest weeds, unmistakable when the red flowers open. A **weak, square-stemmed, hairless annual** with **opposite, ovate leaves** and **single flowers on long slender stalks. The red or pink 5-lobed corolla spreads open in the sun. The ripe spherical capsules split round the middle, and the top falls off**.

A weed of cultivation, also on sand-dunes, throughout much of the British Isles, but mainly coastal in N and W Scotland.
A(P)   30cm   Summer

Chaffweed
Anagallis minima

A **tiny, hairless annual**, with **alternate, ovate leaves and almost stalkless flowers in the upper leaf-axils**. The **whitish corolla is very inconspicuous**, and the plant is best recognised by the capsules opening by a 'lid' as in the other species.

In damp, sandy places, often on disturbed ground near the sea; widespread, but often overlooked, in Britain north to Lewis; rare in Ireland.
A   10cm   Summer

Brookweed
Samolus valerandi

An odd little plant, **yellow-green and hairless**, with **blunt, broadly spoon-shaped basal leaves** and erect stems bearing a **few small white flowers**. The **ovary is remarkable in being half-embedded in the flower-axis**, and the fruit develops with the 5 triangular calyx-teeth on top.

In wet, disturbed ground, especially near the sea, throughout most of Britain and Ireland, but absent from NE Scotland, Orkney and Shetland.
P   50cm   Summer

Sea-milkwort
Glaux maritima

A **small, creeping, hairless, rather fleshy plant with broadly elliptical, more or less opposite leaves** and almost **stalkless flowers in the leaf-axils**. There is **no corolla, but the bluntly 5-lobed calyx is pinkish or white**. The few-seeded, spherical capsule splits into 5 valves.

Rather common in grassy salt-marshes or on rocks around the coasts of British Isles.
P   5cm(tall)   Summer

Trientalis europaea

Anagallis tenella

Anagallis arvensis

Anagallis minima

Samolus valerandi

Glaux maritima

Lesser Periwinkle
Vinca minor

Periwinkles are very familiar in our gardens in spring. The detail of the attractive flower is complicated, with the 5 anthers held tightly round the enlarged head of the style. The long, pointed fruits are rarely produced in Britain.

The lesser periwinkle is a creeping, **evergreen, hairless plant, woody below, with long trailing and rooting stems** bearing **opposite pairs of narrowly elliptic, short-stalked, glossy leaves**. The short, erect flowering stems usually bear only 1 flower, which has a **bluish or white corolla up to 3cm across with a long tube and wide-spreading, asymmetrical lobes**.

Doubtfully native, occurring in woods and hedgebanks throughout Britain except NW Scotland; rare in Ireland.

P   30cm   Spring

Greater Periwinkle
Vinca major

Like a larger version of lesser periwinkle, with vigorous trailing or **arching stems rooting only at the tip**, and **larger, obviously-stalked leaves, heart-shaped at base**. The **large blue-purple flowers** can be as much as **5cm across**.

A garden escape in woods and hedgerows mainly in S England; rare in Wales, Scotland and Ireland.

P   60cm   Spring

Yellow-wort
Blackstonia perfoliata

An **erect, blue-grey, hairless annual**, with a **basal leaf rosette** and **paired stem-leaves fused to make a collar round the stem**. The branched inflorescence bears several **bright yellow flowers unusual in having 6–8 calyx and corolla-lobes**.

Chalk and limestone grassland and coastal dunes; rather common in S and C England, rare and mainly coastal in SW England and Wales, and absent from Scotland; in Ireland mostly in the south and centre.

A   40cm   Summer

Centauries

The centauries are related to yellow-wort and to the gentians. They have simple, opposite leaves and flowers with a tubular corolla and expanded pinkish lobes.

Common Centaury
Centaurium erythraea

Common centaury is a rather variable, hairless **biennial, with a basal rosette of elliptical leaves** and one or more erect stems branching above. The **stalkless flowers are in clusters, forming a more or less flat-topped inflorescence**.

In dry grassland, on sand-dunes etc., throughout England, Wales, Ireland and W Scotland; mainly coastal in E Scotland and absent from N Scotland, Orkney and Shetland.

B   50cm   Summer

Lesser Centaury
Centaurium pulchellum

Differs from the common centaury in being a **smaller, annual plant without a basal leaf rosette**, and in having **stalked flowers not in clusters**. In small specimens (as in the photograph) the **flowers often have only 4 (not 5) corolla-lobes**.

In damp grassy places usually where the ground is disturbed, generally less common than common centaury and mainly near the coast; absent from Scotland and rare in Ireland.

A   10cm   Summer

Seaside Centaury
Centaurium littorale

Like the common centaury, a biennial, with a basal rosette, but with **much narrower, parallel-sided stem-leaves** and **a flat, few-flowered inflorescence**.

Local on sand-dunes especially around the coasts of Scotland, N England and Wales; very rare in S England and Ireland.

B   25cm   Summer

Marsh Gentian
Gentiana pneumonanthe

We associate true gentians more with the Alps than the British countryside, but we have a representative which can compete in size and beauty. The marsh gentian has **erect, simple hairless stems** and **very narrow, opposite leaves**. The **spectacular flowers have a narrowly trumpet-shaped corolla, sky-blue with paler dots and green midribs**, borne singly or few in a dense group.

Very local and decreasing, in wet heaths in England from Dorset to Yorkshire and Westmorland; also in Anglesey.

P   40cm   Late summer and autumn

Vinca minor

Vinca major

Blackstonia perfoliata

Centaurium erythraea

Centaurium pulchellum

Centaurium littorale

Gentiana pneumonanthe

Gentianella

Gentianella species differ technically from the true gentians in having no small extra corolla-lobes between the main ones, and a fringe of long hairs in the corolla throat (see photograph of *G. germanica*). They are **hairless biennial or annual plants with purplish flowers**. The species are not always easy to distinguish; 4 are described here.

Field Gentian
Gentianella campestris
Flowering stems simple or narrowly branched, with paired stem-leaves more or less lance-shaped, and pointed. Flowers with a **calyx deeply divided into 4 unequal pointed lobes, the 2 outer much larger than (and enclosing) the inner pair**. The long, thin corolla-tube has 4 lobes.

Pastures and sand-dunes, common in N Britain, ascending in Scotland to nearly 1000m, but rare in Wales and much of lowland England; scattered in Ireland, but rare in the south.
B 30cm Late summer and autumn

Chiltern Gentian
Gentianella germanica
A rather handsome, **often bushy plant with broadly ovate stem-leaves** and **bluish-purple 5-partite flowers up to 3cm across**.

In chalk grassland in a very confined area of England, mainly the Chiltern Hills.
B 30cm Autumn

Autumn Gentian
Gentianella amarella
Easily distinguished from the field gentian by its **5-partite flowers** in which **the 5 calyx-lobes are more or less equal** and pressed to the corolla-tube.

A variable species, sometimes divided into subspecies, occurring in chalk and limestone grassland and sand-dunes throughout much of the British Isles, but rare in W Scotland and NE Ireland.
B 30cm Autumn

Early Gentian
Gentianella anglica
Best recognised by its early flowering, this small plant has relatively large flowers in which the 5 calyx-teeth are nearly as long as the corolla-tube.

Chalk grassland, dunes and sea-cliffs in S and E England, from Cornwall to S Lincolnshire; not known outside England.
B 20cm Spring to summer

Bogbean
Menyanthes trifoliata
Quite unlike any other wild-flower, the bogbean has **thick, hairless stems bearing large alternate leaves each with 3 elliptical leaflets**. The regular 5-partite flowers are in a raceme; the **corollas open widely, showing the deeply-fringed lobes, pale pink on the outside and white inside**.

In bogs and shallow water, usually acid, throughout British Isles, up to nearly 1000m in mountain lakes.
P 40cm Early summer

Fringed Water-lily
Nymphoides peltata
This remarkable plant is not related to the true water-lilies (p.8), but to the bogbean. It is a **water plant with round 'water-lily' floating leaves, and flowers above the surface, which have 5 broad, bright yellow corolla-lobes prettily fringed at the edges**.

Locally abundant and thought to be native in the Thames river system and possibly in the Fens; introduced elsewhere.
P 10cm (above water) Summer

Jacob's-ladder
Polemonium caeruleum
A very well-known garden plant, also found in the wild. It has a short rhizome and **erect, simple, leafy stems glandular-hairy below**. The **hairless leaves are alternate and pinnate with 6–12 pairs of leaflets**. The **blue (rarely white) flowers are in condensed groups; they have wide-spreading corolla-lobes from a short tube, 5 stamens and 3 styles**.

Locally common in upland limestone country in N England. Recorded elsewhere as a garden escape (though most garden plants are not strictly the same as the wild one).
P 80cm Summer

Gentianella campestris

Gentianella germanica

Gentianella amarella

Gentianella anglica

Menyanthes trifoliata

Nymphoides peltata

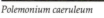

Polemonium caeruleum

Borage Family (Boraginaceae)

Members of the borage family are most easily recognised by the way the flowers open–(see picture of common comfrey). The flowering stalks are tightly coiled and uncurl by growing from the base with only a relatively few flowers open on a stem at one time. Other characteristics are the undivided and untoothed alternate leaves, the calyx of 5 teeth joined at the base and the 5-lobed, tubed flowers, wheel-, funnel- or bell-shaped which frequently change colour between bud, young flower and old flower.

Common Comfrey
Symphytum officinale
A tall, **softly hairy** plant with long, oval leaves: the **leaf-stalks have broad wings which run down the stem to at least the next leaf below**. The drooping, funnel-shaped flowers have a **calyx with teeth about twice as long as the tubular part below** and come in 2 colours – pale yellow (as in the photograph) and carmine red. Intermediates with alternating stripes are frequent in S England.

Ditches, streamsides and marshes throughout lowland British Isles.

P 1.2m Summer and autumn

Russian Comfrey
Symphytum x uplandicum
The most frequent roadside comfrey distinguished from common comfrey by being **roughly hairy** and having **leaf-stalks** which are **either unwinged or in which the wings run only a short way down the stem below** and never reach the next leaf (see drawing). Two main colour forms occur: those with purple buds which change to violet on opening (as in the photograph) and those with red buds which change to pink.

Throughout lowland British Isles.

P 1.5m Summer and autumn

White Comfrey
Symphytum orientale
This **softly hairy** herb is recognisable from a distance by its **pure-white flowers** which first appear in April. Closer inspection shows **leaves without wings running down the stem** and a **calyx** in which the **teeth** are **only about half the length of the tubular part below**.

This introduction from Turkey has escaped from gardens and is well-established and still spreading, often along the base of walls in towns.

P 70cm Spring and early summer

Tuberous Comfrey
Symphytum tuberosum
The **yellow-flowered** comfrey **with no wings on the leaf-stalks running down the stem**. The **leaves in the middle of the stem are larger than those above or below**. The **calyx** is deeply cut into **teeth** which are **3 times as long as the short tube below**. Named 'tuberous' because of the stout, knotted underground stems.

Woodland margins and hedgebanks; frequent in lowland Scotland but rare and perhaps introduced elsewhere.

P 50cm Summer

Hound's-tongue
Cynoglossum officinale
Two characters of this biennial herb relate to its English name: the **long, narrow, softly hairy leaves** may look like a hound's tongue whilst the **rough, barbed surface of the 4 nutlets** produced by each of the **dirty purple flowers** certainly have the feel. The smell of the **leaves crushed** between the fingers produces the **smell of mouse**.

Bare places on dry lime-rich or sandy soils throughout lowland England and Wales, E Ireland and E Scotland north to the Moray Firth.

P 90cm Summer

Borage
Borago officinalis
The **drooping, roughly hairy buds** which develop into **brilliant blue, star-like flowers with a purple/black centre** are unmistakable. The oval, blunt leaves which are also rough have a faint cucumber flavour and can make an interesting addition to a salad whilst a few leaves can enhance a claret cup.

Introduced as an attractive garden plant and culinary herb, it is now established in waste places throughout lowland British Isles but frequent only in the south.

A 60cm Summer

Green Alkanet
Pentaglottis sempervirens
This perennial has rough, hairy stems, **oval, acutely-pointed and strongly-veined leaves** and looks like a big forget-me-not with its **wheel-shaped bright blue flowers with 5 paler 'spokes'**. The **calyx** is **divided almost to the base** whilst the throat of the flower is closed by 5 conspicuous scales which give rise to the name *Pentaglottis* meaning 'five tongues'. The **tube of the flower is straight**.

Introduced from SW Europe, now throughout lowland Britain in hedgerows and on woodland margins; rare in Ireland.

P 90cm Late spring and summer

Bugloss
Lycopsis arvensis
A very **prickly annual** of arable fields **with narrow**, lance-shaped **leaves** and **bright blue, wheel-shaped flowers** which **have a kink in the tube** to which the petals are joined, as can be seen when they are removed from the calyx. The throats of the flowers are closed by 5 conspicuous scales.

Sandy or lime-rich fields throughout lowland British Isles but rare in W Ireland.

A 60cm Summer and early autumn

Symphytum
officinale

WINGS ON
LEAF-STALKS

S. x uplandicum

Symphytum officinale

Symphytum x uplandicum

Symphytum orientale

Symphytum tuberosum

Cynoglossum officinale

Borago officinalis

Pentaglottis sempervirens

Lycopsis arvensis

Lungwort

Pulmonaria officinalis

The **white spotted leaves** looked so much like lungs to our ancestors that they thought it a heaven-sent sign that it would cure lung diseases, especially tuberculosis. Also recognised by the very early **flowers** which are **pinkish when they open but turn blue with age**. This has given rise to a number of double names e.g. Adam & Eve, Joseph & Mary.

Introduced from C Europe but now naturalised in woods and thickets throughout England, Wales and S Scotland.

P 30cm Spring

Forget-me-nots

Forget-me-nots have blue, wheel-shaped flowers in terminal spikes, often forked near the apex, with a single early flower in the axil, clearly seen in the photograph of field forget-me-not. It is not easy to separate the 7 widespread species included here. However attention to the diameter of the flower, the length of the flower-stalk, the hairiness of the calyx and the length of the style compared with the calyx should resolve any problem. Style length is best observed by removing the petals in one piece and viewing the calyx with a lens from the side (see drawing).

Water Forget-me-not

Myosotis scorpioides

There are 3 common forget-me-nots of wet places and all are recognised by the **hairs on the calyx** which **do not stand out** but are laid flat on the surface. However water forget-me-not is the only one of the 3 in which the **style** is **longer than the calyx tube**: the **teeth of the calyx** are **shaped like an equilateral triangle**. Usually **some** of the **hairs on the stem** are **erect**.

Margins of neutral or basic rivers, streams and ponds throughout British Isles mainly in the lowlands but ascending to 450m in the Pennines.

P 45cm Spring to autumn

Creeping Forget-me-not

Myosotis secunda

The aquatic forget-me-not which is abundantly clothed in **hairs at right-angles to the stem**. Like tufted forget-me-not it has a **short style** scarcely visible between the lobes of the **calyx** which is **divided almost to the base**. The **flower-stalks** are **3–5 times as long as** the **calyx** and **turn down as** the **fruits ripen**.

Acid springs and flushes throughout British Isles except E Anglia and the Midlands.

P 60cm Late spring and summer

Tufted Forget-me-not

Myosotis laxa

The aquatic forget-me-not with **all the hairs appressed to the** stem. It has a **style shorter than the calyx tube** and the **teeth of the calyx** are **shaped like an isosceles triangle**. It can usually be identified by the **small flowers less than 4mm across** but beware, later in the season the other aquatic species, which normally have flowers over 4mm across, may also produce small flowers.

Marshes, pond margins and, infrequently, beside running water throughout British Isles to 500m in Scotland.

P 40cm Late spring and summer

Wood Forget-me-not

Myosotis sylvatica

All the terrestrial forget-me-nots have a **calyx covered in hooked hairs** whilst 2, wood and field, have their **flower-stalks** 1½–2 times as long as the calyx. Of these wood forget-me-not has much the larger **flowers – up to 1cm across**. Another difference is that the **style** is **longer than the calyx tube** and clearly visible when viewed from the side after the petals have fallen.

Damp woods in E and C England and S Scotland; rare elsewhere.

P 45cm Late spring and summer

Field Forget-me-not

Myosotis arvensis

The commonest terrestrial forget-me-not, readily distinguished by its small **flowers, less than 4mm across**, the **style much shorter than the calyx tube** and the **flower-stalks** about **twice as long as the calyx**. In fruit the **inflorescence rarely exceeds** in length the leafy part of the stem below.

Arable fields, waste places, roadsides, sand-dunes and woodland margins throughout British Isles to 550m in the Pennines.

A 30cm Spring to autumn

Changing Forget-me-not

Myosotis discolor

In flower the easiest forget-me-not to recognise because, as the name indicates, the **flowers change in colour from yellow or white** when young **to blue** at maturity when the **tube of the flower** is **twice as long as the calyx tube**. Later identified by the style being **longer than the calyx tube** and by being one of only 2 species to have **flower-stalks shorter than the calyx**.

Open grassland, often on light, sandy soils, throughout British Isles to 500m in Scotland.

A 25cm Late spring to autumn

Early Forget-me-not

Myosotis ramosissima

One of only 2 species of forget-me-not with **flower-stalks shorter than the calyx**. Similar to field forget-me-not in having a **style shorter than the calyx tube** but with even smaller **flowers, only c.2mm across** and, in fruit, with **inflorescences** which are **longer than the leafy part of the stem below**.

Dry, shallow, sandy soils throughout lowland Britain; rare and mainly coastal in Ireland.

A 25cm Spring and early summer

Myosotis showing
style longer than calyx
tube as in *M. scorpioides,*
M. sylvatica and *M. discolor*

Pulmonaria officinalis

Myosotis scorpioides

Myosotis secunda

Myosotis laxa

Myosotis sylvatica

Myosotis arvensis

Myosotis discolor

Myosotis ramosissima

Common Gromwell
Lithospermum officinale
This upright, **much-branched** perennial is **covered in hairs** but, except on the calyx, they are mostly **appressed to the stems and leaves**. The latter are oval, pointed, have strong lateral veins and lack any stalk.The **flowers** are like forget-me-not but are **yellowish or greenish-white**. These develop 4 'seeds' at the base of the deeply-divided calyx – they are **white, shining and hard** giving the name *lithospermum* – stone seed – to this plant.

Hedges and woodland margins on lime-rich soils in lowland England, Wales and Ireland.
P 80cm Summer

Field Gromwell
Lithospermum arvense
An erect, **little-branched** annual more **roughly hairy** than common gromwell and with leaves without prominent lateral veins, the lower ones with a short stalk. The **flowers** vary in colour from **white to blue** and are somewhat hidden by the deeply-divided calyx. The 4 'seeds' are not shiny but **warty and greyish-brown**.

An arable weed almost entirely confined to lowland England and most frequent on lime-rich soils.
A 50cm Late spring and summer

Viper's-bugloss
Echium vulgare
This erect, roughly hairy biennial is perhaps the most handsome of all the *Boraginaceae*. Recognised by the **spikes of vivid blue, funnel-shaped flowers** which have a **pronounced lower lip** and some **stamens** which are **longer than the petals**. The bell-shaped flowers are attractive to bees, butterflies and moths. After pollination each produces 4 'seeds' said to resemble a viper's head.

Dry sandy soils inland or on dunes or coastal cliffs throughout British Isles north to the Moray Firth.
B 90cm Summer and early autumn

Oysterplant
Mertensia maritima
Forms large, **circular, purple patches on sand or shingle** shores with the flowers arranged round the circumference. The lower leaves are almost circular – and stalked – whilst the upper ones are narrower and stalkless; all are covered in rough dots. The **flowers** are **pink when young but darken to blue with age** and produce 4 flattened, fleshy 'seeds'.

Northern coasts of British Isles south to Lancashire and Co. Down.
P Prostrate Summer

Hedge Bindweed
Calystegia sepium
All bindweeds have large, showy, **funnel-shaped flowers** and many, like hedge bindweed, climb by twining their stems anticlockwise round other plants in hedgerows or up fences. Species of *Calystegia* are separated from *Convolvulus* by the **2 large, green bracts** which **surround the base of the flower**. In hedge bindweed these are only **c.1.5cm wide** and **do not overlap to hide the true calyx**. The pink or white **flowers** are **up to 7cm long**.

Throughout lowland British Isles to 350m in S Pennines; native in fens and wet woodlands.
P 3m Summer and autumn

Large Bindweed
Calystegia silvatica
Distinguished from hedge bindweed by the, usually, larger **flowers up to 9cm long** which may have alternating pink and white zones, and by the **bracts up to 3cm wide**, swollen and **overlapping to conceal the true calyx**.

Introduced from SE Europe but escaping from gardens and established throughout lowland British Isles.
P 3m Summer and early autumn

Sea Bindweed
Calystegia soldanella
Sea bindweed does not climb like other species but sends runners through the sand and shingle of the beaches on which it grows. At intervals it puts up **glossy, heart-shaped leaves** and beautiful, **funnel-shaped flowers** which are pink with 5 broad, pale yellow, vertical stripes. The **bracts, up to 1.5cm wide, scarcely overlap** and the **true calyx is visible** between them.

All round the coasts of British Isles except N and E Scotland.
P 50cm Summer

Field Bindweed
Convolvulus arvensis
A very persistent and troublesome weed with underground stems which may go down 2m. Any part broken off can form a new plant. Distinguished from *Calystegia* by the **spear-shaped leaves** with outwardly turned lobes and the smaller **flowers, only up to 2cm long**, which have **tiny bracts well below the calyx**. The flowers give off a powerful scent attractive to many species of pollinating insect.

Throughout lowland British Isles but absent from the northern isles.
P 75cm Summer and early autumn

Lithospermum officinale

Lithospermum arvense

Echium vulgare

Mertensia maritima

Calystegia sepium

Calystegia silvatica

Calystegia soldanella

Convolvulus arvensis

Dodder
Cuscuta epithymum
This leafless parasite is a bindweed which no longer relies on roots in the soil as a source of food but instead puts 'roots' (haustoria) into the stems of the plants up which it twines anticlockwise. The **slender, reddish, wiry stems, 0.1mm wide**, are readily recognised, even from a distance. The plant is even more prominent in mid-summer when it produces **clusters of small, pinkish-white tubular flowers**.

Parasitic on gorse, heather, clover and other species in the southern half of lowland England; rare in Wales and E Ireland.

A   Scrambling   Late summer

Henbane
Hyoscyamus niger
This tall annual or biennial is recognised by its **jaggedly divided, glandular, softly-hairy leaves** and the terminal clusters of **livid, tubular flowers, yellow with a strong network of purple veins**. These later develop into a hard **capsule surrounded by the persistent calyx** with 5 acute segments. Seeds poisonous and fatal to cattle but the drug hyoscine is extracted and used as a sedative.

Native on sand near the sea but also a frequent relic of former cultivation on roadsides and in waste places in lowland British Isles.

A or B   1m   Summer

Bittersweet
Solanum dulcamara
The commonest wild member of the potato family and recognised by its **potato-like leaves**, often **with a large terminal lobe and 2 or more** much **smaller ones at the base**, and by the striking **flowers with 5 reflexed, purple petals and** a central core of **bright yellow anthers**. The flowers develop into small, **oval, red berries** which are mildly poisonous to children. The young stems, dried for medicinal purposes, taste bitter at first but become sweeter with age.

Throughout lowland British Isles except extreme N Scotland.

P   2m   Summer and autumn

Potato Family (Solanaceae)
Potatoes and tomatoes are members of the *Solanaceae* and it is their flower type which is characteristic of one genus of wild species which occurs in the British Isles – *Solanum*. The calyx is joined but deeply divided (cf tomatoes) and the petals are also joined making a flat disk with a central core of anthers, often strikingly coloured. Other flowers, such as henbane, are bell-shaped. The fruits also are of 2 kinds – a succulent 'berry' like a tomato or a dry capsule as with henbane.

Black Nightshade
Solanum nigrum
Like a potato which does not produce tubers this more or less **hairless, white-flowered annual** develops, on the upper side of the stem from the leaves, **groups of 5 or 6 short-stalked, globular fruits**, *c*. 8mm diameter, which are green at first but **usually turn black**. A difficult weed to remove from garden beds where it occurs, because the **stem breaks at ground level when pulled** from which it soon grows again.

Lowland England and Wales north to Lancashire and Yorkshire.

A   60cm   Summer and early autumn

Thorn-apple
Datura stramonium
A poisonous annual recognised by the **broad, glossy, spikely-toothed leaves** and the solitary, short-stalked, occasionally **purple, flowers** up to 10cm long. These develop into **prickly fruits** about the size of an unopened horse-chestnut – the thorn-apple. These 'apples' **split into 4** when ripe **releasing dark, kidney-shaped seeds**. All parts of the plant contain poisonous alkaloids.

Appears sporadically in waste places throughout lowland Britain north to C Scotland. Seeds may survive in soil for years.

A   90cm   Summer and autumn

Deadly Nightshade
Atropa belladonna
This perennial, bushy plant may be recognised by its potato-like, dull green leaves which give off a peculiar, heavy smell, and by the **drooping, bell-like, dull purple flowers** underneath the branches. These develop into the juicy **black, cherry-like berries** which are so attractive to children but so deadly poisonous – 3 are enough to kill.

Scattered throughout lowland England in scrub, hedgebanks, and on woodland margins on lime-rich soils and near old buildings; rare elsewhere.

P   1.3m   Summer

Figwort Family (Scrophulariaceae)
The large family *Scrophulariaceae* contains many common wildflowers such as foxglove, speedwell and toadflax. Most of them have showy, irregular and often 2-lipped flowers. The family otherwise resembles the *Solanaceae* in flower and fruit structure, but the fruit is always a dry capsule, not a berry. The mulleins (*Verbascum*), with almost regular flowers and 5 stamens, are unusual for the family, forming a link to the *Solanaceae*.

Cuscuta epithymum

Atropa belladonna

Hyoscyamus niger

Solanum nigrum

Solanum dulcamara

Datura stramonium

Great Mullein
Verbascum thapsus
A stately plant, **covered with woolly hairs**. The **large, oblong basal leaves** can be up to 45cm long, and the **tall, thick leafy stem finishes in a dense 'spike' of yellow flowers** which have a short corolla-tube and 5 spreading, almost equal lobes. The **upper 3 of the 5 stamens have many yellowish hairs, whilst the lower 2 are nearly hairless**.

Common on dry banks and roadsides in much of England and Wales; in Scotland mainly in the south and east and absent from most of the north-west and the islands; scattered in Ireland.
B   2m   Summer

Dark Mullein
Verbascum nigrum
Differs from great mullein most obviously in being **much less hairy, with star-shaped hairs, not woolly ones**, and in having **all 5 filaments of the flowers obviously purple-hairy** (see photograph).

On chalk or limestone soils, common over much of SE England and extending to Cornwall, N Wales and N Lincolnshire; naturalised in places in N England, Scotland and Ireland.
B   1.2m   Summer

Twiggy Mullein
Verbascum virgatum
Differs from both mulleins already described **in having almost hairless stems and leaves** and usually **single flowers in the axils of bracts more widely spaced along the glandular inflorescence.** Like the dark mullein **the flowers have purple-hairy filaments**.

Confined as a native plant to the SW peninsula, but introduced elsewhere including (rarely) both Scotland and Ireland.
B   1m   Summer

Toadflaxes
Toadflaxes and their relatives have 2-lipped flowers in which the 3-lobed lower lip of the corolla has a 'palate' which closes the mouth of the flower. There are 4 stamens attached to the corolla-tube. The toadflax flower (*Linaria* species) has the corolla extended backwards in a slender spur.

Purple Toadflax
Linaria purpurea
The purple toadflax has **hairless stems with very narrow leaves and long, slender racemes with many tightly-packed purple flowers**. The **spur** behind the flower **is curved**.

Often on old walls and near gardens, introduced throughout much of British Isles, though rarer in the north and west.
P   80cm   Summer

Pale Toadflax
Linaria repens
Differs from the purple toadflax in having **whitish or pale lilac flowers much more distantly spaced out**, and a short, **straight spur**.

Widespread on dry, stony ground in much of England and Wales, occasional or rare in Scotland and Ireland; probably not native in Britain.
P   60cm   Summer

Common Toadflax
Linaria vulgaris
The most common toadflax, easily told by its **bright yellow flower**, which has a **more or less straight spur**. It spreads freely by **a creeping rhizome**.

Common on roadsides and in grassy places throughout much of Britain, though rare in N Scotland and absent from Orkney and Shetland; widespread but not common in Ireland.
P   60cm   Summer

Small Toadflax
Chaenorhinum minus
A small, **branching, stickily-hairy annual**, with **narrow, blunt, alternate leaves** and **purplish 'toadflax' flowers singly in the leaf axils**. The corolla spur is short and blunt.

Common on the cinder-tracks of railways, and less commonly on other dry waste ground in S England; less common northwards to C Scotland, and widespread but not common in Ireland.
A   20cm   Summer

Snapdragon
Antirrhinum majus
This familiar garden plant is **somewhat woody at the base**, and the stems, with **numerous narrow leaves**, terminate in a **raceme of showy flowers, usually purplish-red in colour.**

Not uncommon on old walls in many parts of Britain and Ireland, though rarer in the north and west; thought to be native to the Mediterranean, and early introduced into Britain.
P   60cm   Summer

Verbascum thapsus

Verbascum nigrum

Verbascum virgatum

Linaria purpurea

Linaria repens

Linaria vulgaris

Chaenorhinum minus

Antirrhinum majus

Lesser Snapdragon
Misopates orontium
An erect, rather dainty annual plant **usually strongly glandular-hairy**, with **small pinkish 'snapdragon' flowers in the axils of the upper leaves**; the **calyx-lobes are very long and narrow, and unequal in size.**

In cultivated and waste ground, mostly in S England and S Wales, though extending to N England and S Ireland.

A 40cm Summer

Sharp-leaved Fluellen
Kickxia elatine
Like the round-leaved fluellen, but with the **upper leaves spear-shaped and pointed, and straight-spurred flowers on very long, hairless stalks.**

In similar places to (and often mixed with) the round-leaved fluellen, but extending further west, and present in N Wales, the Isle of Man and S and W Ireland.

A 10cm(tall) Late summer to autumn

Round-leaved Fluellen
Kickxia spuria
A distinctive little **glandular-hairy annual with long, trailing stems bearing short-stalked, almost circular leaves**, the lowest up to 5cm. The flowers are borne singly on long stalks in the leaf-axils, and have pretty **corollas, bright yellow with a purple upper lip and a curved spur**.

A rather local weed of arable land, formerly common in corn-field stubble, but now much rarer. In England and S Wales, northwards to Durham.

A 10cm(tall) Late summer to autumn

Ivy-leaved Toadflax
Cymbalaria muralis
One of our prettiest wall-plants, unmistakable with its **delicate, hairless, trailing and rooting stems and ivy-shaped leaves often rather thick and purplish**. The **flowers**, borne singly in the leaf-axils, are **pale lilac with a darker upper lip and yellow palate, and have a short, curved spur.**

Introduced as a garden plant in the seventeenth century, now common on walls (and more rarely on rocks) almost throughout British Isles.

P 5cm(tall) Summer

Figworts

Figworts (*Scrophularia* species) are easily recognised. They have **opposite leaves and square stems** (like many of the Mint Family p.150) and very distinctive **brownish to purple, wasp-pollinated flowers** in which **the corolla-tube is nearly spherical with 5 small lobes**, the 2 upper partially joined. There are 4 proper stamens and the fifth is represented by a **scale-like staminode at the bottom of the upper lip**.

Common Figwort
Scrophularia nodosa
An **almost hairless** perennial with **robust, sharp-angled stems** and **pairs of ovate, pointed, toothed leaves**. The **many greenish-brown, stalked flowers** are in a much-branched, glandular inflorescence. **The calyx-lobes have a very narrow pale border.**

Common in damp woods and hedgerows throughout British Isles except Shetland, ascending to nearly 500m in N England.

P 80cm Summer

Water Figwort
Scrophularia auriculata
(*S. aquatica*)
Like the common figwort, but with **4-winged stems and ovate to elliptical, blunt-toothed leaves**. The calyx lobes of the flowers have an obvious, broad, pale border.

Common in wet places in S England, becoming rarer to the north and west, and extending into Scotland, though absent from NE Scotland, Orkney and Shetland; scattered through Ireland, but commoner in the south.

P 1m Summer

Green Figwort
Scrophularia umbrosa
This rather rare plant has the winged stems and elliptical or ovate leaves of the water figwort, but the **leaf-teeth are sharp** and the **bracts in the inflorescence are larger and more leaf-like**. The best character is in the shape of **the staminode, which is clearly 2-lobed** (in the water figwort it is unlobed).

Rare, in damp shady places scattered through much of England and S Scotland; absent from Wales and the SW peninsula; very rare in Ireland.

P 1m Summer

Misopates orontium

Kickxia elatine

Kickxia spuria

Cymbalaria muralis

Scrophularia nodosa

Scrophularia auriculata

Scrophularia umbrosa

Musks

Musks (*Mimulus* species) are well-known in our gardens, and some have now settled down in the wild. They are **opposite leaved** plants with **large flowers in the leaf-axils**. The corolla has a long tube and a wide-spreading ring of 5 lobes of which the 3 lower lobes are longer and form a landing-stage for visiting insects.

Monkeyflower
Mimulus guttatus

Plant hairless below, but usually somewhat hairy in the inflorescence. The **upper calyx-teeth are unequal, longer than the others**, and the **corolla is bright yellow with small red spots in the throat of the flower. The 'mouth' of the corolla is nearly closed by the palate on the lower lip**.

A native of western N America, introduced as a garden plant and first recorded wild in Britain in 1830; now rather common on streamsides throughout much of Britain and Ireland, though absent from most of E Anglia and C Ireland.

P   50cm   Summer

Musk
Mimulus moschatus

The true musk, again originally a garden plant, is easily told **by being covered with sticky hairs**. The **yellow corollas are without dark blotches or spots**, and **the calyx-teeth are almost equal**.

This plant, a native of western N America, was formerly much grown for its musky scent, but all plants nowadays are scentless. It occurs rather rarely in wet places throughout Britain; very rare in E and N Ireland

P   40cm   Summer

Blood-drop-emlets
Mimulus luteus

Like the monkeyflower, but **hairless** (except for the inside of the flower), and with an **open mouth** to the corolla which usually has **large reddish-brown spots on the lobes**.

Native of Chile, now in similar places to the monkeyflower, but much less common, and most frequent in S and C Scotland.
P   50cm   Summer

Hybrids with *M. guttatus* are now quite common by streams in upland regions of Scotland and N England. They are generally sterile and spread very vigorously by vegetative means.

Foxglove
Digitalis purpurea

One of our most familiar wildflowers, with **long, narrow inflorescences bearing a succession of large, nodding, tubular, pinkish-purple** (rarely white) **flowers on tall, leafy stems**. It cannot be mistaken for any other wild plant when in flower.

Common throughout most of the British Isles on acid soils in heathy and rocky ground and open woodland, rare or locally absent in parts of E Anglia and the Central Plain of Ireland.
B(P)   1.5m   Summer

Speedwells

Speedwells (*Veronica* species) are opposite-leaved plants very easily recognised by the detail of the flower. The **calyx has 4 lobes** and the **corolla has a short tube and 4 broad, flat, unequal lobes of which the uppermost** (representing 2 petals in ordinary 5-petalled flowers) **is the largest**. In the mouth of the flower is a **pair of stamens with long filaments** and between them a single style. Most speedwells have blue flowers.

Brooklime
Veronica beccabunga

A **rather fleshy, hairless plant with creeping and rooting stems**, and **short-stalked, ovate or oblong, toothed, blunt leaves**. The **blue flowers, on slender stalks, are in rather loose opposite pairs of racemes**, and are succeeded by almost spherical capsules.

Common in wet places throughout most of British Isles, but rare in NW Scotland and absent from Shetland.

P   40cm   Summer

Marsh Speedwell
Veronica scutellata

A small, slender, straggling plant, with **narrow, stalkless leaves slightly clasping the stem**, and **alternate, very loose, few-flowered racemes** of whitish or pale blue **flowers borne on long slender stalks. The ripe 2-lobed capsules are flat** and broader than long, with a deep separation between the lobes. The plant is usually hairless, but hairy forms are sometimes found.

Not uncommon in wet places, particularly acid, boggy ground, throughout British Isles, but easy to overlook.

P   15cm   Summer

Mimulus guttatus

Mimulus moschatus

Mimulus luteus

Digitalis purpurea

Veronica beccabunga

Veronica scutellata

Blue Water-speedwell
Veronica anagallis-aquatica
Like brooklime, but more erect, with **rather narrow, pointed leaves, stalkless and clasping the stem at the base, and pale blue corollas.**

Common in wet places, often more or less submerged, throughout much of British Isles, but absent from parts of SW England, Wales and N Scotland.

P   40cm   Summer

FLOWER-STALKS

Veronica anagallis-aquatica

V. catenata

Pink Water-speedwell
Veronica catenata
Very similar to blue water-speedwell and best told by the **pinkish flower colour** and **the flower-stalks spreading at right-angles after flowering** (in *V. anagallis-aquatica* they ascend to an angle of *c*.45°: see drawing).

In similar places to blue water-speedwell, but generally less common; rare in Scotland and N Ireland.

P   40cm   Summer

Vigorous, sterile hybrids between blue and pink water-speedwell are not uncommon in Britain, and are also recorded from Ireland.

Heath Speedwell
Veronica officinalis
A **creeping and rooting, often mat-forming, hairy plant with elliptical, coarsely-toothed, nearly stalkless leaves**, and **long-stalked, dense-flowered racemes** usually alternately in the leaf-axils. The **flowers** are usually **lilac-coloured.**

Common in dry grassland, heaths and open woodland throughout British Isles.

P   15cm(tall)   Summer

Wood Speedwell
Veronica montana
Wood speedwell resembles heath speedwell in being a **strongly hairy, creeping, perennial** plant, but is easily distinguished by its **clearly stalked leaves**, and its **rather few-flowered racemes of bluish-lilac flowers**.

Rather local in wet woodland in England and Wales; scattered throughout Ireland and lowland Scotland, but absent from the Outer Hebrides, most of the north, and Orkney and Shetland.

P   20cm(tall)   Summer

Germander Speedwell
Veronica chamaedrys
A very familiar wildflower, resembling heath and wood speedwell in general appearance and habit of growth, but very readily distinguished by the remarkable distribution of hairs on the stems. In both these species the stems are hairy all round, but here **the stems have 2 opposite lines of long, whitish hairs.** The leaves are very shortly-stalked, and the **loose-flowered racemes have rich blue flowers with an obvious white 'eye'.**

Very common in grassland, hedgerows, etc. throughout British Isles.

P   25cm(tall)   Summer

Spiked Speedwell
Veronica spicata
One of our most handsome wildflowers, shortly-creeping and somewhat woody at base, with ovate lower leaves and **erect flowering stems bearing a long, slender 'spike'** of violet-blue flowers.

The typical, rather small plant is very rare, in dry grassland of the East Anglian Breckland, but the taller subsp. *hybrida* (shown here) grows on limestone rocks in a number of places in Wales and W England.

P   60cm   Summer

Rock Speedwell
Veronica fruticans
A **small rock plant with a woody stock** and numerous ascending branches. The **leaves are more or less oblong, almost stalkless and rather thick** in texture. The **large bright blue flowers with a reddish 'eye'** are borne in loose, few-flowered racemes.

Rare on mountain rocks in the Scottish Highlands, between about 500–1000m.

P   20cm   Summer

Alpine Speedwell
Veronica alpina
A **shortly-creeping plant with ascending, little-branched stems** bearing ovate leaves. The **dull blue flowers are in dense, glandular-hairy heads**, and the whole plant often has a curious metallic grey-blue colour.

Rather rare on mountain rocks in the Scottish Highlands ascending to over 1100m.

P   15cm   Summer

Veronica anagallis-aquatica

Veronica catenata

Veronica officinalis

Veronica montana

Veronica chamaedrys

Veronica spicata

Veronica fruticans

Veronica alpina

Thyme-leaved Speedwell
Veronica serpyllifolia
This common little speedwell has **creeping and rooting stems bearing neat pairs of oblong, hairless, often shiny, leaves.** The stems finish in long, many-flowered racemes borne erect, and the **flowers are whitish or pale blue with violet veins.**

The plant described and illustrated is the lowland plant common in grassland throughout British Isles. On mountains subsp. *humifusa* is occasionally found, a lower-growing plant with glandular-hairy inflorescences bearing **fewer, larger, rich blue flowers.**

P 10cm(tall) Summer

Speedwells (continued)
The remaining speedwells are all 'weeds' familiar to the gardener and farmer. All but the slender speedwell are annuals.

Wall Speedwell
Veronica arvensis
This is the commonest of a group of annual weed speedwells. An **erect, downy annual**, very variable in size, simple or branched from the base, with **more or less triangular, coarsely-toothed leaves narrowing upwards into the flowering part of the stem.** The **flowers are small**, on very short stalks in the leaf-axils; the **blue corollas are shorter than the calyx.**

A common weed of dry soils, often on wall-tops, throughout British Isles.

A 20cm Spring to autumn

Ivy-leaved Speedwell
Veronica hederifolia
An **unmistakable weed**, with **its weak, straggling, hairy stems bearing ivy-shaped leaves broader than long and rather thick in texture.** The **small, usually pale blue, 'speedwell' flowers are on long stalks in the leaf-axils**, and are followed by almost spherical capsules.

Common in cultivated ground in much of England, Wales and S Scotland; rather local in Ireland and rare in NW Scotland.

A 10cm(tall) Spring

Slender Speedwell
Veronica filiformis
A **small, hairy perennial with very slender stems prostrate, creeping and very freely rooting, often forming patches in grassland.** The **relatively large, pale lilac-blue flowers are borne on very long, thread-like stalks.** The capsules hardly ever develop in Britain.

Originally introduced and first recorded as a garden escape as late as 1927; now abundant in lowland Britain in lawns and grazing pasture and recorded throughout British Isles. Its native home is in the mountains of Turkey and the Caucasus.

P 5cm(tall) Spring

Common Field-speedwell
Veronica persica
One of our commonest weeds. It has the branched straggling habit of the ivy-leaved speedwell, but the leaves are tri-angular-ovate. The **relatively large, bright blue flowers with a paler lower lip** are borne singly on long stalks in the leaf-axils, and **2-lobed capsules are nearly twice as broad as long and have long hairs on the rim** (see drawing).

An invasive weed, first recorded in Britain as late as 1825, and now found commonly on cultivated ground throughout British Isles. Its native home is in SW Asia.

A 10cm(tall) All seasons

Grey Field-speedwell
Veronica polita
Similar to the common field-speedwell, but with **smaller flowers that are uniformly bright blue with a white 'eye'.** Best distinguished by the shape and hairiness of the **capsule which is not much wider than long and covered with short, bent hairs** as well as long glandular hairs (see drawing).

A native weed, quite common in lowland England, but local or rare in much of Wales, Scotland and Ireland.

A 10cm(tall) Mainly spring and summer

Capsules

Veronica persica

V. polita

V. agrestis

Green Field-speedwell
Veronica agrestis
Similar to common and grey field-speedwell but with **ovate leaves all longer than broad**, and **small flowers often with all the corolla-lobes white.** Best distinguished from both by the **capsule which is slightly wider than long and covered with long glandular hairs** (see drawing).

Throughout much of the British Isles on cultivated ground, but not usually very common, and perhaps declining.

A 10cm(tall) Mainly spring and summer

Veronica serpyllifolia

Veronica arvensis

Veronica hederifolia

Veronica filiformis

Veronica persica

Veronica polita

Veronica agrestis

Louseworts

The 2 louseworts (*Pedicularis*) introduce us to a remarkable group of *Scrophulariaceae* which constitute a distinct sub-family. They are semi-parasitic herbs living in grassland, where their roots attach themselves to the roots of other plants and derive nourishment from them. They are **green** plants, however, so that they continue to feed in the normal way as well as parasitically.

Lousewort
Pedicularis sylvatica

A **nearly hairless plant with many straggling branches from the base**. The **leaves are deeply and irregularly cut and have a thick, glossy look**. The **handsome 2-lipped pink or reddish flowers are up to 2.5cm long**.

Rather common on damp heath and moorland throughout much of the British Isles, ascending to nearly 1000m; rare in C and E England.

B(P)   20cm   Summer

Marsh Lousewort
Pedicularis palustris

Like the preceding, but **more erect in habit**, often branching from near the base and forming a tuft. Best distinguished by the **calyx** which **is distinctly 2-lipped**, whereas in the ordinary lousewort it is not or very indistinctly 2-lipped.

In wet heaths and bogs, rather common through much of the British Isles, but rare and decreasing through drainage in C and SE England.

B(A)   60cm   Summer

Crested Cow-wheat
Melampyrum cristatum

A very exotic-looking wildflower, with **dense, purplish, 4-sided spikes of flowers with large, folded, pointed bracts with comb-like teeth on the margin**. The corolla is **pale yellow, tinged with reddish-purple, and with a deeper yellow palate**.

Very local, on the edge of seminatural woodland on boulder clay in E England.

A   50cm   Summer

Common Cow-wheat
Melampyrum pratense

A variable annual, with spreading branches, and opposite, entire, narrow leaves. The **yellow flowers are in the axils of pairs of opposite, leaf-like bracts** and **each pair is turned to the same side and held horizontally**. The corolla tube is much longer than the calyx. Each capsule contains 1–4 large seeds.

Common in heaths and dry woodland in many parts of the British Isles, but rare in EC England and parts of Ireland.

A   80cm   Summer

Small Cow-wheat
Melampyrum sylvaticum

Very similar to small plants of the common cow-wheat, and best distinguished by the **calyx, which has long spreading teeth** (in common cow-wheat the teeth do not spread) and **the lower lip of the short corolla which is turned down** (not straight). The flower colour is usually a deeper orange-yellow.

In upland woods, ascending to nearly 400m, mainly in the C Highlands of Scotland, but also in Upper Teesdale in N England; very rare in N Ireland.

A   30cm   Summer

Yellow-rattle
Rhinanthus minor

A variable annual, with **simple or branched, erect, usually black-spotted stem** and **opposite, narrowly oblong to linear, toothed leaves**. The yellow flowers are arranged in spikes and each has **a flattened and inflated calyx with 4 teeth**. The **upper lip of the corolla is flattened from the side** and encloses the 4 stamens.

Common in grassland throughout British Isles, though much reduced in parts of England where permanent pasture is now scarce.

A   50cm   Summer

Eyebrights

Eyebrights (*Euphrasia*) are very difficult to classify, although it is easy to recognise the genus. They are all small annuals with terminal spikes of flowers. The calyx is 4-toothed, the upper lip of the corolla is bent back, and the lower lip is much larger and 3-lobed, each lobe more or less indented. The flowers are often white with yellow throat and purplish lines. We illustrate and describe only the commonest species in England.

Eyebright
Euphrasia nemorosa

A **hairy but not glandular plant** with **relatively large flowers**, variable in habit, but usually with a central erect flowering stem surrounded by ascending branches.

Common in England and Wales in grassland, heaths and wood margins; more local in Scotland and Ireland, where other *Euphrasia* species may be locally more common.

A   40cm   Late summer

Pedicularis sylvatica

Pedicularis palustris

Melampyrum cristatum

Melampyrum pratense

Melampyrum sylvaticum

Rhinanthus minor

Euphrasia nemorosa

Red Bartsia
Odontites verna
A **hairy, often purple-tinted** annual with narrow, stalkless leaves and **dense leafy 'spikes' of reddish flowers all bending over to one side**. Very variable in branching and therefore general appearance.

Common in cultivated ground, field margins, and waste places throughout most of the British Isles, except C and N Scotland where it is mainly coastal.

A   50cm   Summer to autumn

Yellow Bartsia
Parentucellia viscosa
Erect, usually unbranched, grey-green sticky-haired annual with oblong, toothed, stalkless leaves and **large yellow flowers with a long corolla tube and lower lip much longer than the upper.**

Damp grassy places mainly in the S and W of England, S Wales and SW Ireland, but with scattered occurrences further north in NW England, S Scotland and N Ireland

A   50cm   Late summer to autumn

Alpine Bartsia
Bartsia alpina
The famous mourning-flower of Linnaeus, this mountain plant is a **perennial with solitary, glandular-hairy flowering stems**, ovate toothed leaves and **short, few-flowered inflorescences with purplish bracts**. The **large dull purple flowers have an upper lip much longer than the lower.**

On wet places on basic soils and rocks in the mountains in N England and the Central Highlands of Scotland, from *c.*300m to more than 900m; rather rare.

P   20cm   Summer

Toothworts and Broomrapes

Toothworts (*Scrophulariaceae*) and broomrapes (*Orobanchacea*) are total parasites lacking chlorophyll and feeding entirely on the roots of their host plants. The structure of the 2-lipped flowers of broomrapes shows their relationship to the *Scrophulariaceae*.

Toothwort
Lathraea squamaria
This extraordinary **pale flesh-coloured plant** cannot be mistaken for any other. Its **thick, softly hairy flowering stems** bear several flowers in the axil of fleshy scale-leaves; the **short-stalked flowers are all turned to one side of the inflorescence.** Underground is a thick scaly rhizome bearing swollen rootlets attached to the host plant roots.

In damp woods, especially on limestone, parasitic on trees, particularly hazel, throughout much of Britain north to Inverness; in Ireland recent records are confined to the east.

P   25cm   Spring

Common Broomrape
Orobanche minor
Broomrapes differ from toothworts in being short-lived perennials whose attachment to the host plant root is via underground tubers, from which the erect, scaly flowering stems arise. The **common broomrape has an erect stem of a pale reddish-purple (sometimes yellowish) colour with the flowers usually widely spaced below.**

Parasitic in grassland, especially on members of the clover family. Mainly in lowland England and S and E Ireland; formerly widespread as a harmful weed of legume crops.

P   40cm   Summer

Knapweed Broomrape
Orobanche elatior
This robust broomrape is most easily identified by its association with its host, the greater knapweed (*Centaurea scabiosa*). It is a **stouter plant than the common broomrape, with larger, more densely-packed flowers.**

Widely distributed, though rare, in rough pastures, over chalk or limestone in S and E England and S Wales, always associated with greater knapweed; absent from Scotland and Ireland.

P   70cm   Summer

Ivy Broomrape
Orobanche hederae
A **shorter, somewhat stocky and rather few-flowered broomrape exclusively parasitic on ivy** (*Hedera*). The flowers differ from those of the common broomrape in that **the corolla narrows from the rather swollen base**, whereas in the common broomrape the corolla is not narrowed.

Exclusively on ivy, mainly in S and W England and S Ireland, and commonest near the coast.

P   40cm   Summer

Odontites verna

Parentucellia viscosa

Bartsia alpina

Lathraea squamaria

Orobanche minor

Orobanche elatior

Orobanche hederae

Common Butterwort
Pinguicula vulgaris
One of a small group of carnivorous plants in our flora, unmistakable with its **basal rosette of yellow-green, sticky leaves with inrolled margins**, on which small insects are trapped and digested. The pretty, **2-lipped, violet-coloured flowers with a pointed spur are borne singly on long stalks from the centre of the rosette.**

Common in bogs, heaths and wet ground over much of the British Isles; rare or absent from much of S and midland England and SE Ireland.

P   10cm   Summer

Pale Butterwort
Pinguicula lusitanica
Like the common butterwort, but with **smaller, paler leaf-rosettes** and **much smaller pinkish or pale lilac flowers with a short, blunt spur.**

In bogs and wet heaths, locally common in SW England, S Wales, Isle of Man, W Scotland and throughout Ireland, though rare in the Central Plain.

P   10cm   Summer

Greater Bladderwort
Utricularia vulgaris
A **remarkable water plant** whose **submerged, rootless, stems bear finely-divided leaves and small bladders that trap animals and digest them**. The **yellow toadflax-like flowers are on long leafless stalks that emerge above the water surface.**

In still, peaty waters throughout British Isles except NW Scotland.
P   (over-wintering with 'winter buds')   20cm   Summer

Two other bladderworts occur, mainly in the north and west: they differ from the common one in having separate colourless shoots bearing the bladders.

Bear's-breech
Acanthus mollis
A familiar garden plant, with **large, deeply-lobed basal leaves and thick stems bearing terminal spikes of flowers in the axil of ovate, purplish, spiny bracts. The large whitish corollas have only a lower lip, which is 3-lobed.**

Introduced early into gardens from the Mediterranean area, and first recorded as a garden escape in 1820; naturalised especially in SW England.
P   1m   Summer

Vervain
Verbena officinalis
A tall hairy plant with **stiffly erect, branching stems and opposite, deeply-cut leaves.** The **small, pale lilac 2-lipped flowers are in narrow spikes that elongate in fruit.** Each **fruit consists of 4 nutlets that separate when ripe** (like the mint family Labiatae).

Scattered on roadsides and waste ground in England and Wales, north to Cumbria and N Yorkshire.
P   60cm   Late summer

Mint Family (Labiatae)

Labiatae, the mint family, are recognised by their square stems, simple, undivided leaves in opposite pairs arranged at right-angles to those above and below, with groups of flowers often completely surrounding the stem to form whorls. Most genera have irregular flowers with a 5-toothed tubular calyx, 4- or 5-lobed corolla with 2 obvious lips and 2 or 4 stamens often hidden beneath the upper lip. In fruit there are 4 'seeds' at the base of the calyx tube.

Corn Mint
Mentha arvensis
Mints are unlike most *Labiatae* because the flowers are almost regular with a calyx of 4–5 equal teeth and a corolla of 4 nearly equal lobes. Most have a mint-like smell – but not corn mint. This and whorled mint are the only 2 in which there is **no ball or spike of flowers at the top of the stem: all the clusters are amongst the leaves lower down** the stem which has smaller leafy bracts above. 4 **stamens** are usually **longer than the petals** (see drawing).

Arable fields and woodland rides throughout lowland British Isles to 350m in the Pennines.
P   60cm   Spring to autumn

Whorled Mint
Mentha x verticillata
This common hybrid between corn mint and water mint is closer to the former but may be distinguished by having **flowers almost to the top of the stem, with only 1 or 2 small leaf-like bracts above**, and by having **stamens shorter than the petals** (see drawing). It also smells of mint but is much less pungent than the other parent, water mint.

River banks, pond-sides, marshes and field borders throughout lowland British Isles.
P   90cm   Summer and autumn

Pinguicula vulgaris

Pinguicula lusitanica

Utricularia vulgaris

Acanthus mollis

Verbena officinalis

FLOWERS

Mentha arvensis

M. x verticillata

Mentha arvensis

Mentha x verticillata

Water Mint
Mentha aquatica
Easily identified by the smell it gives off when crushed under foot by a marshland walk, but also recognised by the general **reddish** colour of **stems and leaves**, by the **ball of flowers at the top of the stem** with the **stamens longer than the petals** and very visible. Though hairless below, the **upper stems**, the **flower-stalks and calyx** are **hairy**.

River banks, pond-sides, marshes and wet woods throughout British Isles to 450m in mid-Wales.

P 90cm Summer and autumn

Peppermint
Mentha x piperita
This hybrid between water mint and spearmint has the general lack of hairs and **purplish stems** of the former but the **spiked inflorescences** of the latter. Like all mint hybrids the **stamens are shorter than the petals**, not easily visible. Recognised by the characteristic smell of peppermint and by the **absence of hairs on flower-stalks and calyx**. Hairy plants with a weaker smell may also be found.

Ditches and damp roadsides throughout lowland British Isles.

P 80cm Summer and autumn

Spearmint
Mentha spicata
Spearmint is the commonest mint in gardens, recognised by its characteristic smell, **narrow, pointed, hairless leaves with** numerous **prominent teeth** along the margin, and lilac, pink or white **flowers arranged in one or more slender, terminal spikes**. Hairy forms may sometimes occur.

Introduced as a pot-herb and now established on damp roadsides and in waste places throughout lowland Britain; rare in Ireland.

P 1m Summer and early autumn

Apple Mint
Mentha x villosa
Perhaps the second most common mint grown in gardens with **large, round, somewhat toothed leaves** which are **hairy but not white-felted beneath**, and with a handsome, branched **inflorescence of spikes** of lilac or pink flowers. It is a hybrid between spearmint and round-leaved mint and, like other hybrids, the **stamens** are usually **shorter than the petals** and not easily visible.

An escape from cultivation now scattered throughout lowland Great Britain; rare in Ireland.

P 1.5m Summer and early autumn

Round-leaved Mint
Mentha suaveolens
Often confused with apple mint but less robust and recognised by the **smaller leaves** 2–4 × 1.5–3cm (not 3–10 × 1.5–4cm) which are **densely clothed with white hairs beneath** and may appear felted, by the **spikes of flowers rarely exceeding 5cm** (up to 8cm in apple mint) and by the **prominent, showy stamens**.

Native in ditches, on stream sides and in waste places, mainly in SW England and Wales; naturalised elsewhere.

P 90cm Summer and early autumn

Gipsywort
Lycopus europaeus
Looks like a mint with **white flowers** but some of the **strongly-toothed leaves** at the **bottom of the stem are divided into linear segments**. The flowers have only 2 (not 4) stamens though the remains of the 2 others can be seen opposite them. Small female flowers with no stamens may occur. Source of a black dye once used by gipsies to make their skins resemble more closely their supposedly Egyptian origins.

River sides, ditch margins and marshes throughout lowlands except the northern isles.

P 90cm Summer and early autumn

Marjoram
Origanum vulgare
An upright, bushy, purple-tinged and hairy perennial with **inflorescence** branches ending in a **conspicuous roundish cluster of rose-purple flowers**. Distinguished from mints by the markedly **2-lipped flowers with a tube longer than the calyx** and the **characteristic smell**, not mint-like, of the crushed leaves. Separated from wild basil (p.154) by having at least the **longer pair of stamens exceeding the petals**.

Dry grassland, scrub and hedges on lime-rich soils north to Moray Firth.

P 80cm Summer and early autumn

Mentha aquatica

Mentha x *piperita*

Mentha spicata

Mentha x *villosa*

Mentha suaveolens

Lycopus europaeus

Origanum vulgare

Wild Thyme
Thymus praecox
Thymes are low, creeping, somewhat woody plants with **small oval or elliptical leaves emitting a strong odour when crushed**. They have short terminal balls or spikes of flowers, 2-lipped, with the **stamens longer than the petals**. Most easily separated by the distribution of the hairs on the square stems. In wild thyme the **stems** are **hairy only on the 2 opposite sides** or more hairy on 2 sides than on the others (see drawing).

Dry grassland, rocks, heaths and dunes throughout British Isles to 1100m in C Scotland.
P Creeping Spring and summer

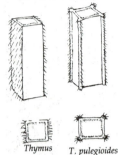

Thymus praecox *T. pulegioides*

Larger Thyme
Thymus pulegioides
Like wild thyme but separated by the **stems with hairs only on the angles** (see drawing) and by the taller, ascending flowering stems with an **elongated, not rounded, head of flowers**. When crushed between the fingers the leaves give off a more **petrol-like smell** than the more characteristic smell of wild thyme.

Lime-rich grassland in S and E England north to Yorkshire, with outlying localities in Wigtown, Angus and C Ireland.
P 2cm Summer

Common Calamint
Calamintha sylvatica
A low-growing perennial recognised by the **flowers** arranged in **2 branched clusters at each node**. The flowers have **straight calyx and corolla tubes**: the **lower calyx-teeth** are longer than the upper all **with long 'eye-lashes'** (cilia) **on the margins** whilst the 2-lobed, reddish-purple corolla has 4 **stamens shorter than the petals**. The whole plant has a strong **mint-like smell**.

On dry, mainly lime-rich banks in the lowlands throughout the southern British Isles north to Co. Down and Isle of Man.
P 60cm Summer and early autumn

Lesser Calamint
Calamintha nepeta
A local plant found mainly east of a line from the Wash to the Solent. Distinguished from common calamint by the much **shorter hairs in the margin of the calyx-teeth**, by the **leaves** on the main stem being **under 2cm long** (not 2–4cm) and by the longer branches of the inflorescence so that there are more **obviously 2 separate clusters of flowers at each node**.

Dry, usually lime-rich, banks.
P 60cm Summer and early autumn

Wild Basil
Clinopodium vulgare
Like marjoram but **lacking** the purple tinge or **any strong aromatic smell**. The whole plant, including the slightly curved calyx, is **covered in long soft hairs** while the stamens are **shorter than the petals** which are not visible as in marjoram. The **flowers** are **not on long branches but** are arranged **in dense clusters** either at the top of the stem or in the axils of the paired leaves.

Woodland margins, scrub and hedge bottoms on dry, lime-rich, soils throughout lowlands, north to Moray Firth and in SE Ireland.
P 80cm Summer and early autumn

Basil Thyme
Acinos arvensis
Closely related to calamint but a **prostrate or ascending** annual with **thyme-sized leaves** and **bright blue or violet flowers with white markings**. The flowers are arranged in relatively few-flowered clusters, usually less than 8, and with a **calyx** which **has a distinct waist in the middle** and is covered in long hairs.

Arable fields and open grassland on dry, usually lime-rich, soils in lowland Britain north to Moray Firth and in SE Ireland.
A(or B) 20cm Late spring to early autumn

Balm
Melissa officinalis
This herb has a distinctive **sweet, lemon scent** and has been widely grown in gardens from which it has often escaped. Also recognised by the almost **hairless, 'blistered' surface of the leaves** which have very **regular**, somewhat **rounded teeth**. The **white or pink flowers** are arranged in tight clusters amongst the leaves: they **have a slightly curved calyx** and a corolla tube widening out above the middle.

Scattered through the southern half of British Isles north to Isle of Man.
P 60cm Summer and early autumn

Thymus praecox

Thymus pulegioides

Calamintha sylvatica

Calamintha nepeta

Clinopodium vulgare

Acinos arvensis

Melissa officinalis

Wild Clary
Salvia verbenaca
Recognised at a distance by the **separate, apparently leafless, whorls of flowers** and the **basal rosette of variously-lobed and toothed leaves with a 'blistered', strongly-veined** surface. The flowers are of 2 sizes – large, open, violet-blue ones over 1.5cm long with 2 stamens protruding from the upper lip and others, much smaller, which never open properly.

Dry grassland and roadside banks mainly in S and E England; very rare and mainly coastal elsewhere.
P   80cm   Late spring and summer

Bastard Balm
Melittis melissophyllum
Recognised immediately by the **large, pink and white flowers up to 4cm**, longer than any other wild British Labiate, on very short stalks in **small clusters of 2–6**. The calyx is also distinctive, 2-lipped and open in fruit, the upper with 2–3 small teeth, the lower with 2 rounded lobes. **Leaves resemble balm** (p.154) **but do not smell of lemon.**

Locally in woods and hedgebanks in England south of the Thames and in SW Wales.
P   50cm   Late spring and summer

Selfheal
Prunella vulgaris
Easily recognised by its **dense, oblong, upright clusters of violet flowers** at the tip of the branches **with a pair of** oval, stalked **leaves at the base** of each. After flowering the usually purple-tinged, markedly 2-lipped calyx closes up but persists. Spreads by short rooting runners and forms **large patches in most old lawns**.

One of our commonest grassland and woodland plants throughout British Isles to 700m in N Pennines.
P   30cm   Summer and early autumn

Betony
Stachys officinalis
Like a selfheal with dense, **oblong clusters of flowers** but much taller and the flowers **bright, reddish-purple** and the clusters often broken below and **showing some bare stem between**. The **leaves** are unmistakable, many in a basal rosette, **oblong, heart-shaped at the base, rounded at the tip, with crinkly teeth** and on long stalks. These leaves, dried, produce a bitter herb tea.

Open woods, grassland and heaths on neutral or acid soils throughout England and Wales; rare in Scotland and Ireland.
P   60cm   Summer and early autumn

Field Woundwort
Stachys arvensis
Woundworts are softly-hairy herbs with 2-lipped flowers in interrupted terminal spikes, often leafless above, which give the genus its name – *stachys* comes from the Greek, a spike. Field woundwort is a **low-growing annual, much-branched from the base** with **small, pale purple flowers** only **about 7mm long in 2–6 flowered whorls**, with all the stamens shorter than the petals.

An arable weed scattered on lime-deficient soils throughout lowland British Isles to 350m on Exmoor.
A   25cm   Spring to autumn

Hedge Woundwort
Stachys sylvatica
One of our commonest hedgerow herbs recognised by the tall spikes of **claret-coloured flowers up to 1.5cm long** with intricate paler markings on the lower lip, by the glandular hairs on the calyx and by the **long-stalked and softly-hairy heart-shaped leaves**, about 1½ **times as long as broad**, which **produce an offensive smell when crushed**. Hybrids with marsh woundwort with short-stalked leaves 2–3 times as long as broad are very frequent.

Woods, hedges and waste places throughout British Isles to 500m in N Wales.
P   1m   Summer

Marsh Woundwort
Stachys palustris
Similar to hedge woundwort but with **almost stalkless** and much **narrower leaves, c.5 times as long as broad**, and **dull purple flowers** with a calyx lacking glandular hairs. The **leaves** are **odourless when crushed**.

Stream banks, ditches, marshes and fens, and in arable fields in the far west, throughout lowland British Isles to 450m in N Pennines.
P   1m   Summer and early autumn

Black Horehound
Ballota nigra
A dusty-looking Labiate with a distinctive and **unpleasant smell when the oval, toothed leaves are crushed**. The smell protects it from being eaten by animals, hence the scientific name which comes from the Greek, *ballo*, to reject. Also recognised by the **compact whorls of purple, hairy flowers with an ice-cream-cornet-shaped calyx** with 5 shortly-pointed, almost equal, teeth, recognisable long after flowering.

Roadsides, wall-bottoms and hedgebanks throughout lowland England and Wales; scattered and introduced elsewhere.
P   1m   Summer and autumn

Yellow Archangel
Lamiastrum galeobdolon
This strikingly beautiful plant has **nettle-like leaves** and **yellow 2-lipped flowers** which make it easy to recognise in woodlands where it forms sheets of colour in spring. *Galeobdolon* comes from 2 Greek words, *galen*, a weasel and *bdolos*, stench, which refers perhaps to the **unpleasant smell of the stems and leaves when crushed** between the fingers.

Common in damp, open woodland and thickets throughout England and Wales; rare in S Scotland and SE Ireland.
P   60cm   Late spring and early summer

Salvia verbenaca

Melittis melissophyllum

Prunella vulgaris

Stachys officinalis

Stachys arvensis

Stachys sylvatica

Stachys palustris

Ballota nigra

Lamiastrum galeobdolon

Dead-nettles

Dead-nettles are so-named because they have the square stems and coarsely-toothed leaves in common with stinging nettles but they do not sting and have large conspicuous flowers. Petals have a well-developed middle lobe often itself markedly 2-lobed: lateral lobes are very small.

Henbit Dead-nettle
Lamium amplexicaule

This annual, arable garden weed is instantly recognised by the **stalkless pairs of leaves which** appear to **encircle the stem**: the **margins** too are distinctive, **wavy-looking** as if nibbled by hens. The reddish-purple flowers have **long, narrow corolla tubes which protrude** obviously **from the short calyx** which is **less than 6mm long** with **teeth** which **close together in fruit**.

Light, dry soils throughout lowland British Isles; rarer in the west.

A   25cm   Spring and summer

Northern Dead-nettle
Lamium moluccellifolium

Like henbit dead-nettle with **upper pairs of leaves stalkless** but they **do not encircle the stem**. The **calyx** is 8–10mm long with **teeth** which **spread open in fruit** and flowers which do not obviously protrude from it.

Widespread in cultivated fields in lowland Scotland, Northumberland and Isle of Man; scattered throughout Ireland.

A   25cm   Late spring and early autumn

Cut-leaved Dead-nettle
Lamium hybridum

Intermediate between northern and red dead-nettle: differs from the former by having **all the leaves stalked** and from the latter by their less hairy surface and their **pointed** rather than rounded, **teeth, especially near the leaf-stalk**. Also recognised by the **distinct ring of hairs inside the corolla** near the base.

Scattered in arable fields throughout lowland British Isles but only frequent in the eastern half of England.

A   45cm   Spring to autumn

Red Dead-nettle
Lamium purpureum

The commonest annual dead-nettle much-branched from the base and recognised by the **stalked, hairy, heart-shaped leaves** with **rounded teeth** on the margin and the **flowers with a** tube protruding **from the calyx** and with a **distinct ring of hairs inside the corolla** near the base.

Arable fields and waste places throughout British Isles to 600m in N England.

A   45cm   Spring to autumn

White Dead-nettle
Lamium album

The only native **perennial** dead-nettle, which spreads by creeping underground stems **forming large patches**. Recognised by its large **white flowers up to 2cm long** in distant whorls with black-tipped buff stamens nestling under a white hood and an **oblique ring of hairs inside the corolla tube** near the base.

Grassland, hedgebanks, arable fields and waste places throughout lowland British Isles but rare in W Ireland and N Scotland.

P   60cm   All year round

Spotted Dead-nettle
Lamium maculatum

An introduced, creeping perennial usually with a large elongated **white blotch on the triangular leaves**. The **pinkish-white flowers** are large, **up to 3.5cm** with the **corolla tube** often longer than the calyx, and **with a transverse ring of hairs** near the base.

Widely grown in gardens and escaping into hedgerows and copses.

P   80cm   Late spring to autumn

Common Hemp-nettle
Galeopsis tetrahit

Hemp-nettles are distinguished by having 2 'humps' near the base of the corolla. Common hemp-nettle is a roughly hairy annual with pink, purple or white flowers, the **corolla tube** scarcely longer than the calyx, and broad, oval **leaves about twice as long as broad** with 10 or more pointed teeth on each margin. The **stems** are distinctly **swollen at the nodes** and most of the hairs below are glandular.

Woods, fens, wet heaths and arable fields throughout British Isles to 400m in Shropshire.

A   1m   Summer and early autumn

Red Hemp-nettle
Galeopsis angustifolia

A softly hairy annual with rose-purple flowers with the **corolla tube much longer than the calyx**, and **narrow, pointed leaves** more than **4 times as long as broad** with 1–4 small serrations on each side. The **stems**, unlike those of common hemp-nettle, are **not swollen at the nodes** and few, if any, of the hairs below are glandular.

Arable fields, mainly on lime-rich soils. Scattered throughout lowland England, Wales and SE Ireland and very rarely in Scotland.

A   80cm   Summer and autumn

Lamium amplexicaule

Lamium moluccellifolium

Lamium hybridum

Lamium purpureum

Lamium album

Lamium maculatum

Galeopsis tetrahit

Galeopsis angustifolia

Large-flowered Hemp-nettle
Galeopsis speciosa
Instantly recognised by the **primrose-yellow flowers with the middle lobe of the lower lip usually mainly violet**, occasionally all yellow, and made more showy by the **corolla tube** being **twice as long as the calyx**. The **stems** are **a little swollen at the nodes** and have yellow-tipped, glandular hairs below.

Arable fields, especially on peat, throughout lowland British Isles except the south-west, to 400m in Shropshire.
A   1m   Summer and early autumn

Cat-mint
Nepeta cataria
A **greyish**, hairy perennial branching from the base with stalked, **heart-shaped**, coarsely-toothed leaves, white beneath and emitting **a strong, pleasant smell when crushed**. The **white flowers** have a fan-shaped lower lip **with a line of small, purple dots**: they are arranged in a compact terminal spike, but below there may be separate clusters in the axils of the paired leaves.

Hedgebanks and roadsides, mainly on base-rich soils, scattered throughout lowland England and Wales.
P   1m   Summer and autumn

Ground-ivy
Glechoma hederacea
A hairy creeping perennial, with erect flowering branches, recognised by the **long-stalked, heart- or kidney-shaped leaves with rounded teeth** (not very ivy-like) and the pretty, **bright blue flowers** with a corolla up to 2cm long **with purple spots on the lower lip**. The flowers are arranged **in 1-sided clusters of only 2–4** and may include some much smaller female flowers.

Woods, hedgebanks and grassland throughout British Isles to 400m in the Pennines; rare in the far north of Scotland.
P   30cm   Spring and early summer

White Horehound
Marrubium vulgare
The hoary horehound, **densely covered in cottony hairs** clothing the stems and **with crinkly, rounded leaves** which are **green above and white below**. The **white flowers**, which are in whorls in interrupted spikes, **have no markings on their lower lips**, but when they wither leave an unusual and unmistakable calyx **with 10 small, hooked teeth**. Grown as a herb valued as a cough cure.

Thinly scattered in waste places and on cliffs throughout lowland England and Wales; a rare garden escape elsewhere.
P   60cm   Summer and autumn

Skullcap
Scutellaria galericulata
A somewhat hairy perennial recognised by the **bright blue flowers** arranged **in pairs pointing in one direction** in the axils of the dark green, **shallowly-toothed leaves up to 5cm long**. The flowers have corolla tubes much longer than the 2-lipped calyx. **This calyx has a large leafy rounded outgrowth on the upper side** said to resemble a *galerum*, a helmet worn by the Romans.

Edges of streams and ponds, and in marshes throughout British Isles to 350m in the Pennines; rare in Ireland and NE Scotland.
P   50cm   Summer and early autumn

Lesser Skullcap
Scutellaria minor
Like skullcap but smaller and less hairy and differing in having **pinkish-purple flowers less than 1cm long**, and by having **leaves less than 3cm long** which **lack teeth** except for perhaps one at the base.

Wet heaths, stream, ditch and pond-sides on acid soils, mainly in the south and west of British Isles, north to Outer Hebrides.
P   15cm   Summer and autumn

Wood Sage
Teucrium scorodonia
This hairy, creeping perennial with crinkly, oval, stalked leaves is recognised by the **pale green colour of the whole plant** and the **yellowish-green of the flowers**. These are arranged in **long, slender, terminal spikes with only 1 or 2 flowers in the axil of leaves** which are shorter than the corolla. The **corolla has a single 5-lobed lip** and lacks a ring of hairs inside the tube; it is longer than the calyx which has the upper tooth larger than the others.

Dry, shady heaths and rocks, on neutral or acid soils to 500m in mid-Wales.
P   30cm   Summer and autumn

Bugle
Ajuga reptans
This creeping, sparingly hairy perennial is superficially similar to selfheal (p.156) with its **short dense spikes of blue flowers**, but bugle has **no upper lip to the corolla** whereas selfheal has a hood above. The **whole plant is suffused with purple** and, in marshes, might be confused with water mint (p.152), but lacks the overbearing aroma of that species.

Damp woods and meadows throughout British Isles to 750m in mid-Wales.
P   30cm   Spring and summer

Galeopsis speciosa

Nepeta cataria

Glechoma hederacea

Marrubium vulgare

Scutellaria galericulata

Scutellaria minor

Teucrium scorodonia

Ajuga reptans

Plantain Family (Plantaginaceae)

The genus *Plantago* provides 2 of our most familiar weeds. Botanically they are very unusual and not closely related to any other group of flowering plants. The leaves are in a basal rosette, and in most species are simple, with parallel veins. The tiny flowers, massed into long spikes at the end of leafless stems, have 4 sepals, a small, 4-lobed, whitish corolla and 4 long, sometimes conspicuous, stamens. All except the hoary plantain are wind-pollinated.

Buck's-horn Plantain
Plantago coronopus
Differs from all other British plantains in **having deeply-lobed leaves** (though small forms are sometimes found with simple, very narrow leaves). The **short inflorescences are usually on stalks that bend upwards from a prostrate base in the middle of the leaf rosettes.**

On dry sandy or gravelly soils, most commonly near the sea, where it may also be found in cracks in rocks. Round all the coasts of the British Isles, and also inland in England. A very variable plant.
B(A or P also)   5cm   Summer

Greater Plantain
Plantago major
One of our most familiar and ubiquitous weeds, with a **basal rosette of ovate or elliptical, 3–9-veined leaves** and **long, brownish or greenish, narrowly cylindrical inflorescences.**

Throughout British Isles on roadsides, lawns and disturbed cultivated ground, also in damp, open ground including the seaside.
P   40cm   Summer

Ribwort Plantain
Plantago lanceolata
The other plantain familiar to all gardeners, with **narrower, lance-shaped, 3–5-veined leaves**, and **much shorter, broader inflorescences on the end of long, grooved stalks.**
Throughout British Isles in grassland, especially on cultivated lawns.
P   30cm   Spring and summer

Hoary Plantain
Plantago media
A much more attractive plant than the 2 abundant weeds, with **greyish, softly hairy leaves** of the general shape of the greater plantain, and a **slightly scented inflorescence with many long purplish filaments bearing pale anthers**, visited and pollinated by insects.

Common in grassland, especially on chalky soils, in S England and the Midlands, becoming rare northwards and westwards; rare and probably introduced in N Scotland and Ireland.
P   30cm   Summer

Sea Plantain
Plantago maritima
Unmistakably a plantain, the sea plantain is easily recognised by its **very narrow, rather fleshy leaves** forming tight rosettes. The inflorescences are quite long and **conspicuous in flower because the stamens are pale yellow.**

Common round the coasts of the British Isles, by streams and on wet rocks on mountains; also on the limestone rocks of the Burren, W Ireland.
P   20cm   Summer

Shoreweed
Littorella uniflora
This remarkable **little waterplant** is a close relative of the plantains. It has **slender, far-creeping runners rooting freely and forming mats of short, narrow, bright green leaves half-cylindrical in section.** There are separate male and female flowers that are only produced in summer when the water-level falls. The **male flowers have 4 long stamens with yellow anthers**, and the female flowers are quite inconspicuous.

On the sandy or gravelly shores of acid lakes and ponds throughout British Isles, but commoner in the north and west.
P   2cm(tall)   Summer

Bellflower Family (Campanulaceae)

The bellflower family, *Campanulaceae*, contains some beautiful and familiar wildflowers, mostly dealt with on the following page. Bellflowers are easily recognised: the joined (often blue) corollas are commonly bell-shaped, with 5 equal lobes at the spreading mouth. The ovary is situated below the rest of the flower and usually develops into a capsule. Two specialised genera, *Phyteuma* and *Jasione*, approach the *Compositae* in having massed heads of small flowers.

Ivy-leaved Bellflower
Wahlenbergia hederacea
One of our really charming wildflowers, shyly blooming in damp, shady places, and quite unmistakable. The **slender, creeping, hairless stems have small, stalked, ivy-shaped leaves and single pale blue flowers on long, delicate stalks.**

In damp places on moors, heaths and woodland, usually on acid soils, most common in Wales, and S and SW England, rare in SE Ireland; absent from the whole of eastern Britain and most of Scotland.
P   15cm   Summer

Plantago coronopus

Plantago major

Plantago lanceolata

Plantago media

Plantago maritima

Littorella uniflora

Wahlenbergia hederacea

Giant Bellflower
Campanula latifolia
A **robust, softly hairy plant** with erect, unbranched, blunt-angled, leafy stems and **large 'bell-flowers' in a leafy raceme**. The lower stem-leaves are ovate and narrowed to a point. The calyx has 5 long-pointed teeth and the **corolla, often 4cm or more long, is blue-purple** (not infrequently white).

Widespread in woods in Britain, but rare in S England and N Scotland; absent from Orkney, Shetland, the Outer Hebrides and the whole of Ireland.
P   1m   Summer

Nettle-leaved Bellflower
Campanula trachelium
Like the giant bellflower, but with **roughly hairy, sharply-angled stems** and a smaller **corolla not longer than 3.5cm**.

In woods in England, E Wales and SE Ireland; not found north of the Humber, and absent from SW England.
P   1m   Summer

Creeping Bellflower
Campanula rapunculoides
As the English name implies, this decorative 'cottage garden' flower is **very invasive, spreading freely by root-suckers**. The **flowers, all directed to one side of the raceme**, can readily be distinguished by the **much more deeply-cut corollas** and in particular by the **calyx-teeth, which are spreading or even turned backwards at flowering time** (in both preceding species the calyx-teeth point forwards).

Naturalised on roadsides, hedgerows and field margins throughout much of the British Isles.
P   1m   Summer

Clustered Bellflower
Campanula glomerata
Aptly named in both Latin and English, this attractive wild-flower has **long-stalked basal leaves and short, erect, hairy stems** bearing stalkless leaves **and terminating in heads of erect, stalkless bellflowers**. The corolla is up to 2.5cm, **bright purplish-blue** (rarely white).

Locally common in chalk grassland, more rarely on sea-cliffs, from S England to E Scotland; absent from Ireland, most of Scotland and Wales, and the SW peninsula.
P   20cm   Summer

Harebell (Scottish Bluebell)
Campanula rotundifolia
The commonest of all the bell-flowers, this **slender, almost hairless plant spreads freely by thin underground runners**. The long-stalked basal leaves (often not observed) are ovate or almost circular, whilst the **stem-leaves are very narrow**. The flowering stems bear **one or more blue flowers on slender stalks, held erect in bud but nodding when open**.

Common throughout Britain (except Orkney) in grassland on shallow soils; in Ireland mainly in the north and west.
P   30cm   Late summer

Venus'-looking-glass
Legousia hybrida
An **erect, roughly hairy annual** with rather wavy, often yellow-green, ovate, stalkless leaves, and small groups of erect, stalkless flowers. The **calyx-teeth** are very obvious and **much longer than the wide, reddish-purple corolla**; below the rest of the flower is **the long cylindrical ovary** which develops into a capsule up to 3cm long.

A weed of arable fields in SE England north to E Yorkshire, formerly not uncommon but much reduced by modern herbicides.
A   30cm   Summer

Round-headed Rampion
Phyteuma orbiculare
An **almost hairless, erect plant** with long-stalked, ovate-oblong basal leaves and few, small stem-leaves. The **flowers are small and massed into heads up to 2.5cm in diameter** with a group of bracts at the base. Each **flower is curved in bud, the violet-blue corolla opening and eventually showing deep, narrow, spreading lobes free nearly to the base.**

A remarkable plant, locally common in chalk grassland south of the Thames from Wiltshire to E Sussex, and unknown elsewhere in the British Isles.
P   40cm   Summer

Sheep's-bit
Jasione montana
Like the rampion, with small flowers in heads, but a **rather spreading, hairy biennial with wavy, narrowly oblong leaves**. The **heads of blue flowers are flattened, and have a very distinct circle of short bracts round the base**. The anthers are joined into a short tube through which the style grows. The pollination mechanism is as in the *Compositae*.

Locally common on light acid soils throughout much of Britain including Orkney and Shetland, but much commoner in the west and absent from N Scotland; in Ireland common in the west.
B(A)   30cm   Summer

Water Lobelia
Lobelia dortmanna
Lobelia is familiar to most gardeners as *Lobelia erinus*, an annual blue-flowered bedding plant. The flowers look very different from bellflowers (though they are quite closely related), because **the corolla is 2-lipped**. The water lobelia is a handsome **aquatic, with long, linear submerged leaves in rosettes from which arise the leafless stems bearing nodding pale lilac flowers above the water.**

In stony, acid lakes in upland Britain, from C Wales northwards; in Ireland mainly in the west and north.
P   60cm   Late summer

Campanula latifolia

Campanula trachelium

Campanula rapunculoides

Campanula glomerata

Campanula rotundifolia

Legousia hybrida

Phyteuma orbiculare

Jasione montana

Lobelia dortmanna

Madder and Bedstraw Family (Rubiaceae)

Madders and bedstraws, which belong to a large family, the *Rubiaceae*, are recognised by having 4-angled stems, whorls of 4 or more, often narrow, undivided leaves and small tubular flowers with 4 joined petals producing a pair of round, 1-seeded fruits.

The genus *Galium* is distinguished from other members of the family by having the tube of the corolla usually shorter than the lobes of the petals.

Field Madder
Sherardia arvensis
A small **trailing** annual **with whorls of 6 oval, pointed, deep green leaves** with prickly margins and **clusters of bright lilac flowers** which have a persistent calyx with 4–6 distinct teeth, enlarging in fruit. There are 2 kinds of flowers – normal bisexual ones and smaller female ones.

Arable fields, meadows, garden beds and old lawns throughout lowland British Isles.

A   Creeping   Spring to autumn

Squinancywort
Asperula cynanchica
A perennial with **trailing stems,** middle and upper **leaves in whorls of 4–6, very narrow,** hairless and unequal in length, with the margins rolled under and ascending branches, terminal or axillary loose clusters of **flowers with tubes twice as long as the petal lobes, white** on the **inside** but delicate **pink outside.**

Lime-rich grassland, dunes and cliffs throughout England, S Wales and W Ireland to 300m in Co. Clare.

P   Creeping   Summer

Crosswort
Galium cruciata
A very hairy, scrambling perennial instantly recognised by the **yellowish-green colour of the whole plant,** the **elliptical leaves, cross-like in whorls of 4,** with **yellow flowers** tightly clustered in their axils which later produce black fruits on turned-down stalks.

Open woods, scrub, hedgebanks and meadows on usually heavy, lime-rich soils throughout England, Wales and S Scotland to 450m in mid-Wales.

P   70cm   Late spring and summer

Woodruff
Galium odoratum
Recognised by the **large patches** it forms **in woods** as it spreads by far-reaching underground runners from which arise **simple stems with whorls of 6–8 linear or elliptical leaves** with prickly margins. The **white flowers** are arranged **in loose, terminal clusters** and produce fruits with hooked, black-tipped bristles. Smells sweetly of hay when dried.

Woods on, usually, base-rich soils throughout British Isles to 600m in Scotland.

P   45cm   Late spring and early summer

Northern Bedstraw
Galium boreale
This almost hairless perennial is, with crosswort, the only *Galium* with **3-veined leaves 4 in a whorl**: each is narrowly elliptical, and **bright green,** not yellowish-green, turning black when dried. The **white flowers,** up to 3mm across, are arranged in conspicuous, much-branched, terminal clusters and produce olive-brown fruits covered in hooked bristles.

Rocky hillsides, stream banks and shingle beds throughout upland Scotland, N England and N and W Ireland; rare in Wales.

P   45cm   Summer

Hedge-bedstraw
Galium mollugo
This is the hedgerow bedstraw with an abundance of **white flowers in a large terminal cluster** and with **smooth,** not prickly, stems which has its **leaves in whorls of 6–8 arising from a** thickened, **swollen area.** The **flowering branches** are **at a wide angle to the stem** and the **flowers are rarely over 3mm across.**

Open woodland, scrub and hedgerows throughout lowland England; scattered elsewhere and not native in Ireland.

P   1.2m   Summer and autumn

Upright Hedge-bedstraw
Galium album
Similar to hedge-bedstraw but with the **flowering branches ascending at an angle of 45°** or less, with **leaves** which are also **ascending** and are, usually, **widest at or below the middle** and narrow into a short point or mucro (more or less horizontal or descending and widest above the middle in hedge-bedstraw) and with larger **flowers, 3–5mm across.**

Grassy banks and meadows, usually on lime-rich soils in lowland England but rare in the north and in Wales and Scotland.

P   1.5m   Summer and early autumn

Lady's Bedstraw
Galium verum
This scrambling or upright perennial is instantly recognised by the **tall, 'fluffy' spikes of bright yellow flowers** smelling of new-mown hay, above the **whorls of 8–12 very narrow, needle-like, dark green leaves** often pointing towards the ground and with turned-down margins.

In all but the poorest grassland throughout British Isles to 600m in Scotland.

P   1m   Summer

Sherardia arvensis

Asperula cynanchica

Galium cruciata

Galium odoratum

Galium boreale

Galium mollugo

Galium album

Galium verum

Heath Bedstraw
Galium saxatile

A creeping, **mat-forming** bed-straw, abundant in acid grass-land and moorland, with **leaves 6–8 in a whorl, broadest near the tip, obtuse, with forwardly directed prickles** on the margin and with a **short terminal mucro** (see drawing). The ascending flowering stems end in small clusters of white **flowers on stalks shorter than the stem between the leaf whorls**.

On acid soils throughout British Isles to 1200m in Scottish Highlands.

P   20cm   Summer

Limestone Bedstraw
Galium sterneri

Like heath bedstraw a creeping, mat-forming plant **but** differs in the **narrower leaves, widest ⅓ distance from the tip** with few to many **backwardly directed prickles** on their margins (see drawing). The ascending flowering stems have clusters of white **flowers on stalks longer than the stem between the leaf whorls**.

Grassland and rocks on hard limestone or basic igneous rocks from S Wales northwards and in W Ireland, to 900m in Scotland.

P   25cm   Summer

Common Marsh-bedstraw
Galium palustre

This is the most frequent bed-straw of wetlands recognised by the **leaves, 4–6 in a whorl, less than 1.5cm long** with **tips** which are **blunt to acute** and **widest in the middle**, but **never have a short point or mucro** (see drawing), and by the **flowers 2.5–4.0mm across** on **inflorescence branches** which are **turned down in fruit**.

Marshes, fens and ditches wet in winter but dry in summer throughout British Isles to 600m in N Pennines.

P   30cm   Summer

Great Marsh-bedstraw
Galium elongatum

Similar to common marsh-bedstraw with **leaves 4–6 in a whorl** without a short point or mucro, but a much taller plant with larger leaves **up to 4cm long** which are **widest near the tip**: the **flowers** are also larger, **3–5mm across**, whilst the **inflorescence branches** are ascending in flower and become **horizontal in fruit**.

Reedswamps with water standing all the year throughout British Isles.

P   1.2m   Summer
[Not illustrated]

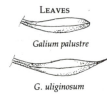

LEAVES

Galium palustre

G. uliginosum

G. saxatile

G. sterneri

Fen Bedstraw
Galium uliginosum

Similar in size and habit to common marsh-bedstraw but with **leaves** usually **6–8 in a whorl with a prominent point or mucro** at the tip (see drawing) and the whole plant rougher, with **downwardly directed prickles on the angles of the stem and backwardly directed prickles on the leaf margins**: the white **flowers** are small, **less than 3mm across**. Smells of new-mown hay.

Lime-rich marshes and fens throughout British Isles to 500m in N Pennines; absent from N Scotland and northern half of Ireland.

P   60cm   Summer

Cleavers
Galium aparine

Cleaves to the passer-by because **stems, leaves and peppercorn-sized fruits all have hooked hairs** which catch on clothing or cling to animal fur. The **leaves** are **in whorls of 5–8 with backwardly directed prickles on the margin**: the **flowers** are tiny, **only 2mm across**. Also called goosegrass because it was chopped up and fed to newly hatched goslings.

In copses, hedgerows, field borders, shingle banks and waste places throughout British Isles to 450m in Shropshire.

A   1.2m   Summer

Wild Madder
Rubia peregrina

This scrambling plant is distinguished from *Galium* by the flowers having 5 (not 4) **petals**, yellowish-green with long cuspidate tips. **The whole plant** is **covered in rough bristles**, down-wardly directed on the angle of the stems and backwardly on the margins of the leathery leaves and on their midribs below. The large **fruits, up to 6mm across** are **smooth and black**: usually only one of the pair develops.

Hedges, thickets and cliff-top scrub in S and W England, and coasts round Wales and southern half of Ireland.

P   1.2m   Summer

Galium saxatile

Galium sterneri

Galium palustre

Galium uliginosum

Galium aparine

Rubia peregrina

Honeysuckles (Caprifoliaceae)

A book on British wildflowers that did not include the honeysuckle would understandably be judged incomplete, so we have stretched our rules about excluding woody plants, and represent the honeysuckle family *Caprifoliaceae* first by the honeysuckle, *Lonicera*. Members of this family are distinguished by having flowers with inferior ovaries, tubular corollas, and stamens, usually 5 in number, attached to the corolla-tube; they are nearly all woody.

Honeysuckle
Lonicera periclymenum
One of our most exotic looking wildflowers, beloved of poets and artists. A **woody climber, with opposite, ovate leaves dark green above and grey beneath, and heads of large, 2-lipped flowers, with long yellow to purplish, glandular-hairy corolla-tube, fragrant in the evening**, and pollinated by large moths. The **fruit is a red berry**.

Common throughout British Isles in woods and hedgerows, and also on shady rocks, ascending to over 600m.
P – Summer

Perfoliate Honeysuckle
Lonicera caprifolium
Like the common honeysuckle, but **with leaves below the inflorescence joined in pairs round the stem (perfoliate)**, and the **corolla-tube not glandular-hairy**.

An introduced garden honeysuckle, found escaped in hedges and scrub, mostly in lowland England.
P – Early summer

Twinflower
Linnaea borealis
This **charming plant has thin, creeping woody stems with opposite pairs of round, stalked leaves, and slender, glandular-hairy flower-stalks each bearing a pair of pendulous flowers**. The **delicate, pink, bell-shaped corolla has 5 short lobes**.

Rare, mainly in native Scots pine forests in the eastern Highlands of Scotland, but recorded from Northumberland to Sutherland.
P 7cm(tall) Summer

Dwarf Elder
Sambucus ebulus
This relative of the common elderberry bush (*Sambucus nigra*) is a **stout, erect, hairless herb with pairs of pinnate leaves with large stipules**. The large flat-topped inflorescence contains many **small white flowers in which the corolla-tube is short with a flat, spreading limb**. The **fruit is a black berry**.

Scattered throughout much of the British Isles on roadsides and waste ground, perhaps native on limestone in England; formerly grown as a medicinal herb.
P 1.2m Summer

Moschatel
Adoxa moschatellina
An attractive and unmistakable little plant **whose greenish flowers are uniquely arranged, 4 in a square at the top of the stalk, with a fifth central terminal flower**. Each basal leaf has 3 lobed leaflets, and the erect, hairless flowering stems bear a single pair of leaves.

Widespread but rather local in Britain in woods, hedgebanks and on shady rocks up to 1100m, from Sutherland southwards; very rare in NE Ireland, and absent from the Isle of Man, the Outer Hebrides, Orkney and Shetland.
P 10cm Spring

Common Valerian
Valeriana officinalis
Like other members of the Valerian family this tall, robust, peculiar-smelling perennial can be recognised by its **opposite leaves** and **clustered heads of small flowers with funnel-shaped corollas**, and its **inferior ovary** forming a **single-seeded nutlet**. The **calyx is inrolled in flower but extends and forms a feathery pappus** (like the Compositae) at the **top of the nutlet**.

Throughout British Isles (except Shetland) in rough grassland, scrub and marshland.
P 1.5m Summer

Pyrenean Valerian
Valeriana pyrenaica
Like the common valerian, but the **basal and lower stem-leaves are broad, simple and coarsely toothed**. The upper leaves just below the flowering branches usually have 1 or 2 pairs of leaflets.

Introduced from the Pyrenees and Spanish mountains as a garden plant, and now naturalised in woodland especially in Scotland; not recorded from SE England and most of Ireland.
P 1m Summer

Marsh Valerian
Valeriana dioica
A smaller plant than the common valerian, with almost hairless, erect flowering stems and **many long spreading runners**. The **long-stalked basal leaves are quite undivided, but the unstalked stem-leaves are pinnately cut**. The plants are **separately male or female**: the photograph shows a male plant, which has a slightly less densely-packed head of flowers than the female.

Not uncommon in fens, bogs and marshes throughout most of England, Wales and S Scotland; unknown in Ireland.
P 30cm Late spring

Lonicera periclymenum

Lonicera caprifolium

Linnaea borealis

Sambucus ebulus

Adoxa moschatellina

Valeriana officinalis

Valeriana pyrenaica

Valeriana dioica

Red Valerian
Centranthus ruber
A familiar garden plant, with **robust, hairless stems and opposite, stalkless, ovate stem-leaves**. The **many scented, red (less commonly pink or white) flowers** are in branched inflorescences. Each **flower has a** spreading ring of 5 corolla-lobes and **slender corolla-tube up to 1cm, with a single spur at the base;** inside is a single stamen. The nutlet fruit is crowned by a feathery pappus.

Widely naturalised on walls, cliffs etc., especially in S and W England and SE Ireland, but recorded up to NE Scotland.
P   80cm   Summer

Common Cornsalad
Valerianella locusta
A **rather brittle, much-branched, nearly hairless annual with spoon-shaped lower leaves and oblong upper ones**. The **tiny flowers, in dense heads, have very small, regular, funnel-shaped, 5-lobed, pale lilac corollas** and in fruit the **calyx persists as a single small tooth on top of the nutlet.**

Throughout much of the British Isles, though rare in Scotland, on arable land, rocky outcrops, sand-dunes etc. Cultivated as a winter salad.
P   30cm   Spring and early summer

Other species of *Valerianella* occur, much more rarely than the common cornsalad. The commonest, *V. dentata*, is easily distinguished by **its much narrower fruit with a conspicuous calyx-tooth on top** (see drawing).

Teasels (Dipsacaceae)

The remaining plants on this page belong to the teasel family, *Dipsacaceae*. They resemble *Compositae* in their dense heads of florets, but are easily distinguished by having 5 free stamens, which protrude on long filaments from the florets. (They are well shown in the photograph of the small teasel.)

Teasel
Dipsacus fullonum
The wild teasel, beloved of flower arrangers, is a tall, **handsome biennial, hairless but prickly.** The rosettes of basal leaves die early in the second (flowering) season, and the **stem-leaves in pairs are joined at the base round the stem.** The **broad cylindrical heads with spiny bracts have many florets with purplish corolla-tube.**

Common in most of England south of the Humber; much less common in Wales, Scotland and Ireland and absent from N Scotland. On roadsides, etc. particularly on disturbed soils.
B   1.5m   Summer

Small Teasel
Dipsacus pilosus
Obviously a teasel, but easily distinguished by **its small, spherical heads of whitish flowers and stalked stem-leaves not joined at the base.**

Rather rare, in damp wood-margins and hedges in England and E Wales; not recorded in Scotland and Ireland.
B   1.2m   Late summer

Field Scabious
Knautia arvensis
A tall, roughly hairy perennial with deeply-cut stem leaves and **long-stalked heads of florets surrounded at the base by a ring of non-spiny bracts.** The **florets have unequally 4-lobed, usually pale bluish-lilac corollas,** the outer florets often markedly irregular. The calyx is represented on the nutlet by about 8 bristles.

Common in dry pastures throughout much of the British Isles, but rare in N Scotland and N Ireland and absent from the Hebrides and Shetland. Favours chalk or limestone.
P   1m   Summer

Small Scabious
Scabiosa columbaria
Like a **smaller version of the field scabious, most certainly distinguished by the 5-** (not 4) **lobed corolla** and the 5 (not *c*.8) calyx teeth. The **conical fruiting head,** (well shown in the photograph) **has a very characteristic 'honeycomb' appearance.** The flowers are usually somewhat darker bluish-lilac than the field scabious.

Locally common on dry chalk or limestone grassland in Britain up to 600m in N England; absent from C and N Scotland, Ireland and the northern isles.
P   60cm   Summer

Devil's-bit Scabious
Succisa pratensis
A small plant, similar in general appearance to small scabious but with very different soil requirements and easily told by the **simple leaves and the small rounded heads of florets with equally 4-lobed corollas of a deeper purplish-blue.**

Common throughout British Isles in marshes, wet meadows and damp woodland.
P   80cm   Summer

Centranthus ruber

Valerianella locusta

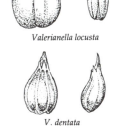

Fruits

Valerianella locusta

V. dentata

Dipsacus fullonum

Dipsacus pilosus

Knautia arvensis

Scabiosa columbaria

Succisa pratensis

Daisy Family (Compositae)

Daisies have small flowers, florets, packed in heads, capitula, surrounded by calyx-like bracts, the involucre. The florets may be tubular with a corolla of 5 equal teeth, or, ligulate, the corolla expanded on one side into a strap-shaped 'petal'. In a head the florets may all be similar, either tubular or ligulate, or those in the centre may be tubular and those at the margin ligulate, 'ray florets'. Each floret has 5 stamens, a single style branched into 2 above and produces a single fruit or achene crowned by a pappus.

Nodding Bur-marigold
Bidens cernua

A slightly hairy annual of water-sides which has rather **drab, brown and yellow flowers** lacking any showy ligulate florets, purplish stems and **opposite pairs of leaves**. Nodding bur-marigold can be recognised by its **drooping heads of flowers** and also by the coarsely-toothed **leaves** being **undivided** and **stalkless**. In fruit the **achenes, with 3–4 barbed bristles, 3mm long**, are unmistakable.

Stream and pond margins, where water lies in winter throughout lowlands, north to Angus.

A   60cm   Summer and early autumn

Trifid Bur-marigold
Bidens tripartita

Similar to, and in similar habitats to, nodding bur-marigold but distinguished at an early stage by the coarsely-toothed **opposite leaves** being **stalked** and having **a pair of narrow lobes at the base**. Later the **less nodding heads of flowers** and, in fruit, the **achenes with only 2 barbed bristles less than 2mm long**, confirm the identification.

Lake, stream and pond-sides, often on bare mud, throughout lowland British Isles north to Perthshire.

A   60cm   Summer and early autumn

Shaggy Soldier
Galinsoga ciliata

Galinsoga, along with *Bidens*, is one of the few genera of Compositae with **opposite pairs of leaves**. These are **oval, pointed, about as broad as long**, and have 3 prominent longitudinal veins. Shaggy soldier is recognised by its **hairy stems** and **numerous glandular hairs on the flowering stalks**, and by the **c.5 conspicuous white ray florets up to 2.5mm long**. In fruit there are small narrow and individual scales between the achenes.

An introduced weed of waste land mainly in the south of England; rare in Scotland and Wales.

A   75cm   Spring to autumn

Gallant Soldier
Galinsoga parviflora

Like shaggy soldier but with almost **hairless stems** and only a **few glandular hairs on the flowering stalks**. The flowers are relatively inconspicuous with **5 dirty white ray florets up to only 1.5mm long**. In fruit there are scales between the achenes cut into 3 acute segments. Gallant soldier is clearly a corruption of the Latin name, *galinsoga*.

An introduced weed of arable fields and gardens especially on sandy soils, mainly in SE England, thinly scattered elsewhere.

A   80cm   Spring to autumn

Ragworts and Groundsels

Ragworts and groundsels belong to the genus *Senecio*. They have yellow flowers with both tubular and ligulate (ray) florets surrounded by an involucre of either a single row of equal bracts or with a few much shorter outer ones as well. The florets produce achenes which develop a pappus of undivided hairs.

Common Ragwort
Senecio jacobaea

This erect biennial or perennial has all its leaves much-divided, a **flat-topped inflorescence** of heads of **bright yellow flowers, 1.5–2cm across**, with *c*.13 conspicuous ray florets and with **2–5 smaller, outer involucral bracts about ¼ the length of the rest**. When **achenes** ripen they can be removed *en masse* by pulling the pappus; the **inner ones** are **hairy** whilst the **outer ones** are hairless, up to **2mm long**.

Abundant in over-grazed pastures, sand-dunes and waste places to 650m in Scotland.

B or P   1.5m   Summer and autumn

Marsh Ragwort
Senecio aquaticus

Distinguished from common ragwort by having some at least of the lowest leaves hardly, if at all, divided and by the **bushy-shaped inflorescence** of larger flower-heads, **2.5–3cm across**, with 13–20 ray florets. These develop into achenes which are **hairless** and up to 3mm long.

Ditches, marshes and wet meadows throughout British Isles to 450m in N Pennines.

B   80cm   Summer

Hoary Ragwort
Senecio erucifolius

As the name implies the stems and leaves are covered in hairs but it may also be distinguished before flowering by the **leaves** which are neatly **divided into more or less equal, narrow, toothed segments**. In flower it is like common ragwort in having a **flat-topped inflorescence** but differs by having **outer involucral bracts only ½ the length of the rest** and, in fruit, by having **all the achenes hairy**.

Grassland on heavy lime-rich soils throughout lowland England and Wales, and around Dublin in Ireland.

P   1.2m   Summer

FLORETS OF
COMPOSITAE

style⌐
stamens

Tubular
(*Doronicum*)

Ray
(*Taraxacum*)

Bidens cernua

Bidens tripartita

Galinsoga ciliata

Galinsoga parviflora

Senecio jacobaea

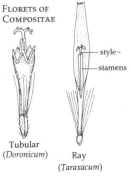

Senecio aquaticus

Senecio erucifolius

Oxford Ragwort
Senecio squalidus
This urban plant of railway lines and waste places is recognised by its **bushy habit**, more or less hairless, **much-divided leaves**, the upper ones clasping the stem, and by having all the **involucral bracts with conspicuous black tips**: the small, **hairy achenes** are 1.5–2mm long.

Introduced from S Italy and first escaping, in Oxford, in 1794, now widespread in lowland England and Wales; rare in Scotland and Ireland.

A or B   40cm   Spring to late autumn

Heath Groundsel
Senecio sylvaticus
Groundsels are annuals differing from ragworts in having very **short ray florets** which soon **turn down and become inconspicuous**, or in having none. Heath groundsel has 8–14 **ray** florets and is a slender, erect **yellowishgreen plant** with narrow, muchdivided leaves, which are **not, or only slightly, sticky**. The **capitula have c.13 involucral bracts**, the outer ¼ the length of **the inner without black tips**; the **stiffly hairy achenes** are *c*.2.5mm long.

Heaths and scrub on dry, limefree soils throughout British Isles.

A   70cm   Late summer

Sticky Groundsel
Senecio viscosus
A **greyish**-looking, **bushy**, very **sticky plant**, stems and deeply dissected leaves covered in glandular hairs which leave a **foul smell** on fingers when rubbed. The **capitula** are **conical** with *c*.20 involucral bracts, the outermost 2 or 3 over ⅓ length of rest: the capitula narrow upwards to a ring of *c*.13 ray florets; the **hairless achenes** are *c*.3mm long.

Railway lines, coastal sands and waste places throughout lowland Britain; rare in the west and almost absent from Ireland.

A   60cm   Summer and early autumn

Groundsel
Senecio vulgaris
This garden weed is the least hairy of the 3 common species of groundsel and is recognised by the **absence of** any **ray florets**. However rayed forms do occur, especially in S and W Britain. Before flowers open the **tight bunching of** the **heads on short stalks**, which only extend later, is diagnostic. The cylindrical capitula have **outer bracts, with black tips**, about ¼ as long as the inner: the **achenes, hairy between the ribs**, are *c*.2mm long.

Arable fields and waste places throughout British Isles to 500m in Scotland.

A   45cm   All year round

Leopard's-bane
Doronicum pardalianches
This robust, **hairy perennial** is easily recognised by its showy, **yellow, oxeye daisy-sized flowering heads** and by its **large, round, toothed leaves heart-shaped and long-stalked at the base, round, and clasping the stem, above**. Usually grows in large patches spreading by stout underground stems with tubers at their tips.

Originally a garden escape, now established in scattered woods and plantations throughout Britain but particularly abundant in E Scotland.

P   90cm   Late spring and summer

Field Fleawort
Senecio integrifolius
Recognised in the lime-rich grassland in which it grows by the **rosette of broad, oval leaves covered in woolly hairs** with a **single**, short, also **woolly, stem** arising from the centre, **bearing a few leaves** diminishing in size, with narrow ones at the top, and **terminating in a cluster of 1–6 yellow flower-heads branching from one point**. The involucral bracts are all the same length: the densely hairy achenes are *c*.4mm long.

Very local in chalk and limestone grassland in southern England with an outlier in N Yorkshire.

P   30cm   Summer

Colt's-foot
Tussilago farfara
Recognised in **early spring**, as in the photograph, by the patches of **golden-yellow heads on short**, scale-covered **stalks** which open on sunny days but close at night, drooping when the florets wither but returning to the upright to release their parachute-born achenes when ripe. **Later** the **rounded**, yet **angular, hairy leaves**, about the size and shape of a colt's foot, appear and persist through the summer.

Arable fields, roadsides, dunes, screes, shingle and waste places throughout British Isles to 1000m in Scottish Highlands.

P   30cm   Spring

Senecio squalidus

Senecio sylvaticus

Senecio viscosus

Senecio vulgaris

Senecio integrifolius

Doronicum pardalianches

Tussilago farfara

Butterbur
Petasites hybridus
Recognised from a distance in summer by the **rhubarb-like leaves** following the course of a lowland stream: they can be 90cm across. Like colt's-foot it **produces flowers** in spring **before the leaves** appear. The heads of reddish-violet flowers are arranged **in a conical spike** of 50 or more: there are separate 'male' and 'female' plants, the former the smaller and more common, the 'female' taller and almost confined to the Midlands.

Wet meadows and copses by streams throughout lowlands except far N of Scotland.
P 80cm Spring

White Butterbur
Petasites albus
Leaves, much smaller than butterbur **about the size of colt's-foot**, are shallowly lobed and have **white woolly** hairs **underneath**. The heads of **yellowish-white flowers**, which begin to expand before the leaves appear, **have no ray florets**, and are arranged **in pyramidal-shaped spikes**.

A garden escape now established on roadsides, in woods, plantations and waste places in scattered localities in England, but frequent and abundant throughout much of lowland E Scotland.
P 30cm Spring

Winter Heliotrope
Petasites fragrans
This vanilla-scented perennial, which usually grows in large patches, **produces leaves and flowers** at the same time and earlier than other *Petasites* species, **often before the end of December**. The leaves are kidney-shaped, toothed but not shallowly lobed, whilst the **outer florets of the lilac heads are** shortly, but distinctly, **ligulate**.

A garden escape widely established on stream sides and road banks and in waste places throughout Ireland and S Britain; scattered and mainly coastal in Scotland.
P 25cm Winter

Elecampane
Inula helenium
This **tall**, perennial, hedgerow plant, **up to 1.5m high**, is unmistakable **with** its **large, ragged, yellow flower-heads** up to 8cm across **with many narrow ray florets** and spreading, leafy, outer involucral bracts, and with its **saw-toothed**, linear, upper **leaves, clasping the stem**, hairless above but **softly hairy beneath**.

An introduction from Europe, formerly grown for medicine, it is established in scattered localities in copses, hedgerows and rough grassland throughout lowland British Isles.
P 1.5m Summer

Ploughman's-spikenard
Inula conyza
A somewhat boring perennial, with upright, simple stems, **leaves like a foxglove, softly hairy beneath**, and a branched, more or less terminal, inflorescence of **green, downy heads, c.1cm across** with **no** conspicuous **ray florets** and the yellow tubular florets shorter than, and almost hidden by, the **involucral bracts** which **have** their **tips turned back**.

Dry banks, rocky slopes, cliffs and scrub on lime-rich soils throughout lowland England and Wales north to Co. Durham.
B or P 1.2m Summer and early autumn

Golden-samphire
Inula crithmoides
This strictly **coastal, hairless plant** is readily recognised by its shining, much-branched, fleshy stems and the **long narrow, blunt leaves, often obscurely 3-toothed near the tip**, as well as, in late summer, by the heads of golden-yellow flowers up to 2.5cm across surrounding orange-yellow tubular florets: the hairy achenes are 2–3mm long.

Salt-marshes and salt-sprayed cliffs and rocks around southern coasts of British Isles from Suffolk to Co. Cork including the Irish Sea.
P 90cm Summer

Common Fleabane
Pulicaria dysenterica
A low-growing, late-flowering, **woolly** perennial with **wrinkled leaves** clasping the stem and bright yellow heads of **many ray florets** surrounding similar-coloured, tubular ones. Separated from *Inula* by the achenes which have a pappus in 2 rows, the outer reduced to a circular, saw-edged cup, the inner of long, fine hairs. The English name is derived from the supposed property of driving away fleas when burnt.

Marshes and wet meadows of England, Wales and Ireland; coastal and south of Fife in Scotland.
P 60cm Summer and autumn

Petasites hybridus

Petasites albus

Petasites fragrans

Inula helenium

Inula conyza

Inula crithmoides

Pulicaria dysenterica

Common Cudweed
Filago vulgaris
A small, densely-hairy, upright annual branching from the base with other **branches arising beneath the terminal clusters of woolly flower-heads**. The **stems are hidden by upwardly-pointing, strap-shaped leaves** with wavy margins. There are **30–40 flower heads in each cluster:** they have no ray florets and the yellow tubular florets are difficult to see: achenes tiny, 0.6mm long.

Heaths, dry grassland, banks and waste ground on acid, sandy soils throughout lowland British Isles except far north.
A   30cm   Summer

Small Cudweed
Filago minima
Separated from common cudweed by having only **3–6 flower-heads in each terminal cluster** and by the more **slender stems** covered by much smaller **leaves, 5–10mm, not 1–2cm, long.**

In acid, sandy fields and on heaths scattered throughout British Isles.
A   15cm   Summer and early autumn

Heath Cudweed
Gnaphalium sylvaticum
This perennial with erect or ascending branches is recognised by its covering of **white, woolly hairs** which contrast with the **dark brown** of the flower-heads which cluster in the axils of the long, **narrow, 1-veined leaves, hairy beneath, hairless above,** in the upper half of the stems. The outer involucral bracts have a central green stripe and a broad, pale, papery margin, brownish towards the tip: the outer ones are woolly below.

Open, heathy woodlands and dry heathland throughout British Isles to 750m in Scotland.
P   60cm   Summer and autumn

Dwarf Cudweed
Gnaphalium supinum
A **densely-tufted perennial**, not more than 12cm high, confined to **acid rocks at high altitudes in** the mountains of **Scotland** where snow lies long into summer. Like other cudweeds a woolly plant but it has very short stems with the **flower heads crowded, 1–7 together**, at the tip: the stems lengthen a little in fruit. The involucral bracts have a central, olive-coloured stripe, and a broad, pale brown, papery margin.

Highlands of Scotland and on Skye, to 1250m
P   12cm   Summer

Marsh Cudweed
Gnaphalium uliginosum
A **bushy**, much-branched, **annual** of damp, muddy places recognised by its long, **narrow leaves covered in dense, woolly hairs** contrasting with the **clusters of 3–10** dark brown **flower-heads** at the tips of the branches. The involucral bracts, enclosing the yellow tubular florets, are pale brown and woolly below, darker and hairless near the tip.

Bare ground in marshland, on tracks, and in arable fields on acid soils throughout British Isles to 350m in the Pennines.
A   20cm   Summer

Pearly Everlasting
Anaphalis margaritacea
This introduced, woolly perennial spreads by short runners and forms **large**, conspicuous **patches** on the waste ground, coal-tips and wall-tops especially in S Wales. The tall, **erect stems** have long, **narrow leaves, woolly**, at least **beneath**, and **terminal clusters of flower-heads**, whose brown involucral **bracts have white, shining, papery tips** which persist for some time. There are separate male and female plants but the latter have a few hermaphrodite florets.

Thinly scattered throughout lowland British Isles.
P   1m   Summer

Mountain Everlasting
Antennaria dioica
A small perennial recognised by the compact **rosettes of basal leaves broadest near the tip,** dark green above but **covered in white, woolly hairs beneath**. The slender **flowering shoots have upwardly pointing linear leaves.** Separate male and female plants have different coloured flowering heads – the **males with white involucral bracts** whilst the **females are usually rose-pink.**

Heaths, dry grassland and mountain rocks and pastures; commoner in the north and declining in the south; to 900m in Scottish Highlands.
P   20cm   Summer

Filago vulgaris

Filago minima

Gnaphalium sylvaticum

Gnaphalium supinum

Gnaphalium uliginosum

Anaphalis margaritacea

Antennaria dioica

Goldenrod
Solidago virgaurea
Aptly named, for it is easily recognised by its upright stems terminating in **spikes of golden-yellow flower-heads** each with **6–12 spreading ray florets** and surrounded by narrow, papery-margined greenish-yellow, involucral bracts in many rows. The **stalked, alternating,** oval **leaves,** hairless above, are usually **toothed and somewhat shining.**

Dry woods, hedgerows, rocks, cliffs and dunes except in the east and centre of both England and Ireland.
P 75cm Summer and early autumn

Hairy Michaelmas-daisy
Aster novae-angliae
Clearly separated from the d ,zen or so species of michaelmas-daisies established in the wild by the **branches of the inflorescence and the involucral bracts** of the flower heads **densely covered in glandular hairs** and by the **purplish-red or pink** colour of the **ray florets** (rarely white), with a smell like a garden marigold.

Commonly grown in gardens and occurring as an escape on river banks and waste places throughout lowland Britain north to Argyll.
P 2m Late summer and autumn

Daisy
Bellis perennis
This beautiful perennial makes a fine display in short grassland everywhere. It forms unmistakable **rosettes of spoon-shaped, glossy leaves,** rounded at the tip and narrowing into a short, broad stalk. The stalks beneath the **flower-heads** are hairy and the heads, **up to 2.5cm across, have numerous, spreading, white ray florets, or pink (especially beneath),** surrounding a mass of bright yellow tubular florets. **Few,** pale, flattened, hairy **achenes** are produced.

Short grassland throughout British Isles to 900m in Highlands.
P 12cm All year round.

Sea Aster
Aster tripolium
Some plants of this species have flowers like a michaelmas-daisy with **blue-purple or whitish ray florets and yellow tubular florets: others have yellow tubular florets only** but all are instantly distinguished by their **fleshy, lance-shaped, undivided** and more or less **toothless leaves** and the flat-topped arrangement of the flower-heads.

Salt-marshes, cliffs, rocks and sea walls of coast of British Isles, estuaries; occasionally in salt pans. The rayless form is rare in N England and Scotland.
B or P 1m Summer and autumn

Blue Fleabane
Erigeron acer
This hairy annual is recognised by its **basal rosette of long, narrow leaves, broadest near the tip,** its numerous, upright, stem-leaves and the branched inflorescence, with **flower heads up to 2cm across** like *Aster* but **with many, short, upright, pale-purple, ray florets** in 2 rows scarcely longer than the yellow tubular florets.

Dry grassland, dunes, banks and walls, usually on lime-rich soils, throughout lowland England and Wales and in SE Ireland.
A or B 40cm Summer

Michaelmas-daisy
Aster novi-belgii
Named from the time of flowering, these are familiar garden plants, mainly introduced from N America, which have often been thrown out and become established in the wild. The commonest is *A. novi-belgii* with **more or less hairless** stems or with hairs in vertical lines, long narrow **upper leaves, 5–10 times as long as broad** somewhat embracing the stem, and **violet-blue or white ray florets.**

Railway lines, river banks and waste places scattered throughout lowland British Isles.
P 1.2m Late summer and autumn

Canadian Fleabane
Erigeron canadensis
An **urban annual** recognised by its **erect, very leafy stems,** up to 1.5m, **much-branched** from below the middle. The **stem leaves** are **long and narrow,** up to 4cm, **without teeth, hairy on both surfaces** and with 'eyelashes' on their margins. The **flowering heads are small, up to 5mm across,** with 25–40 **greenish-white,** inconspicuous, ray florets surrounding pale yellow tubular florets with 4 petals.

Introduced from N America *c.*1690 and now established in much of lowland England and Wales, especially in the SE.
A 1.5m Summer and autumn.

Hemp-agrimony
Eupatorium cannabinum
This is the only common composite with **opposite leaves and tubular, reddish flowers.** The almost stalkless **leaves are divided into 3–5 elliptical, toothed segments** so that **each node appears to have a whorl of 6–10 'leaves'.** Each flower-head has 5–6 florets surrounded by *c.*10 purple-tipped involucral bracts and the **heads are arranged in dense 'fluffy', flat-topped clusters.**

Widespread in wet woods, fens, marshes and on damp cliffs throughout the lowlands, but mainly coastal in Scotland.
P 1.2m Late summer

Solidago virgaurea

Aster tripolium

Aster novi-belgii

Aster novae-angliae

Erigeron acer

Erigeron canadensis

Bellis perennis

Eupatorium cannabinum

Yarrow
Achillea millefolium
A very common grassland flower recognised by its **leaves**, long and narrow in outline but **divided into 'millions' of feather-like segments**. From mid-summer onwards its **flat clusters of white, pink or, rarely, purple flowerheads** are conspicuous: each head, 4–6mm across, has **c.5 ray florets**, as broad as long and only **half the length of the involucral bracts** surrounding creamywhite tubular florets. The achenes are flattened and slightly winged *c.*2mm long.

Throughout British Isles to 1200m in Scottish Highlands.
P 45cm Summer and autumn

Sneezewort
Achillea ptarmica
Immediately recognisable as related to yarrow because of the very similar **white flower-heads**. They are much bigger, **up to 1.8cm across**, and have more, **8–13, ray florets as long as the involucral bracts**, surrounding greenish-white tubular florets arranged in a fewer-flowered laxer inflorescence. However, the **leaves** are quite different, being **long, narrow and undivided with a very fine saw-like edge**.

Damp meadows, marshes and beside streams throughout British Isles, though very rare in southern half of Ireland.
P 60cm Summer

Stinking Chamomile
Anthemis cotula
Chamomiles have strong aromatic scents, **daisy-like flowerheads** with white spreading ray florets and yellow tubular florets in the centre, and **finely divided leaves**. Like mayweeds but differ in having **flat colourless scales between the tubular florets** visible if the latter are gently rubbed away. Stinking chamomile is **hairless**, or almost so, with an **unpleasant smell: scales long and narrow** (see drawing) and the **achenes**, up to 2mm long, are **covered in small tubercles**.

Arable fields and waste places on heavy soils, and rare in north.
A 60cm Summer and autumn

Corn Chamomile
Anthemis arvensis
Similar to stinking chamomile but usually a **hairy** plant with young leaves woolly beneath, **lacking a strong unpleasant smell**. The scales between the yellow tubular florets are **broad, narrowing abruptly into a short point** (see drawing), whilst the achenes are **vertically ribbed, without tubercles**, have a wavy 'frill' at the top and are up to 3mm long.

Locally common in arable fields and waste places on limerich soils mainly in south and east England.
A 50cm Summer and early autumn

Chamomile
Chamaemelum nobile
This low-growing, **creeping perennial** has a **pleasant aroma** and is often used to make a scented lawn, whilst the flowerheads make an excellent tea. The stems and leaves are **hairy** but never woolly; the scales between the tubular florets are **broad but not abruptly pointed** and may be toothed at the top, whilst the **achenes have neither tubercles nor strong vertical ribs** and are only *c.*1.5mm long.

Sandy commons and pastures, mainly in southern England and SW Ireland; rare and introduced elsewhere.
P 30cm Summer

Scales
Anthemis cotula

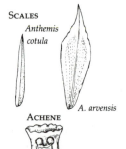

A. arvensis

Achene

Tripleurospermum inodorum

Scented Mayweed
Matricaria recutita
A **pleasantly aromatic** herb with finely-divided leaves, recognised by its **conical dome of yellow tubular florets with the white ray florets drooping** soon after they open. These 'domes' are **hollow** and, if the tubular florets are gently rubbed away, **no colourless scales** remain. The achenes, up to 2mm long, **have 4–5 conspicuous ribs on the inner face** but **no oil glands** on the other side.

Arable fields and waste places throughout lowland England and Wales; rare in Scotland, nearly absent from Ireland.
A 60cm Summer

Pineappleweed
Matricaria matricarioides
Pleasantly aromatic and easy to recognise from a distance. The crushed leaves **smell of pineapple** and the **flower-heads lack** any **ray florets**, consisting of dull, greenish-yellow tubular florets surrounded by **blunt involucral bracts with broad, papery margins**. The achenes, up to 1.5mm long, **have 4 conspicuous ribs on the inner face** and a faint rim at the top.

A **plant of trampled places** on roadsides and paths in gateways. Introduced from America in 1871 and now throughout lowland British Isles.
A 30cm Summer

Scentless Mayweed
Tripleurospermum inodorum
The commonest of all the daisy-like arable weeds, recognised by the **scentless flower-heads**, their large size, **up to 4.5cm across**, with a **flat, not conically domed, area of tubular florets** in the centre, and by the **absence of colourless scales** between the tubular florets. The **achenes** are also unmistakable **with 3 broad ribs on the inner face and 2 dark oil glands**, like a pair of brown eyes, **near the top of the outer face**, with a thin wavy 'frill' above (see drawing).

Arable fields, sea-shores and waste places; to 500m in Scotland.
A or P 60cm Summer and autumn

Achillea millefolium

Achillea ptarmica

Anthemis cotula

Anthemis arvensis

Chamaemelum nobile

Matricaria recutita

Matricaria matricarioides

Tripleurospermum inodorum

Corn Marigold
Chrysanthemum segetum
A handsome **hairless** annual of branching habit, with **large, flat, thick-stalked heads with a ring of bright yellow ray florets, and oblong, stalkless, rather blue-green stem leaves half-clasping the stem. The outer achenes have 2 lateral wings, while the inner ones are plain.**

Scattered throughout British Isles as a weed of acid arable soils and waysides, but rather local and decreasing with modern agriculture.
A   60cm   Summer

Oxeye Daisy
Leucanthemum vulgare
One of our commonest wild daisies, with **almost hairless, erect branching stems bearing large white 'daisy' heads on long stalks**. The stalkless stem-leaves are roughly oblong and variably toothed or cut, with clasping bases; but the (less obvious) basal leaves are more or less spoon-shaped with long stalks.

A common plant of grassland throughout British Isles, though less common in NW Scotland.
P   80cm   Summer

Feverfew
Tanacetum parthenium
A **strongly aromatic**, more or less hairy perennial, **much-branched above, making a large rather flat-topped inflorescence of many small daisy-like capitula**. The deeply-divided,   short-stalked stem-leaves are often yellowish-green.

Probably not native, but frequent on walls, roadsides and waste places throughout much of Britain, though absent from Shetland and scattered and rather rare in Ireland. Originally widely cultivated as a medicinal herb and still seen in and around old cottage gardens.
P   60cm   Summer

Tansy
Tanacetum vulgare
An **aromatic**, almost hairless perennial spreading by runners. **The purplish stems are stiffly erect, bearing flat heads of many button-like yellow capitula. The large, finely pinnately-divided leaves are glandular and strongly aromatic.**

Throughout British Isles on roadsides, hedgerows and waste places, though less common in N Scotland and Ireland. Formerly much cultivated as a medicinal and culinary herb.
P   1.2m   Late summer

Mugwort and Wormwood

The remaining 3 plants on this page are species of *Artemisia*, characterised by their very small, inconspicuous capitula of wind-pollinated flowers (very unusual among *Compositae* in Britain). All these common *Artemisia* species are aromatic, and have a dense greyish-white hair-covering at least on the under-surface of the deeply-cut,   feathery   leaves; related garden plants are often grown for their attractive foliage.

Mugwort
Artemisia vulgaris
One of our commonest roadside plants in late summer, with tall, **erect, sparsely hairy, usually reddish stems bearing stalkless, pinnately divided stem-leaves that are dark green and almost hairless above but densely greyish-white hairy beneath**. The many **ovoid, erect capitula are only about 3mm; there are no ray florets and the heads are dingy in colour.**

Common on roadsides and in waste places throughout most of British Isles; rare and mostly coastal in C and N Scotland.
P   1.2m   Late summer and autumn

Wormwood
Artemisia absinthium
Like mugwort, but more strongly aromatic and **greyish hairy on the stems and both leaf surfaces**. The **drooping capitula are somewhat   larger   (c.4mm),   and broader than long, and the florets are more or less yellow**.

Perhaps native in Britain, quite frequent in waste places to S Scotland; rare and coastal further north; absent from Shetland and introduced in Ireland.
P   80cm   Late summer

Sea Wormwood
Artemisia maritima
Obviously related to wormwood, this **pretty, grey-woolly, much-branched,   spreading   plant occurs on the sea-coast. The strongly aromatic, grey leaves have very narrow segments**, and the **capitula are very small** (*c.*2mm), in leafy inflorescences.

Locally common in the upper part of salt-marshes and on sea-walls of the coasts of E and S England; rarer on the E coast of Scotland and absent from the north and north-west. On the Irish coast only in the Burren and along the east.
P   50cm   Late summer and autumn

Chrysanthemum segetum

Leucanthemum vulgare

Tanacetum parthenium

Tanacetum vulgare

Artemisia vulgaris

Artemisia absinthium

Artemisia maritima

Burdocks

Burdocks (*Arctium*) are very easy to recognise; they are biennials with very large, broad basal leaves and characteristic 'burr' fruits. The 'burrs' develop from the capitula, which consist of a few purplish tubular florets surrounded by a tight involucre of many flat bracts that narrow to a strong hooked point. The hooks are easily entangled in animal hair (and human clothing!), so that the whole more or less spherical head or 'burr' is dispersed, eventually shedding the ripe achenes.

Greater Burdock
Arctium lappa
A large, hairy, much-branched plant with a thick, furrowed stem, and **broad basal leaves up to 50cm with solid stalks**. The **heads are up to 4.5cm across in fruit**, in loose clusters on the main branches.

Roads, hedgerows and waste places throughout lowland England to Humberside; rare in Wales and Ireland, and absent from Scotland.
B   1.5m   Late summer

Lesser Burdock
Arctium minus
Very variable, but generally smaller, less cottony-hairy, and more widely branched than the greater burdock, with smaller, narrower **basal leaves with hollow leaf-stalks**. The **heads are smaller (1.5–4cm across in fruit)** and often arranged in racemes on the branches.

In open woodland, on wood margins, roadsides and waste ground throughout British Isles, but rare inland in C and N Scotland.
B   1.5m   Late summer

Thistles

Thistles are, like burdocks, easy to recognise, with their prickly leaves and purplish heads (white forms are not rare). They constitute a whole Tribe (*Cynareae*), named after that splendid thistle we grow as a vegetable, the globe artichoke, *Cynara scolymus*. Most true thistles in the British flora belong to 2 genera, *Carduus* and *Cirsium*, which differ in a technical character of the pappus-hairs on the achene, fortunately easily observed with an ordinary hand-lens. In *Carduus* the hairs are simple and rough, whereas in *Cirsium* they are branched and feathery (see drawing).

PAPPUS HAIRS

Carduus   *Cirsium*

Carline Thistle
Carlina vulgaris
Our first thistle is strictly biennial, **making in the first year a neat flat rosette of deeply-cut, spiny leaves**. In the second year the stiffly-erect, rather cottony, purplish flowering stems appear and the rosette-leaves die. **The few heads have a ring of very narrow straw-coloured bracts that spread when dry and look like ray florets**, surrounding the many tubular florets.

In chalk and limestone grassland throughout much of British Isles; common in C Ireland, but rare both north and south.
B   60cm   Late summer

Welted Thistle
Carduus acanthoides
A tall thistle with erect, cottony stems somewhat branched above and **with a continuous narrow, wavy, spiny-margined wing stopping just below the flower-heads**. The stem-leaves are stalkless with their bases extended down the stem (decurrent); they are deeply cut, with weakly spiny margins. **The spherical heads are 2–3cm and have very narrow bracts ending in a weak spine**.

Common in lowland England, and extending to NE Scotland and the Inner Hebrides; rather rare in Ireland.
B   1.2m   Summer

Musk Thistle
Carduus nutans
One of our really handsome thistles, quite unmistakable with its **large (up to 5cm), usually single, nodding, reddish-purple, sweet-scented heads. The cottony stems are unwinged for a considerable distance below the head**.

In rough pastures, roadsides and waste places on chalk or limestone soils, locally common through much of England, Wales and SE Scotland with a few records furher north; not recently seen in Ireland.
B(?P)   1m   Summer

Slender Thistle
Carduus tenuiflorus
Easily distinguished by its **cylindrical (not spherical) heads of pale purplish florets, densely clustered together at the ends of continuously spinous-winged stems**. The hairless, ovate bracts surrounding the heads terminate in a spreading spine. The heads fall when the achenes are ripe (unlike in the other species of *Carduus* where the achenes are released).

On roadsides and in waste places, especially near the sea, locally common in England (except the centre) and Ireland; in Scotland mainly on the east coast.
B(A)   1.2m   Summer

Arctium lappa

Arctium minus

Carlina vulgaris

Carduus acanthoides

Carduus nutans

Carduus tenuiflorus

Creeping Thistle
Cirsium arvense
One of our commonest thistles and a serious agricultural weed, **spreading widely by its far-creeping, thin white roots from which both flowering and non-flowering shoots arise**. The erect, furrowed, almost hairless, wingless flowering stems bear stalkless, variably-lobed, prickly leaves. The **many dull pale purple heads up to 2.5cm have appressed ovate bracts, the outer with spreading spiny tips**.

Abundant throughout British Isles in fields and waste places, up to 600m in N England.
P 1.2m Summer

Spear Thistle
Cirsium vulgare
Commonly seen in poor pastures with the creeping thistle, but **biennial with a taproot**, and easily distinguished by **its spiny-winged stem, strongly spiny leaves** and **much larger heads up to 5cm with narrow bracts with spreading spiny tips. The flower colour is usually pale reddish-purple**.

Common throughout British Isles in fields and waste places, like the creeping thistle, up to more than 600m in N England.
B 1.5m Summer

Marsh Thistle
Cirsium palustre
Like the spear thistle, a biennial with a spiny-winged stem, but easily distinguished by its **much smaller heads (not more than 2cm)** with **lance-shaped, sharp but not spiny, appressed bracts**. The florets are usually dark reddish-purple, but white forms are not uncommon.

Abundant throughout British Isles in marshes, damp grassland and wet woodland, up to nearly 800m in Scotland.
B 1.5m Summer

Woolly Thistle
Cirsium eriophorum
A very handsome, robust thistle, biennial with stout, erect, unwinged stem branching above, and **remarkable leaves pinnately divided into 2-lobed segments, one narrow, spiny-tipped lobe pointing upwards, the other downwards**. The **large, erect, solitary heads (up to 7cm) have a very white-cottony involucre of spiny-tipped bracts**.

In grassland and open woods on chalky and limy soils, locally common in England, north to Durham; absent from SW England, most of Wales, and all of Scotland and Ireland.
B 1.5m Summer

Dwarf Thistle
Cirsium acaule
Unique amongst our thistles, as its name indicates, the **few heads in this thistle are at ground level in the centre of a rosette of shiny, spiny leaves**. The **heads are ovoid, with** reddish-purple florets and **hairless, appressed bracts**, the outer with spiny points.

Locally common in grazed chalk and limestone grassland in England and Wales, north to N Wales and Yorkshire; absent from Scotland and Ireland.
P 5cm(tall) Summer

Melancholy Thistle
Cirsium helenioides
A **non-spiny perennial thistle, spreading by runners, with erect, usually simple, cottony, unwinged stems**. The **long-stalked, elliptical, toothed basal leaves and the pointed broad-based clasping stem-leaves are all densely white-felted beneath**. The single heads are up to 5cm and have appressed, almost hairless bracts.

In damp pastures and wet open woodland in upland Britain south to Derbyshire and C Wales; reaching to *c*.1000m in Scotland; very rare in N Ireland, and absent from Orkney and Shetland.
P 1m Summer

Meadow Thistle
Cirsium dissectum
Resembles the melancholy thistle but is shorter, with **smaller heads (up to 3cm) and leaves that are cottony (not densely felted) beneath**.

In peat fens and bog margins in lowland Britain north to mid-Wales and N Yorkshire; common in Ireland, especially in the west. The distribution is almost completely within the area from which the melancholy thistle is absent.
P 40cm Summer

Cirsium arvense

Cirsium vulgare

Cirsium palustre

Cirsium eriophorum

Cirsium acaule

Cirsium helenioides

Cirsium dissectum

Milk Thistle
Silybum marianum
An unmistakable thistle with thick, unwinged, slightly cottony stems and **large, variably cut, spiny-winged, hairless and shiny leaves of unusual pale green colour with white veins.** The solitary, reddish-purple heads are up to 5cm, **and are surrounded by bracts ending in a long, stout, yellowish spine.**

An introduced plant, often seen in and around old cottage gardens, and widely naturalised, though decreasing, in waste places in lowland England and Wales; rare in Scotland and Ireland.
A or B   1.2m   Summer

Cotton Thistle
Onopordon acanthium
Often called, inappropriately, 'Scotch Thistle', this very tall handsome biennial thistle has **a thick, white-woolly stem with a continuous broad, spiny wing, and cottony, spiny-toothed, stalkless leaves.** The solitary, pale purple heads, up to 5cm, have many spiny-tipped, cottony bracts.

Probably not native, but, like the milk thistle, often seen in or near old gardens, and with a similar distribution, though even rarer in Ireland.
B   2.5m   Summer

Saw-wort
Serratula tinctoria
This obviously thistle-like plant is **hairless, with erect, slender, rather wiry stems** and variably-divided, often more or less pinnate, but sometimes unlobed, leaves with small bristle-tipped teeth. The rather **narrow heads of purple florets have closely-appressed purplish bracts.**

Rather rare, in rough grassland, open woodland and damp places on chalk or limestone soils in England, Wales and S Scotland; very rare in SE Ireland.
P   80cm   Late summer

Alpine Saw-wort
Saussurea alpina
A neat mountain relative of the saw-wort, with a **simple, rather cottony flowering stem, and** ovate to lance-shaped basal leaves green above and white-cottony beneath. The purplish, fragrant heads are almost stalkless in a small dense group, and have blunt, hairy bracts.

On mountain rocks and sea-cliffs from near sea-level to nearly 1200m in W and N Scotland, including the Hebrides, Orkney and Shetland; rare in N Wales, the N English mountains and mountains in Ireland.
P   40cm   Late summer

Common Knapweed
Centaurea nigra
An abundant and variable, roughly hairy plant, most easily recognised by its **hard heads of** florets surrounded by triangular bracts with brown or blackish, deeply-cut appendages at their tips. In many forms (such as the one illustrated) the tubular florets are all similar, but not uncommonly forms occur with much larger spreading marginal florets. The leaves are often unlobed, but can be quite deeply cut.

Abundant throughout British Isles (except Shetland, where it is introduced) in grassland, on roadsides and in hedgerows.
P   60cm   Summer

Greater Knapweed
Centaurea scabiosa
A more handsome relative of the common knapweed, easily told by having **most of the leaves, even the stem-leaves, deeply pinnately-divided. The heads are larger and solitary on long, hairless stalks;** they often have large marginal florets.

In dry grassland, hedgebanks, etc. usually on lime-rich soils, throughout lowland Britain. Common in the south but rare in Scotland, absent from the islands and the west. In Ireland frequent on limestone in the Burren and occasional elsewhere but absent from the north.
P   80cm   Summer

Sub-family Cichorioideae
All the remaining *Compositae* on this and succeeding pages belong to the Sub-family *Cichorioideae*, named after the chicory plant, which we describe first. They are easily recognised by a combination of two characters: they have a bitter milky juice in their stems and leaves, and all the florets are ligulate, like the ray florets of a daisy. They are nearly all, with the exception of chicory itself, yellow-flowered, and contain the familiar dandelion-like *Compositae*.

Chicory
Cichorium intybus
The **large, bright blue flower-heads** of chicory are unique among our *Compositae*. The chicory plant has stiffly erect, tough stems usually with some rough hairs, short-stalked, toothed or lobed basal leaves, and small upper stem-leaves clasping at the base. The **heads are stalkless, in small groups in the axils of the upper leaves.**

Not uncommon on roadsides and in grassland especially in lime-rich soils in England and Wales; rare in Scotland and Ireland. Occasionally cultivated on chalk soils.
P   1m   Summer

Silybum marianum

Onoporden acanthium

Serratula tinctoria

Saussurea alpina

Centaurea nigra

Centaurea scabiosa

Cichorium intybus

Nipplewort
Lapsana communis
The easiest of all the yellow 'dandelion-like' *Compositae* to recognise on a simple technical character: the nipplewort **achenes have no pappus**. All other dandelion relatives have an obvious feathery or hairy pappus. The erect, rather hairy stems bear many **small stalked heads**, and the **basal and lower stem-leaves have a large, often heart-shaped, terminal lobe**.

A common weed of roadsides and waste and cultivated ground throughout most of the British Isles, though rather rare in N Scotland, Orkney and Shetland.
A to P   1m   Spring to autumn

Cat's-ear
Hypochoeris radicata
One of the commonest 'dandelion-type' wildflowers, with a **basal rosette of roughly-hairy, oblong to lance-shaped leaves** with a wavy toothed or lobed margin, and **branched, leafless stems enlarged somewhat below the flat, yellow heads**. Best told with certainty from the similar hawkbits (*Leontodon*) by the **presence of scales between the florets on the receptacle**: these are easily seen with a lens if the head is broken open (see drawing).

Common throughout British Isles in meadows, pastures and roadsides.
P   50cm   Summer

Autumn Hawkbit
Leontodon autumnalis
Very similar to the cat's-ear, and because both plants are very variable, best told from it by checking that **there are no scales between the florets**. The branched, leafless flowering stems are slenderer than in the cat's-ear, and less swollen below the heads, and the leaves are often almost hairless. The colour of the back of the florets is often reddish (greyish in the cat's-ear).

Abundant throughout British Isles in meadows, roadsides and mountain pastures and rocks, up to nearly 1000m in Scotland.
P   50cm   Summer and autumn

Rough Hawkbit
Leontodon hispidus
Easily told by the **large, single 'dandelion' heads on obviously hairy stems. With a hand-lens the rough hairs can be seen to be forked** (unlike the simple hairs of the 2 preceding species). Almost hairless forms are occasionally found.

Common in grassland, especially on chalk or limestone, in England, Wales and S Scotland; rare in C and N Scotland, and absent from the Outer Hebrides, Orkney and Shetland; in Ireland commonest in the Central Plain.
P   60cm   Summer

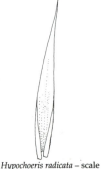

Hypochoeris radicata – scale

Lesser Hawkbit
Leontodon taraxacoides
A small **rosette plant with leafless stems bearing a single head and ascending from the rosette centre**. The leaves and stems usually have **some hairs, which are of the forked type**. Best told by the characteristic **pappus of the outer achenes, which, unlike the inner ones, have only a small crown of scales (not hairs)**.

Locally common over much of the British Isles on dry grassland and on basic soils; mainly on sand-dunes in the north, but absent from N Scotland and the Outer Isles.
P   10cm   Summer

Bristly Oxtongue
Picris echioides
Very easy to recognise by its **prickly hairs set on white swollen bases especially obvious on the leaves, and by the remarkable ring of 5 large heart-shaped outer bracts around each head**. The stems are stout, irregularly branched and covered with short, rigid, forked hairs.

Locally common in lowland England and Wales on roadsides and waste ground, especially on lime-rich clay soils; rare and only casual in Scotland. In Ireland rare and only in the east.
A–B   80cm   Summer

Hawkweed Oxtongue
Picris hieracioides
A **bristly-hairy plant** but without white swollen bases to the bristles. The **stout, erect stems bear rough, wavy-edged leaves and branch above, making a rather narrow, flat-topped inflorescence of yellow, ovoid heads**. The outer involucral bracts are narrow and spreading, much shorter than the inner ones.

Locally common on grassy banks and roadsides, particularly on limestone and chalk, in lowland England and Wales, north to Cumbria and Northumberland; absent from Scotland, and rare and introduced in Ireland.
B–P   80cm   Late summer

Lapsana communis

Hypochoeris radicata

Leontodon autumnalis

Leontodon hispidus

Leontodon taraxacoides

Picris echioides

Picris hieracioides

Goat's-beard
Tragopogon pratensis

An **almost hairless plant with narrow, grass-like leaves which have conspicuous white veins.** The **single yellow heads are on long stalks, leafy only in the lower part.** The **long, conical involucre is made of about 8 long-pointed bracts joined at the base.** The flowering heads only open in sunny weather in the mornings.

In grassland, roadsides and waste places, common in England but less common in the west and Wales, rare in C and N Scotland; in Ireland mostly in the Central Plain.

A–P   60cm   Summer

Lettuces

Our wild lettuces (*Lactuca*) do not produce succulent leaves for salad like the familiar garden plants, which are forms of *Lactuca sativa*, and most people probably do not often see and recognise a garden lettuce when it grows out to produce a tall stem with many small yellow flower-heads. Nevertheless, when garden lettuce does flower, it betrays its close relationship to the wild species, differing most obviously in having no prickles anywhere on stem or leaves.

Prickly Lettuce
Lactuca serriola

An alternative common name for this is 'compass plant', referring to the way in which **the stem-leaves of plants in the sun are held vertically in a north–south plane.** The whitish stems bearing small yellow heads are stiffly erect and almost hairless. The **over-wintering rosette-leaves and the stem-leaves are roughly oblong** (sometimes lobed), **and have small spines on the edges and prickles beneath.**

On waste ground, mainly in SE England, but recorded north and west to Northumberland and Cornwall.

A–B   2m   Late summer

Greater Lettuce
Lactuca virosa

Resembles the prickly lettuce, but the **stem leaves are rather wavy**, not flat, and **are not held vertically**, and the **stems are usually reddish.** Best told by the **ripe achenes** which are **black, not olive-grey** (an easily-seen difference).

Distribution similar to the prickly lettuce, but more often on sand-dunes, cliffs and other natural habitats, and extending to SE Scotland.

A–B   2.5m   Late summer

Wall Lettuce
Mycelis muralis

A **hairless perennial** with **erect, thin stems** and **small, narrowly-cylindrical heads of usually 5 yellow florets in a spreading inflorescence. Basal and lower stem-leaves thin in texture and often reddish, with a large terminal lobe.**

Throughout much of Britain, in walls and rocks, and in woodland, especially on chalk and limestone, but infrequent in SE England and C and N Scotland, and absent from the Outer Hebrides, Orkney and Shetland. Very scattered in Ireland, but common on the Burren limestone in the west.

P   1m   Summer

Sow-thistles

Sow-thistles (*Sonchus*) are usually somewhat spiny-leaved plants with yellow dandelion-like flower-heads and abundant milky juice when the stem is broken. The 3 common species described here are amongst our most abundant weeds.

Perennial Sow-thistle
Sonchus arvensis

A **far-creeping perennial plant** with tall, erect **stems usually strongly yellowish glandular-hairy in the upper part.** The **stem-leaves are stalkless with spiny-toothed margins and a clasping base extended on either side as rounded auricles.** The large, flat flower-heads (up to 5cm) have golden-yellow florets.

On roadsides and in arable land, also on drift-lines by rivers and the sea, throughout British Isles but almost entirely coastal in N Scotland.

P   1.5m   Late summer and autumn

Smooth Sow-thistle
Sonchus oleraceus

A **hairless annual with stout, erect, hollow stems**. The **leaves** are very variable in shape and amount of lobing, but **are always dull and never spiny; the stem-leaves have pointed, spreading auricles.** The heads are up to 2.5cm across, with pale yellow florets, and obconical in shape in the fruiting stage.

Common on cultivated ground and in waste places throughout British Isles.

A (over-wintering)   1.5m   Summer

Prickly Sow-thistle
Sonchus asper

Like the smooth sow-thistle, but the **stem-leaves are usually spiny on the margin, and dark glossy green with rounded, appressed auricles. The florets are a deeper, more golden yellow**. The 3-ribbed ripe achenes are smooth on the surface (in *S. oleraceus* they are rough).

Like the smooth sow-thistle, a common weed throughout British Isles.

A (over-wintering)   1.5m   Summer

Tragopogon pratensis

Lactuca serriola

Lactuca virosa

Mycelis muralis

Sonchus arvensis

Sonchus oleraceus

Sonchus asper

Dandelions

Dandelions (*Taraxacum*) are the most familiar yellow Composites. They share the following characters: they are **perennial with abundant milky juice, a taproot and a basal rosette of leaves**, and the **solitary heads of yellow flowers are borne on unbranched leafless stalks** arising from the centre of the rosette. Most British dandelions are apomictic, setting seed without fertilisation: this situation produces many different 'microspecies'. More than 130 have been described for Britain; we can usefully group these into 4 'species', as we obviously cannot include them all.

Common Dandelion

Taraxacum officinale

Robust plants with leaves usually with a large terminal lobe and triangular side lobes of a characteristic shape: the point of the lobe is facing outwards and downwards. The **outer involucral bracts** of the large heads **are spreading or often strongly curved backwards**.

Abundant on roadsides, waste and cultivated ground, probably throughout British Isles (though records for NW Scotland may partly refer to the next species).
P   30cm   Spring(summer)

Red-veined Dandelion

Taraxacum spectabile

Usually less robust than the common dandelion, **often with rather shallowly-lobed, dark-spotted leaves and typically with reddish colour on the midrib**. The **outer involucral bracts** are shorter and **erect or spreading, not reflexed**.

In damper and less disturbed ground than the common dandelion, often on woodland rides in lowland England, and common in upland areas throughout British Isles.
P   20cm   Late spring

Narrow-leaved Marsh-dandelion

Taraxacum palustre

Easily recognised by its **narrow, often entire, leaves** and the **outer involucral bracts, which are ovate, with a broad, pale margin, and tightly appressed**.

In marshes and fens, particularly when cut or grazed, apparently rare and decreasing through drainage; locally abundant in the Burren in W Ireland
P   20cm   Late spring

Lesser Dandelion

Taraxacum laevigatum

A small, neat plant with **very deeply-cut leaves**. The small heads have **outer involucral bracts with an appendage on the outer side of the tip, so that the tip looks double**.

Common in dry, especially sandy, ground throughout Britain, but mainly coastal in Scotland; in Ireland frequent in parts of the west, and perhaps generally under-recorded elsewhere.
P   15cm   Spring

Hawk's-beards

The hawk's-beards (*Crepis*) are common, **leafy-stemmed yellow Composites. They have 2 rows of involucral bracts, the outer shorter than the inner, and usually more or less spreading. The pappus on the ripe achene is composed of many unbranched white hairs** which protrude very slightly from the involucre in fruit.

Smooth Hawk's-beard

Crepis capillaris

A very variable, usually annual, plant with branched often rather wiry stems bearing several stalkless leaves and many small **heads of yellow florets that close in the fruiting stage and become obconical in shape**. The ripe achenes are only about 2mm. The amount of hairiness is very variable, **but the hairs are never rough in texture**.

Common throughout British Isles in grassland, heaths, roadsides and waste ground.
A(B)   80cm   Summer

Rough Hawk's-beard

Crepis biennis

A **stout biennial herb** with a **roughly-hairy stem** often purplish below. The **heads are twice as large** as in the smooth hawk's-beard, and the **ripe achenes are much larger (7–12mm)**.

Roadsides, pastures and waste ground, not uncommon especially on lime-rich soil in lowland England, but rare in Wales, Scotland and Ireland. Probably native in the south-east, but introduced further north and west.
B   1.2m   Summer

Beaked Hawk's-beard

Crepis vesicaria

This **stout** hawk's-beard is best identified by **its ripe achenes**, which **have a long thin neck or 'beak' at the top below the pappus**. The general appearance is similar to the rough hawk's-beard, but **its much earlier flowering (at least a month) is a useful character**.

An introduced weed of wayside, railway banks and waste ground, first recorded in Britain in 1713, and now common in lowland England and still spreading into Wales, S Scotland and Ireland.
B(A,P)   80cm   Late spring

Taraxacum species

Taraxacum officinale

Taraxacum spectabile

Taraxacum palustre

Taraxacum laevigatum

Crepis capillaris

Crepis biennis

Crepis vesicaria

Marsh Hawk's-beard
Crepis paludosa

A **perennial with rather thin hairless stems**, branching above into a flat-topped inflorescence of yellow heads. The **upper stem-leaves are stalkless with clasping bases and long-pointed auricles; all leaves are hairless, and thin in texture. The involucral bracts are woolly, with many dark glandular hairs**, and the outer, shorter bracts are appressed. The **pappus-hairs are brownish**.

Common in wet places in north Britain and south to S Wales and the Midlands; throughout Ireland; absent from the Outer Hebrides, Orkney and Shetland.

P   80cm   Summer

Leafy Hawkweeds
Hieracium Sects. *Sabauda* and *Foliosa*

The many leafy-stemmed species in these sections are easily distinguished from umbellate hawkweed by the **much broader, often ovate leaves with flat, not turned-back, margins**. They are often tall, robust plants.

Common on hedgebanks, wood margins and roadsides in England and Wales, rarer in Scotland and Ireland.

P   1.2m   Summer

Hawkweeds

The remaining plants on this page are all hawkweeds (*Hieracium*). Like the dandelions, most are apomictic, and very many different microspecies have been described. Our small selection illustrates the wide range in the genus.

Hawkweeds are closely related to hawk's-beards and, indeed, the marsh hawk's-beard has rather intermediate characters. Technically, they differ especially in 2 characters: the involucral bracts are not arranged in 2 rows, as in *Crepis*, and the pappus-hairs on the ripe achene are brownish, not white. (It is in this latter character that the marsh hawk's-beard resembles *Hieracium*.)

Common Hawkweeds
Hieracium Sect. *Vulgata*

A whole group of species **distinguished by the presence of a basal rosette of leaves at flowering time, and stems with few, usually broad and slightly stalked leaves**.

The commonest kind of hawkweed in lowland Britain, containing several widespread, and many local, microspecies; rare in Ireland.

P   80cm   Summer

Umbellate Hawkweed
Hieracium umbellatum

An unmistakable yellow Composite with **slender, erect, very leafy stems, with no basal rosette, terminating in a more or less flat-topped inflorescence of** yellow heads. The **leaves are narrowly lance-shaped with turned-back margins**. The involucral bracts are nearly hairless, with recurved tips. Contains both sexually-reproducing and apomictic variants.

Common in lowland Britain, on heaths and open woodland on acid soils, rather rare in Scotland and Ireland.

P   80cm   Summer

Alpine Hawkweed
Hieracium holosericeum

Many hawkweeds are restricted to small areas of mountain rocks. The true 'alpine hawkweeds' (Sect. *Alpina*) are beautiful plants with almost leafless stems bearing a single large head. Of these the most widespread is *H. holosericeum*, found in the Scottish mountains, the Lake District and Snowdonia.

P   20cm   Summer

Mouse-ear Hawkweed
Hieracium pilosella

This neat, far-spreading little plant is very different from the other native hawkweeds. It produces **long, white runners bearing new over-wintering rosettes of leaves. The rosette-leaves are oblong-pointed, thick in texture, green above and white-felted beneath. The heads are solitary on (usually) leafless stalks**.

Common throughout nearly all British Isles (absent from Shetland) in grassland, heaths, banks and walls.

P   25cm   Summer

Fox-and-cubs
Hieracium aurantiacum

The 'odd man out' among hawkweeds, unmistakable with its **rich orange-brown heads on leafless stalks**. The plant spreads freely by long, leafy runners, and at the base are long, more or less lance-shaped, hairy leaves.

Introduced as a garden plant and now widely naturalised on roadsides, railway banks and waste places throughout much of Britain, and recorded from several places in Ireland.

P   30cm   Summer

Crepis paludosa

Hieracium umbellatum

Leafy Hawkweed

Common Hawkweed

Hieracium holosericeum

Hieracium pilosella

Hieracium aurantiacum

Monocotyledons

The remaining pages are devoted to Monocotyledons, containing 2 large groups, the 'lilies' (*Liliaceae* and related families) and the orchids (*Orchidaceae*). The most important family is the grasses (*Gramineae*), but they are not included in this book.

Most monocotyledons are easily recognised by their very narrow, parallel-veined 'grass-like' leaves. Technically the character which gives the name is that there is only a single seed-leaf (cotyledon) in the germinated seedling, not a pair.

Monocotyledonous flowers have parts typically in **threes**.

Water-plantain
Alisma plantago-aquatica

The common name is very descriptive, because the **large, hairless, ovate basal leaves have the general shape of the greater plantain** (p.162). **The tall, branched, leafless stems bear many small flowers with 3 pale lilac petals and 3 sepals; later a single ring of small achenes develops**.

Throughout most of British Isles by lakes, ponds and slow-moving rivers, often standing in shallow water, but absent from much of N Scotland, the Outer Hebrides, Orkney and Shetland.
P 1m Summer

Narrow-leaved Water-plantain
Alisma lanceolatum

Like the common water-plantain, but with **narrow, lance-shaped leaves gradually narrowed into a long stalk**. The **flowers are usually pinkish, and open (on sunny days) in the mornings**, the petals becoming crumpled by the late afternoon. In the common water-plantain 'new' flowers open each afternoon.

Throughout the range of the common water-plantain and in similar places, but less common.
P 1m Summer

Lesser Water-plantain
Baldellia ranunculoides

A much smaller plant than the preceding, with **narrow, hairless, long-stalked leaves**, and fewer, larger whitish flowers on long individual stalks. **The heads of achenes are more or less spherical resembling those of the buttercups** (*Ranunculus* p.4). Sometimes the stems are more or less prostrate and root freely, producing solitary flowers.

Locally common on muddy and peaty ground, often rooted in very shallow water, throughout most of the British Isles but absent from N Scotland, Orkney and Shetland.
P 20cm(tall) Summer

Arrowhead
Sagittaria sagittifolia

A very handsome **water plant, with large arrow-shaped leaves rising above the water surface, and very different strap-shaped submerged leaves and ovate floating ones**. The white flowers are on leafless stems in small whorls of 3–5; the lower flowers are female and the upper male.

Throughout most of England and E and C Ireland, in shallow water; rare in Wales and almost absent from Scotland.
P 80cm Summer

Flowering-rush
Butomus umbellatus

Undoubtedly one of our most attractive water plants, often grown in garden ponds. The long, thin leaves are as tall as the smooth, leafless flowering stems which terminate in **umbels of handsome large flowers with 6 pink 'petals', the outer 3 rather smaller**. In the centre of the flower are 9 pink stamens and 6 carpels.

In shallow water through much of England, but not very common; in Ireland commonest in the north-east; rare in Wales and absent, except as a garden introduction, from Scotland.
P 1.5m Summer

Frogbit
Hydrocharis morsus-ranae

A remarkable **floating plant with long runners producing bunches of roots and groups of floating leaves at the nodes**. The **leaves are more or less circular, like very small water-lily leaves**, and the white flowers arise on short stalks above the water. There are **separate male and female flowers, both with 3 broad, white, rather crumpled petals with a yellow spot near the base**.

In ponds and ditches in lowland England, but much decreased. Absent from Scotland, rare in Wales and mainly in the Central Plain in Ireland.
P 5cm(above water) Summer

Marsh Arrowgrass
Triglochin palustris

A curious wind-pollinated plant with an odd floral structure, easy to overlook. It has **long, narrow, grass-like, half-cylindrical leaves** and a **very long 'spike' of small pale flowers**. It could be mistaken for a plantain (*Plantago*), but **the flowers can easily be seen with a hand-lens to have their parts in threes** (not fours as in *Plantago*).

In marshy ground, often in tall grass, throughout British Isles but commoner in the north.
P 60cm Summer

Sea Arrowgrass
Triglochin maritima

Like a robust, sea-side version of the marsh arrowgrass, with an even greater general similarity to a plantain (especially the sea plantain, *Plantago maritima*, whose leaves are also very narrow. **The many-flowered inflorescence develops spreading fruits consisting of 6 separate carpels**.

Round the whole of British Isles in coastal turf.
P 60cm Late summer

Both arrowgrasses have a very characteristic smell, not unpleasant, when broken – often an easy way to detect their presence!

Alisma plantago-aquatica

Alisma lanceolatum

Baldellia ranunculoides

Sagittaria sagittifolia

Butomus umbellatus

Hydrocharis morsus-ranae

Triglochin palustris

Triglochin maritima

Lily Family (Liliaceae)

On this and the next two pages we have members of the lily family, *Liliaceae*. They have regular flowers with 6 coloured perianth segments ('petals'), 6 stamens, and a superior ovary which develops into a capsule or a berry. True lilies (*Lilium*) are familiar garden plants, but only one, the Martagon lily, has any claim to be a British native.

Bog Asphodel
Narthecium ossifragum
A very attractive northern 'lily', similar to the famous asphodels of the Mediterranean. **It is a hairless perennial with creeping rhizome and numerous narrow 'iris-like' basal leaves held vertically and in 2 rows. The narrow racemes have bright yellow flowers** which turn deep orange as the capsules develop.

In peat-bogs, moorland and on wet acid rocks on mountains, locally abundant in the north and west of the British Isles, but rare or absent from much of the Midlands and E England.
P   30cm   Late summer

Scottish Asphodel
Tofieldia pusilla
As its common name implies, this small relative of the bog asphodel is a northern plant. The leaves are flat and 'iris-like' but **the small white flowers are densely packed into a head on a long, almost leafless stalk.**

By springs and streams on mountains on basic rock in N and C Scotland; also in Upper Teesdale in N England.
P   20cm   Summer

Lily-of-the-valley
Convallaria majalis
A favourite garden plant familiar to all, **with a long creeping rhizome from which arise hairless, ovate leaves**. The **leafless flowering** stems come from within the wrapped leaf-bases and **finish in a raceme of pretty, scented, hanging, bell-like white flowers. The fruit is a round, red berry.**

In dry woodland especially on limestone, not uncommon in England and E Wales, rare in W Wales and Scotland, and only introduced in Ireland.
P   20cm   Late spring

Solomon's-seal
Polygonatum multiflorum
A familiar garden plant (though the commonest garden plant is a hybrid of this and angular Solomon's-seal). The **long, creeping rhizomes send up smooth, hairless stems with several ovate leaves along the length and attractive, drooping, tubular white flowers in the leaf axils.** The fruit is a berry, blue-black when ripe.

Local in limestone woods in England and Wales, and often introduced from gardens, not native in Scotland and Ireland.
P   80cm   Early summer

Angular Solomon's-seal
Polygonatum odoratum
Like the common solomon's-seal, but **with a shorter angular stem, and somewhat larger flowers singly or in pairs in the leaf-axils** (in the common species the flowers are grouped in 3–5).

Rather rare in limestone woods in W and N England and S Wales (Brecon).
P   25cm   Summer

Fritillary
Fritillaria meleagris
Often called 'snake's-head fritillary' this strikingly-beautiful wildflower is also often grown in gardens and the grounds of large houses. The **hairless stem arises from a small bulb and bears a few very narrow leaves and** at the top **a single, large bell-shaped nodding flower** which is purple mottled with pale spots (rarely white).

In wet meadows in England and Wales, very local, but abundant in a few places; introduced widely.
P   50cm   Spring

Meadow Saffron
Colchicum autumnale
Often also called 'autumn crocus', this remarkable flower is not related to the true crocuses (p.210). The **large crocus-like pale reddish-purple flowers arise from a swollen corm in the late summer,** and are succeeded the following spring by **very large, stalked capsules. The more or less oblong glossy-green leaves appear in spring and are withered by flowering-time.**

Damp pastures and woods usually in basic soils in England, Wales and SE Ireland; rare and introduced in Scotland. Much reduced by ploughing of pasture.
P   15cm   Late summer

Martagon Lily
Lilium martagon
The tall stems of the martagon lily arise from **large bulbs and bear several widely-separated whorls of lance-shaped leaves with some smaller, alternate leaves near the inflorescence.** The **large, nodding flowers have pale purple, dark-spotted perianth segments curled backwards, below which hang free the red-brown anthers.**

Commonly grown in gardens and certainly introduced in many woods in England and Wales, but possibly native in Surrey and Gloucestershire.
P   1m   Late summer

Narthecium ossifragum

Tofieldia pusilla

Convallaria majalis

Polygonatum multiflorum

Polygonatum odoratum

Fritillaria meleagris

Colchicum autumnale

Lilium martagon

Star-of-Bethlehem
Ornithogalum umbellatum
A hairless plant arising from a bulb, with a group of **long, narrow, basal leaves with a white stripe down the midrib,** and **leafless flowering stems terminating in a rather flat-topped raceme of 5–15 flowers.** The 6 white perianth segments have a broad green stripe down the back, and open widely only in the sun. The fruit is a capsule.

Perhaps native in grassland in E England, but widespread in Britain as a naturalised garden plant and extending to NE Scotland; absent from Ireland.
P 30cm Spring

Spiked Star-of-Bethlehem
Ornithogalum pyrenaicum
Like Star-of-Bethlehem, but **the leaves wither early,** and **the many flowers are on long stalks in an elongated raceme.** The petals are very narrow and greenish-white.

A very local woodland plant in England from Bedfordshire to W Somerset, common enough in the area round Bath to yield the young shoots sold as 'Bath asparagus' in the market.
P 80cm Summer

Yellow Star-of-Bethlehem
Gagea lutea
This charming little woodland plant is obviously related to *Ornithogalum*. It has a single, often curled, narrowly lance-shaped basal leaf and a delicate flowering stem with 1–5 pretty yellow flowers and (usually) 2 small, leafy bracts. The perianth segments are green-backed.

Apparently shy of flowering and so often overlooked. Throughout much of Britain, in damp woods and pastures on lime-rich soils, very local, and commonest in N and C England; absent from Ireland.
P 25cm Spring

Bluebell
Hyacinthoides non-scripta
(Endymion non-scriptus)
In many ways our most characteristic 'British' wildflower, producing **sheets of blue in woodlands in spring.** The narrow leaves arise from the bulb and are followed by **the juicy, leafless stems with blue (rarely white) bell-shaped flowers.** Later in the year the rather large capsules (up to 1.5cm) form, ripen and shed their seed, persisting on dried pale brown stalks.

Common in woods and hedgerows throughout nearly all the British Isles.
P 50cm Spring

Spring Squill
Scilla verna
An attractive little plant with **3–6 narrow, shiny, often twisted leaves arising** from the bulb **before the short, stocky, leafless stem bearing 2–12 pale violet-blue flowers with bracts.** The perianth segments spread widely (quite unlike the related bluebell).

Locally abundant in coastal grassland in N and W Britain from Shetland to Devon; rare on the E coast, and only on the E coast in Ireland.
P 15cm Spring

Autumn Squill
Scilla autumnalis
Looks quite different from the spring squill, although it is closely related. The **numerous small flowers are in a rather dense raceme, and there are no bracts. The leaves appear after the flowers, in the autumn.**

A very local plant of coastal grassland in S England, commonest in Devon and Cornwall.
P 25cm Late summer

Grape Hyacinth
Muscari neglectum
This plant is familiar in gardens as an early-flowering 'bulb' (though, strictly, garden plants are usually not the same as the the wild one). Its **dense head of small, rich blue, drooping flowers have a characteristic pitcher-shape, with a narrow white-fringed mouth.**

Dry grassland, especially in Breckland in E Anglia; widely recorded elsewhere (but probably mostly plants of garden origin).
P 25cm Spring

Herb-Paris
Paris quadrifolia
This extraordinary plant needs no description, only a photograph: there is no other British wildflower with which it could possibly be confused. **The hairless stems** arise from a creeping rhizome and **bear a ring of usually 4 quite broad leaves** from the middle of which arises **the single terminal greenish flower with its parts in fours.**

Local in damp woodland on lime-rich soils throughout much of Britain, though absent from W Scotland, Orkney and Shetland, and Ireland.
P 40cm Early summer

Butcher's-broom
Ruscus aculeatus
Our only woody member of the lily family, quite different from all others. The true leaves are reduced to small brownish scales, and **the evergreen, thick 'leaves' are actually flattened stems. The small, white, 'lily-type' flowers sit stalkless in the middle of these 'leaves',** and are succeeded (in female plants) by red berries.

Widespread in dry woodland. Commonest in S England, extending north to N Wales and Norfolk, but commonly cultivated and recorded much further north; not native in Ireland.
P 80cm Early spring

Ornithogalum umbellatum

Ornithogalum pyrenaicum

Gagea lutea

Hyacinthoides non-scripta

Scilla verna

Scilla autumnalis

Muscari neglectum

Paris quadrifolia

Ruscus aculeatus

Onions and Garlics

Everyone knows the genus *Allium*, in the shape of the familiar onions and leeks of our vegetable garden. They all have bulbs, with or without rhizomes as well, and have the familiar smell of garlic or onion when the leaves or stems are broken. The flowers have the typical 'lily' structure, and the 6 perianth segments are hardly joined at the base. Several species are wild in the British Isles.

Chives
Allium schoenoprasum

The wild plant is the same as the cultivated chives, a **tufted perennial with long, thin, cylindrical leaves** and **spherical heads of pretty pale purple or pink flowers on leafless stems**. The **leaves are often characteristically twisted** in the wild plant (shown well in the photograph).

Native in rocky pastures and on rocks by streams usually on limestone, sometimes locally abundant, with a scattered distribution in England and Wales, S Scotland and (very rare) Ireland. Occasionally also recorded as a garden escape.
P   40cm   Summer

Wild Onion
Allium vineale

An 'onion' with leaves similar to chives, but somewhat grooved on one side, and **long, leafless flowering stems bearing curious, rather greenish heads, often with** flowers replaced by **small bulbous plantlets (bulbils)**. Flowers, if present, stalked, pinkish or pale green. At the base of the mature head is a **pale brownish bract (spathe) which covers the young head, and falls off early**.

On roadsides and field margins. Widespread in British Isles, formerly a common weed in parts of E England. Absent from Orkney and Shetland.
P   80cm   Summer

Field Garlic
Allium oleraceum

Rather like the wild onion, and commonly with bulbils as well as flowers, but **with a spathe of 2 very long-pointed, persistent, green bracts sheathing the base of the flower-head**. The pink flowers are on long, slender stalks.

Perhaps originally introduced; in similar places to the wild onion, but less common, and absent from W and N Scotland and most of Ireland (except the south-east).
P   80cm   Summer

Three-cornered Leek
Allium triquetrum

Easily recognised **by its head of large, white, rather bluebell-like nodding flowers early in the spring**, and – as the name implies – its **3-angled stem**. The few basal leaves are narrow, flat, and rather pale green.

A native of the W Mediterranean, now rather common in hedgebanks and waste ground in SW England, S Wales and S Ireland; still rare elsewhere, but increasing.
P   50cm   Spring

Few-flowered Leek
Allium paradoxum

Rather like three-cornered leek, but with **very few flowers hanging out from the head on long slender stalks** and **many small, stalkless yellow bulbils like eggs inside a pale brownish spathe**. The single basal leaf is narrow, flat, bright green and shining.

This odd-looking onion relative comes to us from the Caucasus region. It is a not uncommon weed of gardens and waste ground in Britain, particularly in E Anglia and SE Scotland, and seems to be spreading.
P   50cm   Spring

Ramsons
Allium ursinum

Although obviously an 'onion' by its smell, ramsons is quite different from all the rest. It has **stalked, narrowly ovate, pointed basal leaves** with a general resemblance to those of the lily-of-the-valley, and a **rather flat-topped inflorescence of open, white, star-like flowers on long stalks**.

Rather common in wet woodland throughout most of the British Isles, though rare in NE Scotland, and in Ireland mainly in the north and east.
P   45cm   Late spring

Allium schoenoprasum

Allium vineale

Allium oleraceum

Allium triquetrum

Allium paradoxum

Allium ursinum

Wild Daffodil
Narcissus pseudonarcissus
Daffodils and their relatives (Family *Amaryllidaceae*) differ from lilies in one important character: the ovary is inferior, that is, it can be seen below the rest of the flower. The wild daffodil is unmistakable in spring **with its deep yellow 'trumpet' and 6 pale yellow, spreading perianth segments.** Garden daffodils are mainly hybrids of this and other species.

In damp grassland and woods, throughout England and Wales but commoner in the west; only a garden introduction in Scotland and Ireland.
P 35cm Early spring

Snowdrop
Galanthus nivalis
Our favourite winter-flowering 'bulb', with its charming **single, nodding white flowers. The 3 outer perianth segments are pure white and spread somewhat; the inner 3 form a bell-shaped centre, white with a green spot.** There is no 'trumpet' as in daffodil.

Perhaps native in damp woods in Wales and W England, but widely naturalised in Britain; very rare in Ireland.
P 20cm Winter

Summer Snowflake
Leucojum aestivum
A beautiful plant with a misleading name (it flowers in spring!), obviously related to the snowdrop, but **taller, with 3–7 flowers on the flowering stalk, and all 6 perianth segments alike, forming a bell-shaped, hanging flower.** The tips of the white 'bell' are marked with a pale green dot.

Sometimes called 'Loddon Lily' after the tributary of the R Thames where it grows and is a native plant in wet meadows and willow thickets. It is also native along the R Shannon in Ireland. Elsewhere in England, Wales and Ireland it may be introduced.
P 60cm Spring

Yellow Iris
Iris pseudacorus
Irises are so familiar in gardens they need no description. Members of the Family *Iridaceae* differ from lilies in having inferior ovaries and only 3 stamens, and often also have 'iris'-type leaves flattened in one plane. Our common yellow iris is a very handsome wild representative. It has a **thick rhizome and large yellow flowers, several on a smooth leafless stem.** The flower, though easy to recognise, has a complicated structure.

Common throughout British Isles in marshes, wet woods and by rivers and ditches.
P 1.5m Summer

Stinking Iris
Iris foetidissima
Our other wild iris is characterised by a **curious, unpleasant smell when its evergreen leaves are bruised,** and its **much smaller flowers,** though obviously 'irises', **are a rather dull purplish colour usually with pale yellow inner perianth.** In fruit, however, this iris comes into its own, producing **capsules that split open to reveal large orange-red seeds.**

Quite common in woods and hedgebanks on chalk and limestone in S and C England and Wales; only naturalised in Scotland and Ireland.
P 80cm Summer

Spring Crocus
Crocus vernus
No crocus is native, but the common purple, spring-flowering crocus of gardens is occasionally naturalised. The crocus flower resembles the meadow saffron, *Colchicum* (p.204), but they are not closely related, and technically they differ in stamen-number (3 in *Crocus*, 6 in *Colchicum*). **Crocus leaves are very narrow and channelled, with a white stripe on the back.**

In short turf in scattered localities in England and Wales; very rare in Scotland and Ireland. Native in European mountains, and long cultivated in Britain.
P 15cm Early spring

Montbretia
Tritonia x *crocosmiflora*
Formerly included by botanists in the genus *Montbretia* (hence the gardener's name), this very pretty garden plant has **flattened 'iris-type' foliage and long, spike-like 1-sided inflorescences on leafy stems.** The **orange-red flowers have a long, slightly curved tube and spreading perianth segments.**

Though the montbretia is a garden hybrid artificially produced by crossing two S African plants as recently as 1880, it is now widely grown and, especially in Ireland and the west of Britain, very widely naturalised.
P 80cm Late summer

Black Bryony
Tamus communis
Our only wild member of the very important tropical yam family *Dioscoreaceae*, the black bryony is unrelated to white bryony (see p.104), and indeed easily distinguished by its **undivided heart-shaped leaves**. It is a **vigorous climber from a large, swollen underground stem, producing groups of small greenish flowers succeeded** (on the female plants) **by pale red berries**.

Common in much of England and Wales in woods and hedgerows; very rare (and probably introduced) in Scotland and Ireland.
P – Summer

Narcissus pseudonarcissus

Galanthus nivalis

Leucojum aestivum

Iris pseudacorus

Iris foetidissima

Crocus vernus

Tritonia x *crocosmiflora*

Tamus communis

212 Helleborines

Orchid Family (Orchidaceae)

Orchids flowers consist of 3 sepals and 3 petals alternating with them. Two of the petals resemble the sepals but the third, the lip or labellum, has developed an immense range of shape and colour: some mimic insects like the bee and fly orchids, others, such as man orchid, may resemble us. Often the base of the labellum is extended into a tube or spur: short and broad in marsh-orchids, long and narrow in fragrant orchid. The inside of orchid flowers consists of male and female parts joined together in a central column with the stamens above the stigmas whilst the pollen grains are gathered into pollinia or pollen masses containing thousands of individual grains stuck together. Part of each pollinium is sticky and when an insect visits the flower it adheres to the top of its head. During flight the pollinium moves from vertical to horizontal and when the insect visits another flower it is in position to make contact with the stigma below the stamen and pollination occurs. Orchids have very light seed carried long distances by the wind: thus species often occur in new places miles from the next nearest plant (see drawings).

Narrow-leaved Helleborine
Cephalanthera longifolia
Another white helleborine, but taller with long, **narrow leaves**, often folded longitudinally, and held upright, when the upper may overtop the spike of flowers. In contrast the **bracts** amongst the flowers are short, **never longer than** the seed **pods**, whilst the 3 **sepals** of the somewhat smaller flowers are **pointed**, not rounded, **at the tip**.

Deciduous woods and shaded places thinly scattered throughout lowland British Isles, especially on lime-rich soils.
P   60cm   Late spring and summer

Violet Helleborine
Epipactis purpurata
Recognised by its clustered habit, **6–10 stems** growing **together**, each frequently **tinged with violet** and covered with short hairs above. The spirally arranged **leaves** are usually **at least twice as long as broad** in the middle of the stem and **violet-tinged**, at least beneath. The numerous flowers have the lower bracts exceeding them in length. The **outer part of the lip** is **as long as broad**, whitish with a down-turned tip, and an elongated, faintly violet, central boss.

Woods on lime-rich soils in England north to Shropshire.
P   70cm   Summer and autumn

White Helleborine
Cephalanthera damasonium
Species of *Cephalanthera* are recognised by their **stalkless flowers**, the **absence of a spur** and the **short lip with a constriction in the middle**. This lip is **hidden by the sepals and the petals** except for a brief period. White helleborine has **oval leaves**, leaf-like **bracts** amongst the flowers which are **longer than** the seed **pods**, and **sepals with rounded tips**.

Deciduous woodlands, especially beech on the chalk, in England north to about Cambridge, with an outlier in E Yorkshire.
P   50cm   Spring and early summer

Marsh Helleborine
Epipactis palustris
Like *Cephalanthera* species of *Epipactis* are recognised by the **absence of a spur** and by having the **lip constricted in the middle**, but the **flowers** are much more showy, spreading or hanging down **on a stalk** and with the **lip not concealed by the sepals** for most of the flowering period. Marsh helleborine **spreads by long underground stems**. The **outer part of the lip** has a delicate **frilly** margin and is **joined to the inner by a very narrow hinge**.

Fens and wet dunes scattered throughout lowlands but only in SE Scotland.
P   45cm   Summer

Dark-red Helleborine
Epipactis atrorubens
Instantly separated from other species of helleborine by the **leaves arranged in ranks on opposite sides of the densely hairy stem** and by all the parts of the flowers being a dull reddish-purple. The **outer part of the lip**, which is about **twice as long as broad**, has a turned-down tip, **with a bright red, warty area near the base**.

Thinly scattered on limestone rocks from Derbyshire northwards and in the Burren and Connemara areas of W Ireland.
P   30cm   Summer

Broad-leaved Helleborine
Epipactis helleborine
The commonest and tallest helleborine with **1–3 stems together**, **spirally-arranged oval leaves**, **almost as broad as long** in the middle of the stem but much narrower above, and spikes of up to 50 flowers with green to deep purple sepals and a rosy or greenish-white **outer part to the lip** which is **broader than long**.

Woods, copses, wood margins and screes on a wide range of soils throughout lowland British Isles but rare and only coastal in N Scotland.
P   80cm   Summer and autumn

Autumn Lady's-tresses
Spiranthes spiralis
This small orchid, flowering from August onwards, cannot be mistaken for any other with its **glandular hairy stems and white flowers arranged in a single row, spirally twisted round the stem** like a braid of lady's hair. The tiny flowers have a **frilly lip** and produce a sweet scent by day attractive to pollinating bumble bees.

Frequent in short grassland, especially on lime-rich soils, in the southern half of the British Isles, but less predictable near its northern limits.
P   20cm   Late summer and autumn

dorsal petaloid sepal
lateral petaloid sepal
lateral petal
pollinia (stamens)
lip or labellum

Orchid flower – from front

lateral petal
pollinium (stamen)
central column
stigma
lip or labellum
spur
twisted ovary

Orchid flower – from side

Cephalanthera damasonium

Cephalanthera longifolia

Epipactis palustris

Epipactis helleborine

Epipactis purpurata

Epipactis atrorubens

Spiranthes spiralis

Common Twayblade
Listera ovata
One of our commonest orchids, recognised by the conspicuous 'tway blades', the **single pair of round**, more or less **opposite leaves, up to 20cm across**, somewhat **below the middle of the hairy stem** which carries a **long spike**, up to 25cm, **of yellowish-green flowers** which look like a man. The flowers lack a spur but have **lips up to 1.5cm deeply divided to almost half way into 2 parallel segments**.

Woods, hedgerows, damp pastures and sand-dunes on lime-rich soils throughout British Isles to 600m in N Pennines.
P 60cm Summer

Lesser Twayblade
Listera cordata
A secretive plant found under old heather bushes with *Sphagnum* moss round their roots. Readily recognised by the **pair of small**, more or less opposite, **rounded leaves, up to 2.5cm across, about ⅖ the way up the stem**. The slightly hairy stem carries a **short spike**, less than 6cm, **of 6–12 reddish-green flowers** with **lips c.4mm long divided into 2 diverging segments**.

Mountain woods, and moors, locally common in Scotland, where it ascends to 800m, and scattered throughout Ireland, the northern half of Wales and

England, with outliers in New Forest and Exmoor.
P 20cm Summer and autumn

Bird's-nest Orchid
Neottia nidus-avis
English and scientific names both refer to the blunt, fleshy roots which radiate from a solid core like an untidy nest. A **leafless, brownish saprophyte** feeding on humus in the soil. Erect **stems covered in** numerous **brown scales** carry **spikes of pale brown flowers** with a **lip c.1.2cm long divided into 2 diverging, round-tipped lobes**. The spike persists – the skeleton may stand for a full year.

In woods on lime-rich soils throughout lowlands, but only common in southern half of England.
P 45cm Summer

Creeping Lady's-tresses
Goodyera repens
Like autumn lady's-tresses (p.212) it has **small white flowers in a slightly twisted spiral** but differs in having long, **creeping underground stems**, net-veined leaves and a **lip** in which the **outer part is narrow and spout-shaped** not frilly and down-turned as in *Spiranthes*.

Occasional in pine and birch woods in N England and in Scotland to over 300m; locally also in E Anglia, the only area of overlap with autumn lady's-tresses.
P 25cm Summer

Coralroot Orchid
Corallorhiza trifida
A **small, brown saprophyte** named after the coral-like, cream or pale yellow, much-branched, fleshy underground stems. The **slender, hairy aerial stems** have only **2–4 sheathing scales, in the lower half**, and carry a **lax spike of 2–12 inconspicuous flowers** with a small **lip, up to 5mm long**, which is **3-lobed**, though the 2 lateral ones are often hard to see or even absent: the lip is **whitish with crimson lines or spots**.

Thinly scattered in damp, mossy woods from Yorkshire to the Moray Firth: mainly lowland.
P 25cm Late spring and summer

Musk Orchid
Herminium monorchis
A small, fragrant **greenish-yellow orchid** recognised by **having a pair of basal leaves** like twayblade, but **elliptical with acute points** and 1–2 smaller ones on the stem above. The **spikes are many-flowered, each flower with sepals almost forming a hood** and all the **petals strap-shaped with pointed lateral lobes** in the middle of each side.

Short grassland on chalk and limestone in England from Bedfordshire southwards.
P 15cm Summer

Frog Orchid
Coeloglossum viride
One of our commonest orchids but easily overlooked because green flowers and green leaves are camouflaged in grassland. Recognised by its cluster of **oval basal leaves, narrow stem leaves** and the **conspicuous bracts amongst the flowers**. The **sepals** almost join to **hide the narrow lateral petals: the lip has parallel sides with a** pronounced **notch at the tip**. Smells faintly of honey attractive to insects.

Short turf, sand-dunes, and mountain rocks, usually lime-rich, throughout British Isles to 900m in Scottish Highlands.
P 25cm Summer

Listera ovata

Listera cordata

Neottia nidus-avis

Goodyera repens

Corallorhiza trifida

Herminium monorchis

Coeloglossum viride

Fragrant Orchid
Gymnadenia conopsea
One of our most colourful orchids, recognised by the tall, **dense, cylindrical spikes of reddish-violet, very fragrant flowers**, smelling of clove carnation, each with a **long, slender, curved spur** almost twice as long as the ovary. The upper sepal and lateral petals are close together forming a hood, whilst the **lip** of the flower is **divided to half way into 3**, more or less equal, lobes.

Lime-rich grassland throughout British Isles to 600m in Scottish Highlands. A large form, up to 80cm, with darker flowers and broader leaves grows in marshes.
P   40cm   Summer

Small-white Orchid
Pseudorchis albida
A small, greenish-white orchid with a **short, cylindrical spike of flowers with broad, blunt conical spurs** with **5 sepals and petals** close together **forming a hood** and the lip close to the hood so that the **flowers** appear **bell-shaped**. The **lip** is distinctive **with 3 pointed lobes**, the central one longer than the other two. The flowers are faintly vanilla scented.

Pastures in the upland parts of British Isles to 500m in Scottish Highlands.
P   30m   Summer

Greater Butterfly-orchid
Platanthera chlorantha
Butterfly-orchids are recognised by their tall spikes of large, **white flowers** with long, slender spurs and long, narrow lips. Greater butterfly-orchid is the **taller, up to 40cm**, with a **longer spur, 1.9–2.8cm, curved downwards and forwards** sometimes forming a semi-circle; when the flower is seen from the front the **pollinia** are **diverging** – 2mm apart above, 4mm apart below (see drawing).

Woods and grassland, especially on lime-rich soils, throughout British Isles except N and E Scotland, to 450m in N Pennines.
P   40cm   Spring and summer

Lesser Butterfly-orchid
Platanthera bifolia
Similar to greater butterfly-orchid but **shorter, up to 30cm** high, with flowers having **shorter spurs, 1.5–2.0cm, held horizontally**, and with lips only 6–10mm long. When viewed from the front the **pollinia** are seen to be **parallel**, *c.*2mm apart both above and below (see drawing).

Wood, grassland and heather moors on lime-rich and acid soils throughout lowlands to 400m in Lake District; commonest in N and W.
P   30cm   Spring and summer

Both species are fragrant, the scent strongest at night attracting moths which dip their probosces into the nectar-filled spurs.

Bee Orchid
Ophrys apifera
Recognised by its **beautifully marked lip**, about 1.5cm long, **resembling** the velvety body of a female **bumble bee**. The lip is 3-lobed, the **lateral lobes** small, **hairy, protruding** forwards and upwards, easily seen in the upper flower in the picture. The 2 other petals are small, narrow and pinkish-green: in contrast the **3 sepals are large, rose-pink or whitish** in the front and greenish on the back.

Copses, banks and grassland on lime-rich, often disturbed soils throughout lowland England, Wales and Ireland.
P   45cm   Summer

Early Spider-orchid
Ophrys sphegodes
Though the **lip** is similar in shape and size to the bee orchid it is distinguished by **having** a **shiny, bluish H or horseshoe-shaped mark on its velvety, purplish-brown surface**, frequently **poorly developed lateral lobes**, **3 sepals** which are **green**, not rose-coloured, and lateral petals which are greenish-yellow and blunt, often with wavy margins.

A rare plant confined to lime-rich grassland in the extreme south of England from Dorset to Kent.
P   35cm   Spring and early summer

Fly Orchid
Ophrys insectifera
A difficult species to see in woodland shade but easily distinguished by the **long and purplish-brown, apparently 4-lobed, lip with a transverse patch of shining blue across the middle**: this together with the **other 2 petals**, reduced to narrow purplish-brown protrusions which **look like antennae**, give the whole a fly-like appearance. The **3 sepals are oval and a pale yellowish-green**.

A local plant of woods, scrub, grassy hillsides and fens on lime-rich soils in England, N Wales and central Ireland.
P   60cm   Spring and summer

Gymnadenia conopsea

Pseudorchis albida

Platanthera chlorantha

Platanthera bifolia

POLLINIA

Platanthera chlorantha

P. bifolia

Ophrys apifera

Ophrys sphegodes

Ophrys insectifera

Lady Orchid
Orchis purpurea
All species of *Orchis* can be recognised by the **flowers having short, fairly broad spurs**, and **all the sepals and the 2 lateral petals** close together **forming a helmet** or hood, or only the 2 lateral sepals spreading: the **lip** is usually 3-lobed. Lady orchid is separated by the **helmet** being blotched **dark reddish-purple** whilst the **pink lip** is **covered in** darker, **papillose spots**. The **spur** is c. **half as long as the ovary**.
Open woods on chalk in SE England.
P 40cm Spring

Burnt Orchid
Orchis ustulata
An *Orchis* in which sepals and petals, except the lip, form a helmet and which has a **descending spur** and a **lip which is man-shaped** with a central lobe much longer than the 2 lateral 'arms', and divided at the tip into 2 'legs'. The lip is c.**6mm long, white, and reddish-purple spotted**: the spur is c. **¼ the length of the ovary**.
Scattered in limestone grassland throughout England but declining.
P 20cm Late spring and early summer

Green-winged Orchid
Orchis morio
Though having all the sepals and petals except the lip forming **a helmet**, the **lip is not man-shaped but broader than long** with **3 equal lobes**, the lateral reddish-purple and reflexed, the central paler with dark spots: the 'green wings' refer to the **conspicuous green veins on the sepals**. The spur is **almost as long as the ovary**.
In damp, lime-rich meadows throughout lowland England and Wales and in central Ireland, but declining through drainage.
P 40cm Late spring and early summer

Early-purple Orchid
Orchis mascula
A common orchid of woodland, and of grassland in the west, recognised by the rosettes of **glossy, blunt leaves with round black spots** and blotches and by the **purple flowers with a stout ascending spur as long as or longer than the ovary**. The **lateral sepals** do not join the other sepal and 2 petals to form a helmet but are **spreading or folded back**. The **3-lobed**, reddish-purple **lip** is **about as broad as long**, paler at the base and dotted with darker purple.
Lime-rich soils throughout British Isles to 900m in Scottish Highlands.
P 60cm Spring and summer

Common Spotted-orchid
Dactylorhiza fuchsii
Spotted-orchids are recognised by their **spotted leaves**, and lips **covered in a network of reddish lines or dots** on a paler pink background. Common spotted-orchid is separated by its **7–12 leaves** and by its **leaf-spots being transversely elongated**, by the **central lobe of the lip** being **triangular-pointed** and **longer than the lateral lobes** and by the markings being a symmetrical pattern of lines. **Spur** c.**1.5mm across**.
Woods, meadows and marshes, usually lime-rich, throughout British Isles to 900m in Scottish Highlands.
P 60cm Summer

Heath Spotted-orchid
Dactylorhiza maculata
Like common spotted-orchid but distinguished from it by the **leaves** being **marked by dark, circular spots, or without any**, and by the **lip** which **has a very small central lobe shorter than the lobes on either side**, whilst the **markings are a mixture of dots and short lines** on a, usually, pale background. **Spur less than 1mm across**.
Damp acid open woods, heaths and peaty grassland throughout British Isles but rare in E England; to 900m in Scotland.
P 50cm Late spring and summer

Early Marsh-orchid
Dactylorhiza incarnata
The marsh-orchids are difficult to separate: not only are species similar in appearance but they vary within themselves so that, in one damp meadow, the lips of no two plants are alike. Early marsh-orchid can, however, be distinguished from the rest by **beginning to flower in May**, several weeks before others, and by the lateral lobes of the **diamond-shaped**, usually pink, **lips** which are **strongly folded back** towards the stem. **Spur over 2mm across**.
Marshes, fens and damp dunes throughout British Isles.
P 60cm Late spring and summer

Southern Marsh-orchid
Dactylorhiza praetermissa
As the name implies this is the commonest marsh-orchid in southern England and S Wales coming into flower in June. Recognised by its **height, up to 60cm**, its long, unspotted **leaves, up to 20cm**, and the rich, reddish-lilac flowers with **lips up to 1.4cm across**, variously 3-lobed or undivided and **marked with dots and lines in a central elliptical area**. **Spur very stout up to 3mm across**.
Wet meadows, marshes and fens, usually lime-rich, north to Lancashire and S Northumberland.
P 60cm Summer

Northern Marsh-orchid
Dactylorhiza purpurella
Totally replaces southern marsh-orchid in the northern half of British Isles A shorter plant, usually **under 25cm high**, with **leaves** which may **have** small, circular spots in the upper half and **broadly hooded tips**. The smaller flowers are rich purple with diamond-shaped **lips up to 1cm across**, 3-lobed or undivided, **marked with dark red loops and spots** over most of the surface. **Spur stout** but not exceeding **2.5mm across**.
Wet meadows, marshes and fens north of a line from Pembrokeshire to E Yorkshire.
P 25cm Summer

Orchis purpurea

Orchis ustulata

Orchis morio

Orchis mascula

Dactylorhiza fuchsii

Dactylorhiza maculata

Dactylorhiza incarnata

Dactylorhiza praetermissa

Dactylorhiza purpurella

Man Orchid
Aceras anthropophorum
So called because the **greenish-yellow lip** of each flower **strongly resembles** the body of **a man**, complete with arms and legs, **hanging by his head**, which is **'hidden' by** all the sepals and petals, except the lip, being close together forming **a helmet or hood**. Unlike other 'helmeted' species man orchid has **no spur**. Develops a smell of new-mown hay on drying.

Lime-rich grassland in SE England north to Derbyshire, but declining.
P 40cm Summer

Pyramidal Orchid
Anacamptis pyramidalis
A frequent and unmistakable orchid with its **pyramid-shaped heads of flowers** varying in colour from pale pink to deep purplish-red but usually **pale rose**, each with a **prominent, unmarked lip divided into 3 equal lobes** and a fine **spur only 0.5mm wide and c.1.2cm long**, longer than the ovary. Emits a foxy smell attractive to day- and night-flying moths.

Scattered in open woodland, scrub, and grassland on lime-rich soils throughout England, Wales and Ireland but very rare, and only coastal, in Scotland.
P 50cm Summer

Sweet-flag
Acorus calamus
Well-named as it has **leaves like a flag** and all parts give off a fragrant, somewhat sickly, **smell of tangerines** when crushed. The **leaves** can be distinguished from all others which are long, narrow and flat by **having undulations along the margin**. The tightly-packed spike of **yellowish-green**, hermaphrodite flowers, the **spadix, held at an angle of 45°**, is unmistakable. Ripe seed never produced here.

Introduced in 17th century. Now established on the margins of rivers, canals, lakes and ponds throughout lowland England; rare elsewhere.
P 1m Late spring and summer

Lords-and-Ladies
Arum maculatum
Recognised by the **glossy, arrow-shaped leaves** which begin to **grow in spring**. Later a **large green and purple** sheath or **spathe** appears, tapering to a point and twice as long as, and **enclosing, a long, fleshy, purple** (rarely yellow) **organ, the spadix**, with separate male and **female flowers** in rings at the base, the female **at the bottom**. The latter **develop red berries which are poisonous**. Forms with spotted or unspotted leaves occur.

Woods, copses and hedge-banks throughout British Isles except northern half of Scotland.
P 50cm Spring

Italian Lords-and-Ladies
Arum italicum
Differs from Lords-and-Ladies by having the **leaves growing in the autumn** and persisting through the winter and by the sheath or spathe being 3 times as long as the **orange-yellow spadix** which it encloses. The leaves are variable, some having conspicuous white veins, some with darker spots.

A plant of light shade in rough places, usually near the sea, along the S coasts of England and Wales.
P 30cm Spring

Aceras anthropophorum

Anacamptis pyramidalis

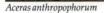

Acorus calamus

Arum maculatum

Arum italicum

Index

	PINK/ROSE	RED/PURPLE	BLUE/VIOLET
	This includes all flowers which are called pink, deep pink or rose. See also RED/PURPLE	With red and purple are all those flowers which are bright red, carmine or reddish-purple. When in doubt, look also at PINK/ROSE.	Within blue and violet are included all those flowers in which blue is the predominant colour with only a tinge of redness.
0–2 petals irregular flowers		Honeysuckle *171* **xxi**	Common Milkwort *29* **xix**
4 petals regular flowers	Water Mint *153* **xxiv**	Common Poppy *11* **xxi**	Dame's-violet *23* **xix**
4 petals irregular flowers	Common Fumitory *13* **xxiv**	Rose-bay Willowherb *91* **xxi**	Germander Speedwell *143* **xix**
3 or 6 petals regular flowers	Flowering-rush *203* **xxv**	Martagon Lily *205* **xxi–xxii**	Pasqueflower *3* **xix**
3 or 6 petals irregular flowers	Indian Balsam *57* **xxv**	Pyramidal Orchid *221* **xxii**	Violet Helleborine *213* **xix**
5 or 7 petals regular flowers	Red Campion *33* **xxv**	Common Mallow *51* **xxii**	Field Forget-me-not *131* **xix**
5 or 7 petals irregular flowers	Water Lobelia *165* **xxvi**	Snapdragon *137* **xxiii**	Monk's-hood *3* **xx**
8 or more petals regular flowers	Butterbur *179* **xxvi**	Greater Knapweed *193* **xxiii**	Sea Aster *183* **xx**
tubular	Bilberry *117* **xxvi**	Bell Heather *115* **xxiii**	Grape Hyacinth *207* **xx**